Jane Austen
Writer in the World

... an old grievance .... "What, my dear, are you
you talking of; cried the Husband with sturdy
vanity - We are always at home before
midnight. They would laugh at Osborne Castle
to hear you call that late; they are but just
rising from dinner at midnight. -- "That is
nothing to the purpose. - retorted the Lady calmly.
Osbornes are to be no rule for us.
n had met every night, & break up two

So far, the subject was very
ten carried; - but Mr & Mrs Edwards were wise
as never to pass that point; & Mr. Edwards
med to something else. - he had lived
enough
this long in the Idleness of a Town, to
become a little of a Gossip, & having some
riosity to know more of the two
circumstances of
his young guest
began
than had yet reached him, he
with
"I think Miss Emma, I remem-
very well
w your aunt about 30 years ago;
I am
in the old.
tty sure I danced with her
ms at Bath, the year before I married --
was a very fine woman then - but like
people I suppose she is grown somewhat
er since that time. - I hope she is likely

Jane Austen

Writer in the World

Edited by
Kathryn Sutherland

Bodleian Library
UNIVERSITY OF OXFORD

First published in 2017 by the Bodleian Library
Broad Street, Oxford OX1 3BG

www.bodleianshop.co.uk

ISBN: 978 1 85124 463 8

Front cover: unknown artist, *Portrait of a lady*,
hollow-cut silhouette, c1810–15. © National
Portrait Gallery, London.
Back cover: Frontispiece from *The Universal Letter
Writer or Whole Art of Polite Correspondence*, 1808.
© Bodleian Library, University of Oxford.
Image opposite: Endsleigh from *Humphrey
Repton, Fragments on the theory and practice
of landscape gardening*, 1816. Oxford, Bodleian
Library, Arch. AA c.13
p. 6 Circulating Library from *Poetical Sketches
of Scarborough* (1813), with plates by Thomas
Rowlandson. Oxford, Bodleian Library, G.A. Yorks
4° 253
p. 186 Lyme Park © Snowshill / Shutterstock

Cover design by Dot Little at the Bodleian Library
Designed and typeset by 11/14pt Monotype
Baskerville by Dot Little at the Bodleian Library
Printed and bound by Great Wall Printing Co.
Ltd., Hong Kong on 157gsm Matt Gold East paper

British Library Catalogue in Publishing Data
A CIP record of this publication is available from
the British Library

Contents

Introduction

every scrap of information and every ray of light on Jane Austen are of national importance

CAROLINE SPURGEON, Shakespeare scholar and first woman professor in London University, 1927

I hear such different accounts of you as puzzle me exceedingly

ELIZABETH BENNET speaking to Mr Darcy, *Pride and Prejudice*, ch. 18

In a letter to the *Times Literary Supplement*, 6 January 1916, Reginald Farrer, plantsman and explorer, proposed a memorial edition of Jane Austen's novels to appear in 1917, exactly one hundred years after her death, as a fitting means to pay off a portion of England's 'national debt' to her. He further suggested that the edition be associated with a fund in Austen's name for the support of retired governesses, the Miss Taylors and Jane Fairfaxes of *Emma* and of the new twentieth century. Farrer signed his letter as from 'Ingleborough, Yorkshire' and 'the Valley of Rocks and Wolves, Tibet', two points on the world map unexpectedly conjoined. In 1917, Robert W. Chapman, a commissioned officer in the Royal Garrison Artillery, was serving in Macedonia and in off-duty moments preparing *Mansfield Park* and *Emma* as Oxford schools' editions. The project had been planned before the outbreak of war and was a joint enterprise with his wife, Katharine Metcalfe, whose *Pride and Prejudice* of 1912 provided the model. Reconceived and eventually published in five volumes in 1923, Chapman's Clarendon Press edition of *The Novels of Jane Austen* may have missed her centenary but it inaugurated the modern critical engagement with the English novel. This edition remained the standard Austen text until the end of the twentieth century; its faux-Regency production values and illustrations 'from contemporary sources' represented a recovered authenticity or equivalent of an early nineteenth-century reading experience.

Chapman's visual packaging of Austen's text, its careful incorporation, through selective annotation, into a canon of high male company (plenty of references to Shakespeare, Milton and Dr Johnson – almost none to her female novel-writing

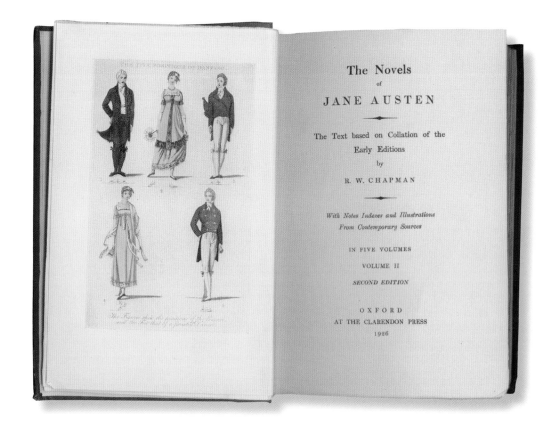

contemporaries), its total silence over matters of politics and history, influenced
generations of readers, whether they encountered Austen on page, screen or over
the airwaves. Screen adaptations from the late 1940s onwards, overwhelmingly of
Pride and Prejudice and *Emma*, were made as television plays or serials, usually for the
Sunday tea-time slot and its school-age audience. Inspired by radio dramatizations,
they obeyed the same principles of fidelity and reliance on dialogue, and they carried
over techniques from the stage: artificial indoor sets; little or no outdoor action; fixed
cameras; shots dominated by close-ups of talking heads; a consciously theatrical
dialogue and period-style aesthetic.[1] The exhibition to celebrate the bicentenary of
Austen's birth, mounted in the King's Library, British Museum, from 9 December 1975
to 29 February 1976, stands as a conspectus of the idealizing interpretations of Austen's
life and works up to this point in the twentieth century. Its overall design, by which
the visitor moved through biography and teenage writings, to the six major novels
in order of their publication, followed by the holograph manuscript of the last novel,
Sanditon, and final sections on 'Portraits' (three of Austen and one of her niece Anna
Lefroy) and 'Illustrations' (old images of Lyme Regis, Portsmouth harbour and Bath),
paid respectful homage to Austen's honorific place inside a particular, cloistered view

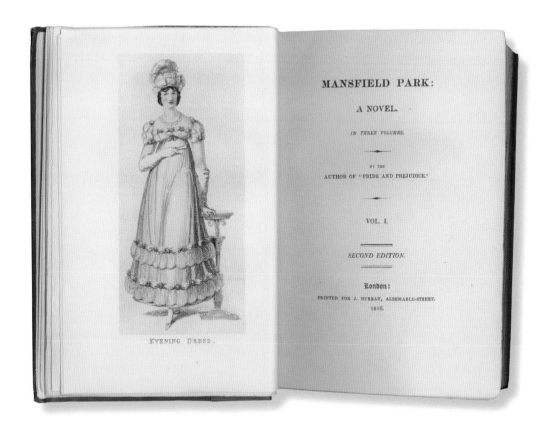

of literature. But in the same bicentenary year Marilyn Butler's *Jane Austen and the War of Ideas* shook our Austenian assumptions to their foundations. Butler challenged Austen's protected status among 'the band of dead writers that modern academic literary critics agreed to idolize',[2] showed her in conversation with a startling range of contemporary voices, male and female, and refused to extract her from the contentious historical times through which she lived and wrote. In the process, Butler burst open the doors of the claustrophobic drawing rooms in which Austen's heroines sat talking while the world and its events appeared to pass them by.

From this moment, Austen's novels and their interpretation became political and, by extension, politics included feminist or gendered readings and an alertness to material conditions – Austen's and our own. As Butler wrote in a new introduction for the book's paperback reissue in 1987, 'I thought it obvious that criticism would benefit, in range of comprehension and in stimulating difficulty, if Austen and her art-form were brought on to a plane where they were more examinable, which meant more assailable, like things of this world.'[3] 'Things of this world' could serve as the watchwords for this volume of essays compiled in advance of the bicentenary exhibitions in the Weston Library, Oxford, and the Discovery Centre, Winchester. Where nostalgia or the urgent search

Type-facsimile title page to *Mansfield Park* from the same edition with facing period illustration, again displaying Chapman's concern to simulate Regency production values. Oxford, Bodleian Library, 256 E.15000 – 15003.

for shared moral values once justified a historically defended reading of Austen's artistic and social detachment, it has now long seemed impossible to separate our practices and pleasures as readers from a sense of her as a writer in the world – in her world and in our world. Twenty years on from Butler's book, in 1995, three screen adaptations of Austen novels (the BBC miniseries *Pride and Prejudice*, Columbia Pictures' *Sense and Sensibility* and the BBC telefilm of *Persuasion*) again shifted the ground of our understanding as they reinforced through sheer visual specificity our sense of Austen as, indeed, a writer of 'things': a novelist of 'real estate literature'[4] or material romances of sex, money and handsome male leads.

This book is a tale drawn from two exhibitions and considers yet again Jane Austen's life and writings through a world of things. Several essays engage with objects associated intimately with Austen: her teenage notebooks, her music books, an item of clothing, a selection of her letters, the homemade booklets into which she composed her fictions, the portraits made of her during her life and afterwards. Others explore, through yet more objects, her filiations with wider social and political worlds: the Regency novel, other voices heard in letters, newspaper articles and naval logbooks, contemporary political cartoons, a stained glass window in Winchester Cathedral. These 'things' map Austen's immediate space of writing, the threads that connect her (from India to Bath and from North America to Chawton) to those on the world stage during the wars with France – wars that measured her own lifetime; finally, they chart her reputation over the 200 years since her death.

Each essay uses objects to invite us to reconsider what we think we know and love about Jane Austen, and challenges our familiarity through new configurations of things and fresh contexts: her early collaborative fiction-making and lifelong commitment to family writing; her enduring love of music-making; her immersion in a world of fashion and shopping; the impact of war on her novels; her habits and materials as a writer; her professionalism; her changing appearance within the portfolios of amateur artists; shifts in Austen's legacies. In these essays and their illustrations, Jane Austen's famous art of the social miniature is itself reconfigured and reimagined through other objects and other artefacts. Jane Austen's pelisse-coat, her portraits, her letters, the revised and patched pages of her fiction manuscripts – all are items with strong visual and emotional appeal and the power to stimulate new insights. Looking anew at objects and groupings of objects, many of them unfamiliar or associated here for the first time, will, we hope, provoke new ways of thinking about things we think we know so well – even too well. What did Jane Austen look like? How do we reconcile her anarchic teenage writings with their riotous display of narcissistic freeloaders, drunks and even murderers, to her realist romances of English village life? In what sense was she a wartime novelist? And at the heart of all stands Jane Austen herself, infinitely and richly unknowable.

The objects examined and illustrated in our essays have been drawn from many collections, both private and public; their generous support has been essential. The

Bodleian Library, Oxford, has extraordinarily rich Austen holdings: it houses one of the world's major collections of Austen materials; so, too, the British Library, London. Other contributors of images to this volume and of artefacts to the exhibitions in Winchester and Oxford include the National Portrait Gallery, the Victoria and Albert Museum, Hampshire Cultural Trust, King's College, Cambridge, Chawton House Library, Hampshire, Jane Austen's House Museum, Hampshire, the Murray Archive, National Library of Scotland, Edinburgh, the National Maritime Museum, Greenwich, London, the Houghton Library, Harvard, Cambridge, Massachusetts, and many private collectors. To all we send our grateful thanks.

Kathryn Sutherland
St Anne's College Oxford, July 2016

1   See Robert Giddings and Keith Selby, *The Classic Serial on Television and Radio*, Palgrave Macmillan, Basingstoke and New York, 2001.

2   Marilyn Butler, *Jane Austen and the War of Ideas*, 1975; new introduction, Clarendon Press, Oxford, 1987, p. x.

3   Butler, *Jane Austen and the War of Ideas*, 1987, p. xiv.

4   The phrase is Marjorie Garber's, 'The Jane Austen Syndrome', in *Quotation Marks*, Routledge, New York, 2003, pp. 199–200.

Note on Short Titles and References

Jane Austen's novels are referred to by chapter numbers as they appear in any continuously numbered modern edition; thus, *Pride and Prejudice*, ch. 45, not vol. 3, ch. 3.

All quotations from and references to Jane Austen's letters are taken from *Jane Austen's Letters*, ed. Deirdre Le Faye, 4th edition, Oxford University Press, Oxford, 2011; letters are identified throughout by letter number as assigned by Le Faye and by date.

J.E. Austen-Leigh, *A Memoir of Jane Austen and Other Family Recollections*, ed. Kathryn Sutherland, Oxford University Press, Oxford, 2002 is referred to throughout in abbreviated form as Austen-Leigh, *Memoir*, ed. Sutherland.

Georgian
Life

Edgar and Emma

a tale.

Chapter the first.

"I cannot imagine," said Sir Godfrey to his
Lady, "why we continue in such deplorable
"Lodgings as these, in a paltry Market-town,
"while we have 3 good Houses of our own
"situated in some of the finest parts of En:
"gland, & perfectly ready to receive us!"

"I'm sure Sir Godfrey," replied Lady Marl
"it has been much against my inclination

I

Teenage Writings
Amusement, Effusion, Nonsense

Thomas Keymer*

We know Jane Austen's teenage writings or juvenilia from three grandly labelled manuscript notebooks ('Volume the First', 'Volume the Second', 'Volume the Third') in which she transcribes a total of twenty-seven items, all originally written between 1786 and 1787, when she was 11 or 12, and 1793, when she was 17. These were not merely personal or private writings, however. They remained unknown outside the Austen family circle for many decades, but they played an energizing role within it, and each item seems to have started life as a free-standing manuscript booklet dedicated and presented to another member of the family (in the extended eighteenth-century sense of that word: the dedicatees include cousins, nieces and friends as well as brothers, parents and Austen's sister Cassandra). The notebook transcriptions all appear to have been completed, if we set aside Austen's later revisions and material added by others in the next generation, by June 1793. We might think of the notebooks, then, as a mock 'collected edition' in which Austen playfully trumps the century's leading poet (whose sumptuous, audacious *Works of Mr. Alexander Pope* came out when he was 29), and mimics certain aspects of print publication: these include the running speech marks in the margin of 'Edgar & Emma' (fig. 1.1) and the swell rule separating Austen's po-faced dedication of 'Sir William Mountague' from the spoof genealogy that follows (fig. 1.2). The whole enterprise is carried through with characteristic style and wit, though perhaps this kind of childhood gambit was more frequent in future novelists than we now know. There is an arresting parallel with the juvenilia written, illustrated and hand-stitched into mock-book form by the young Margaret Atwood in the 1940s, now in the Thomas Fisher Library, University of Toronto (fig. 1.3).

A generation later, the three manuscript notebooks were still in use, or were in use again, as animators of domestic sociability in the Austen family. It was in 1815 or thereabouts that Austen's teenage nephew James Edward Austen entered his own continuation of one item in *Volume the Third* (the micro-novel 'Evelyn'), and topical

Figure 1.1 Jane Austen, *Volume the First*, opening page of 'Edgar and Emma'. Oxford, Bodleian Library, MS. Don. e. 7, fol. 76.

Sir William Mountague

an unfinished performance

is humbly dedicated to Charles John
Austen Esqre, by his most obedient humble
Servant

The Author.

Sir William Mountague was
the son of Sir Henry Mountague, who was the
son of Sir John Mountague, a descendant of Sir
Christopher Mountague, who was the nephew
of Sir Edward Mountague, whose ancestor was
Sir James Mountague a near relation of Sir Robert
Mountague, who inherited the Title & Estate from Sir

reference points make clear that revisions were inserted into another story ('Kitty, or the Bower') at about this time. On Austen's death in 1817 the notebooks were preserved by Cassandra, and when Cassandra died in 1845 they were dispersed through different branches of the family, at last reaching their present homes – the Bodleian Library (*Volume the First*) and the British Library (*Volume the Second, Volume the Third*) – in the twentieth century. The only item from the notebooks to be published in the nineteenth century was one of the most insubstantial, 'The Mystery, An unfinished Comedy', which was included by James Edward Austen-Leigh – then a bewhiskered septuagenarian and noted authority on fox-hunting – in the 1871 edition of his *A Memoir of Jane Austen*.[1] Though embarrassingly 'puerile' in their content, these early writings, he suggested, at least had the merit of 'pure simple English'. Austen-Leigh offered this 'juvenile effusion ... as a specimen of the kind of transitory amusement which Jane was continually supplying to the family party'.[2]

This is language worth dwelling on. As Peter Sabor astutely notes, the term *effusion* has clung to the juvenilia since the inscription probably pencilled by Austen's father in *Volume the Third* ('Effusions of Fancy By a very Young Lady Consisting of Tales in a Style entirely new') at a time when the word typically conveyed respectable literary meaning, even special prestige, as a spontaneous or otherwise authentic outflow of genius.[3] Coleridge and Wordsworth called some of their poems 'Effusions', and Austen used the 'effusions of fancy' formula herself in *Northanger Abbey*'s famous chapter in defence of the novel genre (ch. 5). In Victorian usage, however, *effusion* grew more pejorative in connotation, suggesting the fatal absence of disciplining intelligence or structuring art. *OED* cites a dismissive contrast in *Fraser's Magazine* for 1842 between literary masters and serial hacks: 'All great novelists ... were men of genius and learning. The popular monthly effusionists nowadays are neither.' This same anxiety about juvenile effusiveness could still be heard when a complete edition of *Volume the First* at last appeared in print in 1933. Even as he composed his preface, the pioneering Austen scholar R.W. Chapman worried that 'it will always be disputed whether such effusions as these ought to be published; and it may be that we have enough already of Jane Austen's early scraps'.[4] Chapman's allusion was to the prior publication of *Volume the Second* in 1922; *Volume the Third* would follow in 1951.

The other telling phrase in Austen-Leigh's account is 'transitory amusement', which also looks back to, but at the same time darkens, the view taken of the juvenilia by those closest to them at the time. 'For my *Brother Charles*: I think I recollect that a few of the trifles in this Vol: were written expressly for his amusement', wrote Cassandra in a note pasted to the front endpaper of *Volume the First*, perfectly catching the lightness of the contents as agents of playful sociability. Yet *to amuse* is not only to entertain but also, at least potentially, to distract or even mislead – a double meaning very much at work with the 'unsafe amusements' of play-acting at Mansfield Park (ch. 20). It was just this possibility that preoccupied Austen's heirs as they sought to manage her Victorian

Figure 1.2 Jane Austen, *Volume the First*, opening page of 'Sir William Mountague'. Oxford, Bodleian Library, MS. Don. e. 7, p. 106.

reputation. In the *Memoir*, Austen-Leigh quotes an anecdote from his sister Caroline, who – protesting authenticity just a fraction too much – recalls a conversation in which Aunt Jane warns her against teenage writing, and half-regrets her own:

> She said—how well I recollect it!—that she knew writing stories was a great amusement, and *she* thought a harmless one, though many people, she was aware, thought otherwise ... that if I would take her advice I should cease writing till I was sixteen; that she had herself often wished she had read more, and written less in the corresponding years of her own life.[5]

Yet Austen-Leigh refrained from quoting a rather more interesting and perceptive document by Caroline, a letter of 1869 in which she suggests he consider including the surreal 'Evelyn' ('the story, I beleive in your possession, all nonsense') in his memoir-in-progress. Here anxiety about the potential of the juvenilia to jeopardize Austen's reputation as a serious novelist, a proto-Victorian domestic realist, coexists with real alertness to the literary qualities that would do the damage. The teenage writings, Caroline suggests, do not anticipate the mature novels but run clean counter to them:

> I have always thought it remarkable that the early workings of her mind should have been in burlesque, and comic exaggeration, setting at nought all rules of probable or possible—when of all her finished and later writings, the exact contrary is the characteristic. The story I mean is clever nonsense but one knows not how it might be taken by the public, tho' *some*thing must *ever* be risked.[6]

Keen as he was to pad out the *Memoir*, Austen-Leigh chose not to run this risk, though a trace of Caroline's guarded recommendation survives as he characterizes Austen's juvenilia as a whole: 'Her earliest stories are of a slight and flimsy texture, and are generally intended to be nonsensical, but the nonsense has much spirit in it.'[7]

Nonsense is of course a term of disparagement: literally a negation of sense, that cardinal virtue of Austen's novels, or so a surface reading of *Sense and Sensibility* would have us believe. Yet 'clever nonsense' suggests something more, whether or not the parallel was intended, at a time when nonsense was emerging as a distinctive, sometimes startlingly innovative, literary mode. We associate this mode especially with Lewis Carroll, whose games with language, logic and representation in *Alice's Adventures in Wonderland* (1865) find fullest expression in *Through the Looking Glass* (1871) – which contains, for example, 'Jabberwocky' and a dizzying analysis of its nonce-words by Humpty Dumpty – and in Carroll's extended nonsense-poem *The Hunting of the Snark* (1876). The term was used most emphatically by Edward Lear, whose zanily inventive *A Book of Nonsense* (1846) was followed, as Austen-Leigh's *Memoir* went into its second

edition, by the verbal pyrotechnics of *Nonsense Songs, Stories, Botany and Alphabets* (1871), where 'The Owl and the Pussycat' first appeared.

Nonsense literature was also beginning to be theorized at this time, the classic formulation being Edward Strachey's in an 1888 essay on 'Nonsense as a Fine Art'. Here nonsense, 'the proper contrary of Sense', is a mode that 'sets itself to discover and bring forward the incongruities of all things within and without us'. Though associated with a destabilizing topsy-turvydom, with suspension of moral norms and with elements of the satirical grotesque, it limits itself for the most part, in Strachey's account, to a register of unthreatening amusement. Nonsense injects 'confusion into order by setting things upside down, bringing them into all sorts of unnatural, impossible, and absurd, but not painful or dangerous, combinations'.[8] Modern accounts go somewhat further, and emphasize the disconcerting quality of the contradictions, collisions and ruptures left unexplained or unresolved in nonsense literature. Linguistic havoc, irrational logic and representational muddle are among the most commonly cited forms of disruption. For Noel Malcolm, who finds the mode already alive and well in the seventeenth

Figure 1.3 Margaret Atwood, 'Annie the Ant', cover illustration and stitching. Toronto, Thomas Fisher Library, MS. Coll. 00547, Box 1, Folder 2.

century, there is a self-conscious literariness about nonsense – distinct, then, from the anarchic energies of popular writing – which makes parody its central technique for putting standard ways of seeing, thinking and writing at an ironic distance. We might extend to the conventions of fiction the point made by Roderick McGillis about the relationship between nonsense literature and mainstream Victorian verse: 'By subverting sense and the depth of thought in the poetic canon, by standing sense on its head in order to draw attention to it, nonsense challenges a thoughtless acceptance of reality and a language that purports to reflect reality.'[9]

If Austen's teenage writings were nonsense by these criteria,[10] not just empty trifles but texts inimical in their very mode to the mature novels' fidelity to morality and truth, it becomes easy to see why the Victorian custodians of her reputation kept them under wraps. Yet it also becomes possible to see why, at the height of 'Janeite' enthusiasm in the interwar years of the twentieth century, the juvenilia seemed so refreshing to their earliest readers outside the family. In his introduction to *Love & Freindship and Other Early Works* (the title used in 1922 for *Volume the Second*), G.K. Chesterton proposed a radical realignment of Austen's place in literary tradition, likening the contents to 'the great burlesques of Peacock or Max Beerbohm' and locating her in a line of exuberant, carnivalesque satire that ran from Rabelais to Dickens. Suddenly everything looked different; now the real wellspring of her writing was that 'of Gargantua and of Pickwick; it was the gigantic inspiration of laughter'.[11] Reviewing the Chesterton edition, Virginia Woolf seized the opportunity to throw off the suffocating blanket of Janeism and instead celebrate the transgressive fun, the gleeful cruelty, the 'sheer nonsense' of the contents. Above all, Woolf celebrated *Volume the Second* for its clear-eyed refusal to be decorous or deferential in the interests of politeness or taste. 'Never, even at the emotional age of seventeen, did she round upon herself in shame, and obliterate a sarcasm in a spasm of compassion, or blur an outline in a mist of rhapsody. Spasms and rhapsodies, she seems to have said, end here.'[12]

Woolf concludes her review by saying that to read this volume is 'to listen ... to Jane Austen practising', and the teenage writings do indeed offer thematic and rhetorical anticipations of the published novels, especially the three we know to have started life just a few years later (*Sensibility and Sensibility*, *Pride and Prejudice* and *Northanger Abbey* were all drafted in one form or another in the later 1790s). Woolf's verb 'listen' is exactly right, and we should remember that these works, though fashioned in imitation of print conventions, were also unmistakably designed as scripts for oral performance. In Austen's day the rise of silent reading had by no means yet eclipsed convivial practices of recital in groups, and as Elspeth Jajdelska points out, 'for centuries, the word "aloud" was not needed to indicate that reading meant speaking'.[13] Just how strong this practice remained for the mid-century novelists whom Austen most admired is clear from many sources: one sees it in Susanna Highmore's pencil sketch of Samuel Richardson reading *Sir Charles Grandison* to his coterie in 1751 (fig. 1.4); one hears it in Elizabeth

Carter's disapproval a year later when the Bishop of Gloucester, pleading a cold, insists on 'reading [Henry Fielding's] Amelia in silence', so violating the standard practice of 'read[ing] en famille after supper'.[14] Reading *en famille* was no doubt more fun in the Revd George Austen's household than it had been in the Bishop of Gloucester's, but the norm was the same, and a new lease of life was probably given to the practice by the new generation of nieces and nephews during Austen's Chawton years (from July 1809). Another editor of *Volume the Second*, Brian Southam, attributes 'the carelessness of some of the writing ... to the fact that Jane Austen intended these pieces to be heard, not read'. The earliest family memoir, written by Austen's brother Henry shortly after her death, notes her virtuosity as a performer of her own prose, which was 'never heard to so much advantage as from her own mouth; for she partook largely in all the best gifts of the comic muse'.[15]

Figure 1.4 Susanna Highmore (later Duncombe), *Mr. Richardson reading the MS History of Sir Cha. Grandison at North End* (1751) reproduced in *The Correspondence of Samuel Richardson*, ed. Anna Laetitia Barbauld (London, 1804). Oxford, Bodleian Library, (Vet.) 2569 e.53, frontispiece.

Yet if Woolf was right to hear a speaking voice in *Volume the Second*, was she also right to talk of Austen practising for the author she would become? Recent scholars have been struck more by discontinuities between the early manuscripts and the published novels than by links between them, and in this respect they resume Caroline Austen's insight of 1869, albeit without Caroline's alarm. Probably the most influential modern account is by Margaret Anne Doody, for whom, if the teenage writings are rehearsals for anything at all, they are rehearsals for the road not taken. Central to Doody's reading are the long years of frustration and blockage endured by Austen until she at last broke into print in 1811, a process Doody represents in terms of capitulation to, or at least compromise with, the limiting norms of published fiction at the time. The conformist, even didactic genre to which Austen was forced to adapt 'was not the appropriate home of social criticism or free aesthetic play—still less of moral questioning', and as she effected this necessary adaptation, the challenge was 'how to sustain some of her own deeper interest while submitting to the restrictions of the domestic and moral courtship novel as the only available form'. In this context, for Doody, the special value of the juvenilia lies in the trace they leave of the wayward literary instincts that Austen had to suppress in order to get published at all. 'Her early writing is rough, violent, sexy, jokey'; it tells us 'what Austen might have sounded like without such domestication'.[16] In other words, the Austen we listen to here is not the author she would become; it is the one she wouldn't.

More evolutionary accounts have been offered, and for Juliet McMaster the achievements of the novels ('all that restraint in the service of exactness and the *mot juste*, all the fine moral imagination that can trace the delicate intricacies of an evolving relationship') seem all the more impressive for their origins in 'the uninhibited gusto of youthful creativity'. Yet McMaster is no less struck than Doody by the contrast, and as she notes, it has become second nature in Austen critics more broadly to characterize the two bodies of work in binary terms: on the one hand, the 'irreverent, rollicking, spontaneous, hyperbolic, violent, indecent, indecorous, outrageous' early manuscripts; on the other, the 'balanced, measured, understated, disciplined, decorous, nuanced' published novels.[17]

McMaster's own account of the contrast turns on parody, and she enumerates many ways in which the juvenilia send up the conventions and clichés of the mainstream novel, a genre much satirized at the time for its high circulation levels and its low literary standards (note which shelves have been emptied out in fig. 1.5). There are specific connections to the disposable circulating-library fiction that Austen and her siblings clearly binge-read in the Steventon years, and at one level *Love and Freindship* is a cruelly accelerated burlesque of Eliza Nugent Bromley's *Laura and Augustus* (1784), a 500-page epistolary tear-jerker that was hailed on publication by one world-weary reviewer as 'frequently interesting'.[18] More generally, the juvenilia target the tired formulae and creaking conventions of the genre as a whole, though with unmistakable relish

Figure 1.5 *The Circulating Library*, watercolour by Isaac Cruikshank (Laurie & Whittle, London, 1804). © Yale Center for British Art, Paul Mellon Collection.

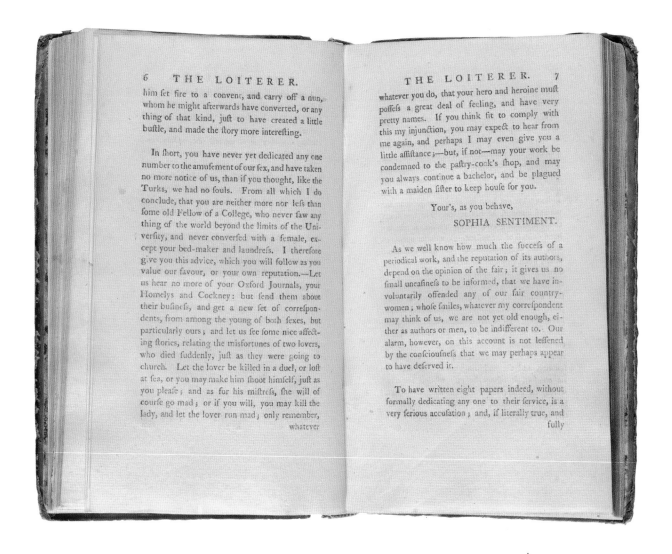

him set fire to a convent, and carry off a nun, whom he might afterwards have converted, or any thing of that kind, just to have created a little bustle, and made the story more interesting.

In short, you have never yet dedicated any one number to the amusement of our sex, and have taken no more notice of us, than if you thought, like the Turks, we had no souls. From all which I do conclude, that you are neither more nor less than some old Fellow of a College, who never saw any thing of the world beyond the limits of the University, and never conversed with a female, except your bed-maker and laundress. I therefore give you this advice, which you will follow as you value our favour, or your own reputation.—Let us hear no more of your Oxford Journals, your Homelys and Cockney: but send them about their business, and get a new set of correspondents, from among the young of both sexes, but particularly ours; and let us see some nice affecting stories, relating the misfortunes of two lovers, who died suddenly, just as they were going to church. Let the lover be killed in a duel, or lost at sea, or you may make him shoot himself, just as you please; and as for his mistress, she will of course go mad; or if you will, you may kill the lady, and let the lover run mad; only remember, whatever

whatever you do, that your hero and heroine must possess a great deal of feeling, and have very pretty names. If you think fit to comply with this my injunction, you may expect to hear from me again, and perhaps I may even give you a little assistance;—but, if not—may your work be condemned to the pastry-cook's shop, and may you always continue a bachelor, and be plagued with a maiden sister to keep house for you.

Your's, as you behave,

SOPHIA SENTIMENT.

As we well know how much the success of a periodical work, and the reputation of its authors, depend on the opinion of the fair; it gives us no small uneasiness to be informed, that we have involuntarily offended any of our fair country-women; whose smiles, whatever my correspondent may think of us, we are not yet old enough, either as authors or men, to be indifferent to. Our alarm, however, on this account is not lessened by the consciousness that we may perhaps appear to have deserved it.

To have written eight papers indeed, without formally dedicating any one to their service, is a very serious accusation; and, if literally true, and fully

Figure 1.6 A page from *The Loiterer*, showing Sophia Sentiment's letter, 28 March 1789, p. 7. Oxford, Bodleian Library, Hope 8° 582, vol. 1, no. 9, p. 7.

alongside the ridicule, and with no trace of the lofty put-downs – 'Let us leave it to the Reviewers ... to talk in threadbare strains of the trash with which the press now groans' – from which Austen would distance herself in *Northanger Abbey* (ch. 5). It is entirely in a spirit of fun that she satirizes the oleaginous dedications and flatulent prefaces that routinely accompanied eighteenth-century novels (one dedication offers deadpan *sententiae* to her niece Anna, who 'will derive from them very important Instructions, with regard to your Conduct'; Anna was seven weeks old at the time); the gratuitous interpolated tales ('Will you favour me with your Life & Adventures?', a young lady is asked as she writhes with a broken leg in a gamekeeper's trap; she cheerfully obliges); the prestige of debilitating sensibility ('It was too pathetic for the feelings of Sophia and myself—We fainted Alternately on a Sofa'—Austen is channelling Sheridan's play *The Critic* (1779) here); the crippling formal self-consciousness of epistolary novels

('Dear Maud | Beleive me I'm happy to hear of your Brother's arrival. I have a thousand things to tell you, but my paper will only permit me to add that I am yr affect. Freind | Amelia Webster').[19] It is worth adding that many of these conventions and clichés were still limping on in 1815–16, the likely date of Austen's tongue-in-cheek 'Plan of a Novel', which trains its fire on the recycled plot devices and rhetorical platitudes of sentimental-didactic fiction ('the poor Father ... after 4 or 5 hours of tender advice & parental Admonition to his miserable Child, expires in a fine burst of Literary Enthusiasm, intermingled with Invectives against Holder's of Tythes').[20] In this respect, we may see the teenage writings as giving notice, parodically, of a vein of satire that would run throughout Austen's oeuvre, and as mocking tastes and expectations to which – albeit with surpassing creative intelligence – she would later have to adjust.

Two early works outside the manuscript volumes participate in this pattern, albeit with uncertainties of attribution in each case. The first is a letter of 28 March 1789 contributed by 'Sophia Sentiment' to a student-generated essay-periodical in the Addisonian tradition entitled *The Loiterer*, published every Saturday in Oxford for sixty weeks in the period 1789–90; the editor was Austen's brother James, and between them he and his younger brother Henry contributed thirty-eight of the sixty essays.[21] With a lightness of touch that neither brother could reach elsewhere, 'Sophia Sentiment' announces herself an avid reader ('some hundred volumes of Novels and Plays') and berates the authors for producing essays on manners and morals instead of fiction ('not one sentimental story about love and honour ... Not one Eastern Tale full of Bashas and Hermits'). The only way *The Loiterer* can hope to reach female readers is to include 'some nice affecting stories, relating the misfortunes of two lovers, who died suddenly, just as they were going to church', and to this end Sophia offers the editors her own assistance. If they refuse – one hears brothers being teased here by a witty younger sister – 'may you always continue a bachelor, and be plagued with a maiden sister to keep house for you' (fig. 1.6).[22]

The second item is a dramatic skit on Richardson's *Sir Charles Grandison* (1753–4), probably composed with Austen's encouragement by her niece Anna (she of the 'very important Instructions') after 1800, though Brian Southam's attribution of the opening section to Austen herself, probably in 1791–2, is still sometimes repeated.[23] One way or another (and in this respect like the *Loiterer* venture), 'Sir Charles Grandison' forms part of a corpus of family entertainments with Austen herself at its heart, and joins a long line of *Grandison* jokes running through her oeuvre (see fig. 1.7, where the little booklets into which the 'Grandison' play has been written may echo the original manuscript booklets of the juvenilia). Her admiration for the moral and literary seriousness of Richardson's achievement takes smart ironic form in *Northanger Abbey*, whose characters, in thrall to Gothic sensationalism, find *Grandison* 'amazing horrid ... Miss Andrews could not get through the first volume' (ch. 6). But *Grandison* was also notorious for its exhaustive circumstantial realism and its glacial narrative pace, a point nicely caught in Walter Scott's anecdote of an old lady who liked having it read to her "'because," said she, "should I drop asleep in course of the reading, I am sure when I awake, I shall have lost none of the story'".[24] This same joke takes the form of burlesque acceleration in the 'Grandison' playlet, which condenses Richardson's seven volumes into a few brisk minutes of family entertainment, no doubt for domestic staging as well as reading. In a neat display of amused impatience, Richardson's slow-motion plot is drastically quickened to the rate of an afterpiece farce (or think, alternatively, of Adam McNaughton's three-minute *Hamlet*), with the same frenzy of staccato dialogue, hectic stagecraft (*'Exit Bridget. & Mr. Reeves at a different door.—calls behind the Scenes—'*)[25] and arbitrary lurches of plot.

Yet we must probe beyond the fairly stable categories of parody and burlesque to get the full measure of Austen's 'clever nonsense' in these precocious texts. The play of wit in the juvenilia runs far in excess of satirical function, and one obvious example lies in Austen's extravagant wordplay. There are the outlandish names of her fictional locations: Crankhumdunberry ('Frederic & Elfrida'), Pammydiddle ('Jack & Alice'), or the charmed environment where Sir William Mountague falls multiply in love 'with the 3 Miss Cliftons of Kilhoobery Park'. There are her risqué character names: in 'Frederic & Elfrida' alone, the inspired 'Jezalinda' (part sentimental heroine, part biblical whore) and 'Captain Roger of Buckinghamshire' – perhaps an innocent name, but with so many counties to choose from, did Roger really have to be from Bucks? In general, there is too much sexual innuendo to explain away, and as in *Mansfield Park*, with Mary Crawford's notorious gag about *'Rears,* and *Vices'* in the navy (ch. 6), sodomy comes into view in 'The History of England', which zanily casts the upstart page boy Lambert Simnel as 'Widow of Richard [III]' and praises James I for the 'keener penetration' he shows when cultivating, with royal favourites, 'that amiable disposition which inclines to Freindships'. Beyond these deft touches of obscene periphrasis or roundabout phraseology, it may have been Austen's cornucopian list-making that reminded Chesterton of Rabelais, generated more by the play of sound than by any internal logic. Witness Mr Clifford's carriage collection – 'a Coach, a Chariot, a Chaise, a Landeau, a Landeaulet, a Phaeton, a Gig, a Whisky, an italian Chair, a Buggy, a Curricle & a wheel barrow' ('Memoirs of Mr Clifford') – or the meat feast consumed by Charlotte – 'a young Leveret, a brace of Partridges, a leash of Pheasants & a Dozen of Pigeons' ('Frederic & Elfrida') – shortly after inadvertently accepting two separate marriage proposals; she drowns herself a paragraph later. The effect spills into verse with the pile-up of picturesque settings in the 'Ode to Pity' closing *Volume the First* – 'The hut, the Cot, the Grot, & Chapel queer' – and elsewhere Austen highlights her enjoyment of ill-placed cliché by generating bogus proverbial phrases of her own: 'Tho' … Frederic was as bold as brass yet in other respects his heart was as soft as cotton' ('Frederic & Elfrida'). She revels in jarring mismatches between polite and demotic language

Figure 1.7 Manuscript of 'Sir Charles Grandison'. © Chawton House Library.

He did once you know. And I do
not know what you mean by my
~~being~~ called upon.

Miss G. Why, when
to be married.
not get on Lo
will be worsted
come is not it
at her watch
four.

Lord L. Lyou
- lotte,
dine a
Miss G. Li
did no
Jarda
Lit
Lord L. line
But

Act 2.— Scene 1st
~~Eh~~ The Curtain drawn
discovers
Miss Kexpron Mrs Burke

Mrs. R. But my dear your
Lady, think what a la
fortune Sir Hargrave

Sir Charles
The happy
a Comedy
Dramatis Personæ
Men
Sir Charles Grandison
Sir Hargrave Polleren Harm
Lord L.
Mr Beever Lady
Mr Selby

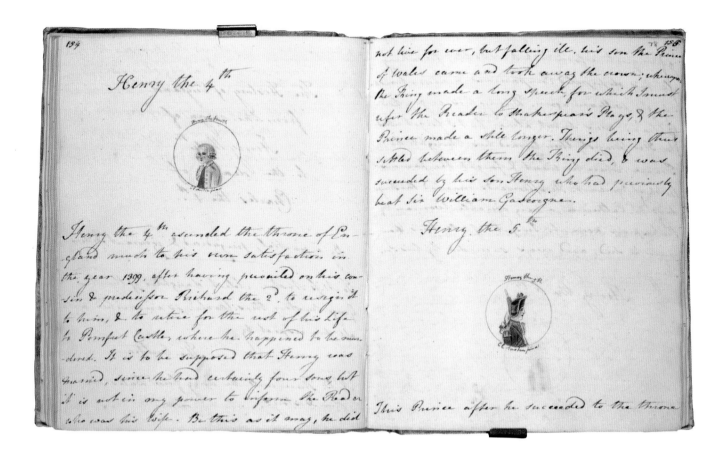

Figure 1.8 Medallion portraits of Henry IV and Henry V by Cassandra Austen in Jane Austen, *Volume the Second*, London, British Library, Add. MS. 59874, pp. 154–5. © British Library Board.

registers – 'I shall trouble Mr Stanly for a Little of the fried Cow heel & Onion' ('The Visit') – and gratuitous intrusions of epic diction: one hero is 'of so dazzling a Beauty that none but Eagles could look him in the Face' ('Jack & Alice'). Again and again it is as though, to misquote *Northanger Abbey*, Austen is aiming for the worst-chosen language.

Similar incongruities are at work on the level of representation, typically with no explanation. In gleeful violation of formal realism, indeed even rudimentary standards of literary competence, there is absurd hyperbole – 'Emma … continued in tears the remainder of her Life' ('Edgar & Emma'); ironic understatement – 'Our neighbourhood was small, for it consisted only of your Mother' ('Love and Freindship'); self-contradiction – 'his name was Lindsay … I shall conceal it under that of Talbot' ('Love and Freindship'); tautology – 'Tho' Benevolent & Candid, she was Generous & sincere' ('Jack & Alice'); bathos – 'A Grove of full-grown Elms sheltered us from the East—. A Bed of full-grown Nettles from the West—' ('Love and Freindship'); sheer gratuitous nonsense – 'he regularly sent home a large Newfoundland Dog every Month to his family' ('The Generous Curate'). Two lovers are unable to marry 'on account of the tender years of the young couple, Rebecca being but 36 & Captain Roger little more than 63'; a few pages later, 'That plea can be no more, seven days being now expired' ('Frederic & Elfrida'). A frequent device is one Laurence Sterne called 'the Cervantic humour ... of describing silly and trifling events with the circumstantial pomp of great ones',[26] and elaborate narrative attention is forever being bestowed on the wrong thing: a suspenseful elopement tale is interrupted by a long debate about the pros and cons of red-cheeked complexions ('Jack & Alice'); paragraphs are devoted to the exchanges of a family deciding whether or not to open a door ('Love and Freindship'). Without registering the slightest surprise, 'Henry & Eliza' (its title a joking allusion to Jane Austen's brother, Henry, and their cousin Eliza de Feuillide)[27] merges wildly incompatible narrative settings, presided over by 'the Dutchess of F.', who fluctuates between alternative roles as enlightened modern aristocrat and medieval warlord: in the first she attends assemblies and arranges advantageous matches; in the second she builds dungeons and plans tortures for her enemies, and 'sent out after them 300 armed Men, with orders not to return without their Bodies, dead or alive'. This may have been a joke about the first tentative historical novels of the late eighteenth century, still incongruously couched in a modern rhetoric of sensibility, before the genre hit its stride

Figure 1.9 Medallion portrait of Edward IV by Cassandra Austen in Jane Austen, *Volume the Second*, London, British Library, Add. MS. 59874, p. 158. © British Library Board.

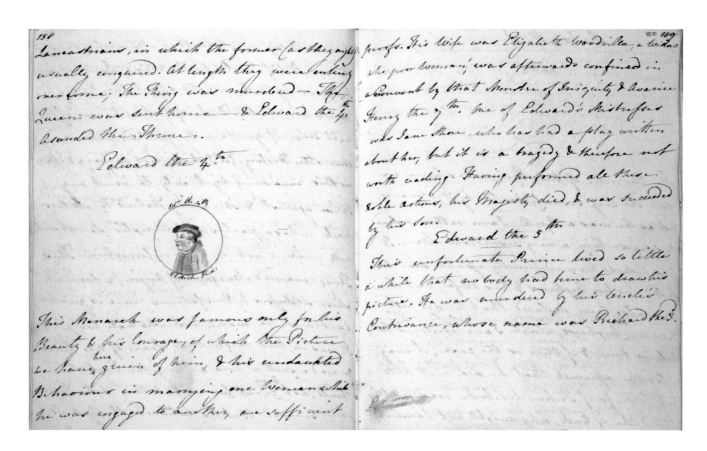

with Walter Scott a generation later. It is a joke resumed in the madcap anachronisms of the medallion portraits contributed by Cassandra to 'The History of England', which represent Henry IV as a rouged, peruked fop in frock coat and ruffles (fig. 1.8), and Henry V as a preening naval officer with tricorn hat and gold epaulettes. Edward IV – 'This Monarch was famous … for his Beauty' – looks like a slovenly eighteenth-century farmer; David Nokes nicely describes his 'ugly porcine face, wide snout, flabby cheeks and double chin' (fig. 1.9).[28]

Highlighting these effects of incongruity and absurdity is Austen's staunch refusal to recognize that anything is awry at all. Her characteristic narrative stance is one of deadpan neutrality, of unsurprised, even uninterested, acceptance of cruelty and violence, of cheerful, moral insouciance and emotional anaesthesia. It is a matter of mere report, not comment, when one character grotesquely mangles the eighteenth-century 'beauties of the mind' trope:

> Lovely & too charming Fair one, notwithstanding your forbidding Squint, your greazy tresses & your swelling Back, which are more frightfull than imagination can paint or pen describe, I cannot refrain from expressing my raptures, at the engaging Qualities of your Mind, which so amply atone for the Horror, with which your first appearance must ever inspire the unwary visitor. ('Frederic & Elfrida')

The addressee takes no offence at this, and no other character sees anything amiss. The same is true when, with a beautifully Johnsonian switch from abstract Latinate generalities to concrete Anglo-Saxon particulars, Austen explodes the pastoral idyll of 'Henry & Eliza', which opens with 'Sir George and Lady Harcourt … superintending the Labours of their Haymakers, rewarding the industry of some by smiles of approbation, & punishing the idleness of others, by a cudgel'. 'Cudgel' is the perfect narrative ambush on Austen's part, its approach hidden by elegant parallelism ('rewarding the industry … punishing the idleness') and the vapid clichés of benevolent paternalism ('superintending', 'smiles of approbation'). But Austen makes no more of the word than this, and instead moves briskly on to the next irruption of chaos. This is a world of random, abrupt violence, in which lovers are casually shot by their rivals and jealous ladies murder their friends, but no one seems to mind, or even much notice. The narrator is always interested in something else, whether the happy consequences for her marriage plot ('Sir William shot Mr Stanhope; the lady had then no reason to refuse him' ('Sir William Mountague')) or the requisite forms of commemoration:

when one heroine dies – 'Sukey … jealous of her superior charms took her by poison from an admiring World' – we might almost miss the operative word 'poison' amidst the surrounding fluff ('superior charms', 'admiring World' ('Jack & Alice')). Yet other characters enjoy cartoon-style immunity from harm, and this too offers no grounds for remark. When a romantically roaming lover has her leg broken 'in one of the steel traps so common in gentlemen's grounds', she is perfectly healed in an instant by a passer-by with no surgical experience – a circumstance the narrator points out, but feels no need to explain. Steel traps are recognized as inappropriate in courtship – 'Oh! cruel Charles to wound the hearts & legs of all the fair' ('Jack & Alice') – but Austen is no harder on Charles than she is on the heroine of 'The beautifull Cassandra', a fond caricature of her beloved sister, who bilks tradesmen and beats them up during the course of 'a day well spent'. Sometimes – a trick from Henry Fielding's *Jonathan Wild* (1743) – criminal conduct is slyly endorsed by a rogue adverb or a switch from moral to aesthetic criteria. In 'Love and Freindship', the hero and heroine enjoy 'a considerable sum of Money which Augustus had gracefully purloined from his Unworthy father's Escritoire'; 'The History of England' applauds Henry VIII for dissolving the monasteries, an act 'of infinite use to the landscape of England in general'.

For Anthony Burgess, 'the British nonsense tradition, like the surrealist one that succeeded it, is only a bizarre way of making sense'.[29] The 'clever nonsense' of Austen's early manuscript mock-books (to return to her niece's formulation of 1869) is bizarre indeed in the sense it makes. Yet the distinguishing features of this nonsense – stylistic exuberance; radical incongruity; unexplained or unresolved paradox; suspended norms of perception and judgement; arbitrary subversions of narrative logic; unruffled acceptance of narrated chaos – are aspects of Austen's repertoire that we do well to remember.

* With thanks to Sushani Singh for skilful research assistance.

1 James Edward Austen added 'Leigh' to his family name in 1836 when he inherited the estate of his great-aunt Jane Leigh Perrot.

2 Austen-Leigh, *Memoir*, ed. Sutherland, p. 40.

3 Jane Austen, *Juvenilia*, ed. Peter Sabor, Cambridge University Press, Cambridge, 2006, p. li.

4 Jane Austen, *Volume the First*, ed. R.W. Chapman, Clarendon Press, Oxford, 1933, p. ix.

5 Austen-Leigh, *Memoir*, ed. Sutherland, p. 42.

6 Caroline Austen to James Edward Austen-Leigh, letter of 'Wednesday Evg. [1869?]', in Austen-Leigh, *Memoir*, ed. Sutherland, Appendix, p. 186.

7 Austen-Leigh, *Memoir*, ed. Sutherland, p. 40.

8 *Quarterly Review*, no. 167, July–October 1888, p. 335, quoted in Wim Tigges, *An Anatomy of Literary Nonsense*, Rodopi, Amsterdam, 1988, pp. 7, 8.

9 Noel Malcolm, *The Origins of English Nonsense*, HarperCollins, London, 1997; Roderick McGillis, 'Nonsense', in Richard Cronin, Alison Chapman and Antony H. Harrison (eds), *A Companion to Victorian Poetry*, Blackwell, Oxford, 2002, pp. 155–70 (p. 164).

10 So far as I know, this suggestion has been made just once before in Austen scholarship. Discussing Austen's use of syllepsis, Kathryn Sutherland notes that this device 'connects Austen's youthful sketches with a whole tradition of English nonsense or absurdity, from Charles Lamb and Dickens to Edward Lear, in which the world is turned upside down and different kinds of reality collide in a lunatic logic of their own' (Jane Austen, *Volume the First*, intr. Kathryn Sutherland, Bodleian Library, Oxford, 2013, p. xiv).

11 *Love & Freindship and Other Early Works*, intr. G.K. Chesterton, Chatto & Windus, London, 1922, pp. xi, xiv.

12 Virginia Woolf, 'Jane Austen Practising', *New Statesman*, 15 July 1922.

13 Elspeth Jajdelska, *Silent Reading and the Birth of the Narrator*, University of Toronto Press, Toronto, 2007, p. 37.

14 *A Series of Letters between Mrs. Elizabeth Carter and Miss Catherine Talbot*, ed. Montague Pennington, London, 1809, vol. 2, pp. 65, 71.

15 Jane Austen, *Volume the Second*, ed. Brian Southam, Clarendon Press, Oxford, 1963, p. xi; Henry Austen, 'Biographical Notice of the Author' (1818), in Austen-Leigh, *Memoir*, ed. Sutherland, p. 140.

16 Margaret Anne Doody, 'The Early Short Fiction', in Edward Copeland and Juliet McMaster (eds), *The Cambridge Companion to Jane Austen*, 2nd edition, Cambridge University Press, Cambridge, 2011, pp. 72–86 (pp. 83–4, 85, 86).

17 Juliet McMaster, 'Young Jane Austen: Author', in Claudia L. Johnson and Clara Tuite (eds), *A Companion to Jane Austen*, Blackwell, Oxford, 2009, pp. 81–90 (p. 81).

18 Peter Garside, James Raven and Rainer Schöwerling (eds), *The English Novel 1770–1829: A Bibliographical Survey of Prose Fiction Published in the British Isles*, Oxford University Press, Oxford, 2000, vol. 1, p. 336, quoting the *Critical Review* for March 1784.

19 Jane Austen, *Teenage Writings*, ed. Kathryn Sutherland and Freya Johnston, Oxford University Press, Oxford, 2017, 'To Miss Jane Anna Elizabeth Austen', 'Jack & Alice', 'Love and Freindship', 'Amelia Webster'.

20 Jane Austen, 'Plan of a Novel', in Jane Austen, *Minor Works*, ed. R.W. Chapman, Oxford University Press, Oxford, 1954, p. 430.

21 For arguments for and against its attribution to Jane Austen, see *Teenage Writings*, ed. Sutherland and Johnston, Appendix.

22 *Teenage Writings*, ed. Sutherland and Johnston, Appendix.

23 For this debate see Jane Austen, *Later Manuscripts*, ed. Janet Todd and Linda Bree, Cambridge University Press, Cambridge, 2008, pp. cxi–cxviii.

24 Ioan Williams (ed.), *Sir Walter Scott on Novelists and Fiction*, Routledge, London, 1968, p. 31.

25 *Jane Austen's Sir Charles Grandison*, ed. Brian Southam, Clarendon Press, Oxford, 1980, p. 69.

26 Laurence Sterne, *The Letters, Part I:* 1739–64, ed. Melvyn New and Peter de Voogd, University Press of Florida, Gainesville, 2009, p. 92.

27 In 1781, at the age of 19, Eliza had married a French soldier; he was guillotined in Paris in 1794. In December 1797, she married Henry. A decade earlier, in December 1787, they were flirting and acting together in family performances of Susanna Centlivre's popular comedy *The Wonder: A Woman Keeps a Secret!* (1714). The play sees the hero Don Felix (played by Henry) and the beautiful Violante (played by Eliza) contend with parental opposition, impish servants and various misfortunes and misunderstandings before they are finally united forever. 'Henry & Eliza', probably written in 1788, oddly predicts Eliza de Feuillide's widowhood and removal from France to England.

28 David Nokes, *Jane Austen: A Life*, Fourth Estate, London, 1997, p. 125.

29 Anthony Burgess, 'Nonsense', in Wim Tigges (ed.), *Explorations in the Field of Nonsense*, Rodopi, Amsterdam, 1987, pp. 17–21 (p. 21).

Queen Mary's Lamentation

I sigh and lament me in vain These walls can but echo my
moan Alas it increases my pain when I think of the days that are gone — Thro' the
grate of my prison I see the birds as they wanton in air my heart how it pants to be
free my looks they are wild with despair

2.
Above tho' oppress'd by my fate
I burn with contempt for my foes
Tho' fortune has alter'd my state
She ne'er can subdue me to those
False woman in ages to come
Thy malice detested shall be
And when we are cold in the tomb
Some heart will still sorrow for me

3.
Ye roofs where cold damps & dismay
With silence & solitude dwell
How comfortless passes the day
How sad tolls the evening bell
The pilots from the battlements cry
Hollow winds seem to murmur around
Oh Mary prepare thee to die
My blood it runs cold at the sound

2

Making Music

Jeanice Brooks

From the balls in *Pride and Prejudice* to the concert in *Persuasion*, from Mary Crawford's harp in *Mansfield Park* to Jane Fairfax's piano in *Emma*, Jane Austen's novels evoke a rich and meaningful world of musical sound. Austen's surviving music books have provided opportunities to explore connections between the repertoire she performed and the musical episodes she imagined, helping to reconstruct the soundscape of sociability that her own contemporaries took for granted.[1] Less attention has been paid to her music books as physical objects: to how making music includes not only performance but also the crafting of musical materials. The Austen music albums are literally gatherings in that they bring together disparate items of music into a single book, and they are also gatherings in a more abstract sense: they have a pronounced collective, social dimension. Austen's engagement with the material culture of music provides us with unexpected insights into her social and artistic world.

The Austen family's music books display patterns characteristic of domestic music collection among the gentry from the mid-eighteenth century onward.[2] Many such albums figure in libraries amassed by wealthy landowning families. The Austen books instead provide a window onto the lives of a more diverse group that included prosperous merchants and farmers, and professional people such as lawyers, doctors, schoolmistresses and clergymen, as well as the minor gentry. Although there are some differences, not only in the size of libraries but also in music choice, the Austen volumes also show considerable overlap with libraries of much wealthier families, demonstrating how the material practices of gentility figured in larger concepts of politeness and taste that made the 'nobility and gentry' (as they were styled in concert announcements during the period) a legible social grouping despite variation in income.

Like music collections further up the economic scale, the Austen books bring together a broad range of music. Eighteen albums compiled by members of the Austen family are known today, including a total of approximately six hundred

Figure 2.1 Jane Austen"s vocal manuscript of Tommaso Giordani, 'Queen Mary's Lamentation', text by Anne Hunter. See Austen's letter of 8–9 February 1807 (letter 50) for a mention of this song. © Jane Austen's House Museum. Image by the University of Southampton Digitisation Unit.

pieces.[3] Although all the music is suitable for domestic performance, there are significant differences in format, scoring, level of difficulty, language and register. The books mainly contain solos and duets for voice, keyboard and harp, though many pieces feature optional parts for other instruments (especially flute and violin), and some theatrical and operatic music is notated in score rather than with keyboard accompaniment. The genres range from short overtures, songs, glees and dances to longer multi-movement works such as keyboard sonatas and more complex vocal music drawn from Italian opera. And although I will refer to them as the Austen music 'collection', the surviving volumes were owned by different members of the extended family, and copied or compiled over a long period between roughly 1750 and 1825.

The Austen collection includes binder's volumes – compilations of individually purchased sheet music, subsequently bound together in a personal album – each of which may contain thirty or more separate items. It also features manuscript copybooks, purchased as blank, ruled music books into which users entered pieces by hand, usually over a period of several months or years. Other manuscript books were compiled from separate items copied onto loose sheets of printed music paper, subsequently bound together, and there are a few examples of volumes mixing manuscript and print. Jane Austen owned books of several types: she filled two manuscript copybooks (fig. 2.1); owned binder's volumes of printed sheet music that she may have assembled herself; and her ownership marks also appear in a 'scrapbook' of mixed print and manuscript items that was probably begun by older relatives before it came into her possession (fig. 2.2). She also certainly knew volumes copied or compiled by other family members, including her sisters-in-law Elizabeth Bridges (who married Austen's brother Edward in 1791) and Eliza de Feuillide (Austen's cousin, and wife of her brother Henry, whom she married in 1797).

The volumes reflect larger currents of geography and musical availability, as well as the biographies, choices and abilities of individual copyists and compilers. For example, Eliza de Feuillide's years in Paris, where she began to study the harp, are reflected in her copies of French periodical publications for the instrument.[4] Elizabeth Bridges, daughter of a baronet, was educated at an exclusive London boarding school where music played an important role; her books include more difficult keyboard music as well as the greatest amount of Italian operatic music, by this time long connected with aristocratic taste.[5] Austen's own books show familiarity with an international repertoire that complicates notions of a limited provincial outlook that are still sometimes applied to her work.

Although the books yield perspectives on personal identities and circumstances, they speak equally eloquently of connections between their owners. Several books include material associated with more than one user. Austen's hand appears amid many others in a volume of miscellaneous manuscript items copied on different papers, possibly representing loose material bound up after Jane's death by her sister Cassandra. The

Contents

inscription 'Miss Finch' on an item in a binder's volume that belonged to Elizabeth Bridges indicates that this piece once belonged to Anne Finch, a musical friend in the Kentish Finch/Finch-Hatton family.[6] New annotations and signatures show that books made by the previous generation were reused, and material copied or purchased by older relatives was bound up in younger family members' albums. For example, one Austen family scribe – possibly Austen's niece Fanny Knight – created the manuscript indices to several volumes compiled by other family members. Henry Austen's second wife Eleanor Jackson's book of songs includes pieces with dedications to her mother, suggesting that Eleanor inherited these items before having them bound with her own music. Here again the Austens' practice matches that of other, sometimes much grander, collections. For example, binder's volumes owned by successive duchesses of St Albans show that Maria Nelthorpe, second wife of the eighth duke, bound up items purchased by her husband's first wife, Charlotte Carter Thelwall, in volumes stamped with her own name. Maria's volumes were in turn annotated, and supplied with new bookplates, by her son's second wife Elizabeth Gubbins. Women inherited music not just from first wives and mothers-in-law, but from unmarried or widowed female relatives: Jane Austen's music books were inherited by her sister, and probably arrived at the Knight family library through a subsequent gift to a niece. Similarly, at Killerton House in Devon, Mary Erskine – wife of Sir Thomas Dyke Acland, 11th baronet – inherited music from her mother-in-law, her unmarried maternal aunt and her husband's unmarried sister.[7] That music was considered a properly feminine possession is clear from volumes preserving the marks of several generations of women, while the collections as a whole demonstrate how the patrilinear superstructure created and organized material connections between them.

Overlapping material traces create the impression of a conversation through and about music that involved a wide circle of family and friends. This conversation began early in Jane Austen's life. Music making featured strongly in eighteenth-century debates over the accomplishments, the suite of tasteful attainments considered desirable for elite girls. Contemporary opposition often represented the accomplishments as at best a form of mere ornament, a waste of valuable time that might be spent on more serious study (fig. 2.3).[8] Much modern scholarship has followed this negative assessment in considering musical training as a form of constraint.[9] Accounts of the accomplishments often also figure music as an asset on the marriage market to the exclusion of other uses, with sisters and acquaintances vying for attention from potential husbands. While music could certainly serve as a field for comparison and competition – as in *Pride and Prejudice*, where Austen contrasts Caroline Bingley's showy virtuosity with Elizabeth Bennet's easy gentility – music as a sociable practice had many roles beyond the attraction of suitors.

Music copying and collection could serve to form and maintain bonds between women that often pass uncommented in accounts of the accomplishments and their

Figure 2.3 James Gillray, 1798, satirical cartoon entitled *Country concert, or an evening's entertainment*. Oxford, Bodleian Library, John Johnson Collection, Concert bills folder 2 (52).

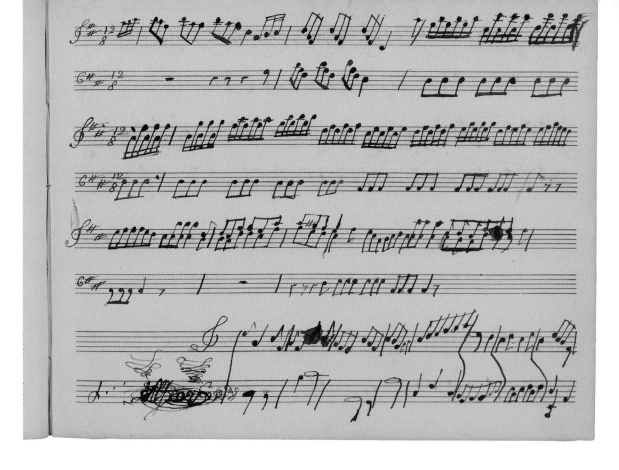

uses, fostering intergenerational ties as well as those with sisters and friends. Older women often used the blank pages in their own manuscript albums to instruct children. Two of the Austen music books were originally copied in the mid-1750s by Ann Cawley, a relative of Jane Austen's mother.[10] Probably in March 1783, Jane and Cassandra Austen and their cousin Jane Cooper – aged 7, 10 and 12 respectively – were sent to Oxford to be taught by the childless Mrs Cawley, who had been widowed in 1777 and may have begun taking in pupils at that time. Mrs Cawley apparently used her old music copybooks to provide musical instruction, noting dates in the early 1780s for lessons, payments and harpsichord tuning. Both books contain pages of practice music writing, some fairly accomplished, as if made by a child already reasonably skilled with a pen, while others were done by a younger writer – possibly the 7-year-old Jane – whose entries are both musically nonsensical and graphically inexpert, with unsteady lines and ink blots testifying to relative inexperience in writing of any kind (fig. 2.4).

Skill in writing out music grew along with instruction in performance. Austen probably continued music study at the Abbey House School in Reading in 1785–6, as music lessons were offered there; but her family did not yet own a piano. They borrowed one in 1786 when Eliza de Feuillide came to visit the Austen's Steventon vicarage for the Christmas season: a letter from Mrs Austen describes how Eliza played to the family every day.[11] It was perhaps her French cousin's example that encouraged Jane's own musical efforts, and Eliza may have provided some instruction during her

Figure 2.4 Children's writing in a manuscript book originally copied by Ann Cawley. © Richard Jenkyns. Image by the University of Southampton Digitisation Unit.

regular visits to Steventon in subsequent years. The Austen family acquired a piano for Jane – always referred to as hers in letters and memoirs, rather than as a general family instrument – and by the mid-1790s she was receiving lessons from George Chard, assistant organist at Winchester Cathedral.[12] Jane's Ganer square piano was kept in an upstairs sitting room that was converted from a bedroom in 1795 for Jane and Cassandra's use; they called it the dressing room. On 1 December 1798 (letter 13) Austen wrote to her sister that she felt 'more elegant' there than in the parlour.[13] Such semi-intimate feminine spaces were frequently used for music-making as well as for reading books and writing letters: in *Lady Susan* (letter 17), the 'small pianoforté' is moved into the dressing room so Frederica can practise there all day – a ruse to keep her away from Mrs Vernon – and in *Pride and Prejudice* (ch. 55), Mary Bennet retires to her upstairs piano in the same way that her father retreats to his library.[14]

At around this time Jane Austen seems to have begun two copybooks, devoted to keyboard and vocal music respectively. Both are notated in oblong folio music manuscript books produced by London publishers in the late eighteenth century. Featuring repertoire that appeared in printed publications from *c.*1790 onward, they suggest that copying began in the early to mid-1790s. A teasing exchange with her sister-in-law Elizabeth Bridges in a letter of 8 January 1799 (letter 17) suggests that Austen was spending significant amounts of time copying music. Austen's copybooks resemble other manuscript music books compiled by contemporaries, such as those made between 1796 and 1801 by Elizabeth Sykes of Sledmere and her cousin Mary Egerton of Tatton Park.[15] Copyists might obtain printed sheet music for this purpose from circulating libraries, but also – and perhaps more usually – they borrowed music from friends and relations. This could be a way of making sheet music stretch to more players: pieces that appear in one family member's album in print sometimes show up in another's in manuscript, perhaps a reflection of the copyist's relatively modest means, the difficulty of obtaining music in the provinces, or both.

But even when expense or availability posed no problems, exchanging music served to form or cement social bonds: young women of the early nineteenth century swapped notated music as today's teenagers exchange music downloads, with manuscript copybooks and sheet music compilation acting similarly to the personal collection of music on a tape, CD or media player in the recording age. Blank manuscript copybooks were popular gifts for young women, and one or both of Austen's copybooks may have been such a present. This seems particularly likely for CHWJA/19/2, whose title page features an engraved cherub holding a billowing label inscribed 'Juvenile Songs and Lessons' with, in smaller writing underneath, 'For young beginners who don't know enough to practise' (fig. 2.5). While the second line is in Austen's hand, the main inscription seems to have been written by someone else, possibly Eliza de Feuillide. Whether or not the book was a gift from Eliza, she was the source for a portion of the contents: for example, the overture to Jean-Baptiste Le Moyne's opera *Les Prétendus*

Figure 2.5 Austen's keyboard manuscript, showing the publisher's engraved title page with manuscript inscription. © Jane Austen's House Museum. Image by the University of Southampton Digitisation Unit.

p. 46 **Figure 2.6** Jane Austen's copy of Jean-Baptiste Lemoyne's overture to *Les Pretendus* (1789), arranged by Pierre Dufeille, known as Blattman, in her keyboard manuscript. © Jane Austen's House Museum. Image by the University of Southampton Digitisation Unit.

p. 47 **Figure 2.7** Eliza de Feuillide's harp music in a binder's volume of Parisian periodical publications. Jean-Baptiste Lemoyne, overture to *Les Pretendus* (1789), arranged for harp by Pierre Dufeuille, known as Blattman; published in the *Feuilles de Terpsichore* 5e année, no. 37 (July 1789). © Richard Jenkyns. Image by the University of Southampton Digitisation Unit.

(1789), which Austen faithfully copied from a harp arrangement originally owned by Eliza (figs 2.6 and 2.7).

Such interactions through sharing and copying music were widespread among gentry women. Elizabeth Sykes's 1801 manuscript album, for example, contains pieces copied for her by Mary Egerton, two years before Elizabeth's marriage made her Mary's sister-in-law. By the 1820s it had become increasingly common for girls to record the dates and donor names for sheet music they were given or pieces that they copied. Another volume at Tatton Park, possibly owned by Elizabeth Sykes's daughter Charlotte, has both printed sheet music and manuscript copies labelled with donor names mixed together in a single book. Many girls kept entire manuscript albums devoted to such exchanges: one of Elizabeth Gaskell's manuscripts, dated 1825 from Avonbank where she was at school, labels dozens of pieces with the names of classmates from whom she obtained them.[16] The exchange of music could also serve as material conveyance for other forms of emotional communication. In November 1814, Fanny Knight, desperate for her aunt Jane's advice about a marriage proposal but unwilling to have other family members aware of the discussion, sent a letter – possibly enclosing one from her suitor as well – to Austen in a parcel of music.[17] The incident has obvious parallels with the transmission of Robert Martin's letter to Harriet Smith in *Emma* (ch. 7): the young farmer puts his marriage proposal into a parcel of songs that his sister Elizabeth had borrowed from Harriet for copying.

In *Emma*, the exchange of music takes a minor role in comparison with Harriet's compilation of a book of charades and riddles, but both activities connect to a broader domestic culture of feminine craft. Harriet collects items for her book from friends and acquaintances in the same way that women collected music; she has 'a very pretty hand' and decorates the pages with figures and monograms (ch. 7). Fancy writing often appears in manuscript music albums, and many women included decorative titles and text hands to increase the attractiveness of their work. Caroline Austen remarked that her Aunt Jane's music manuscripts were copied 'so neatly and correctly, that it was as easy to read as print'; she connected this quality of neatness to Austen's fine embroidery, her excellent handwriting and the handsome finish of her letters.[18] Austen's music copying can be linked to her other craft activities of the 1790s; for example, the compilation of her manuscripts of teenage writings, including 'The History of England', with its watercolour portraits by Cassandra. Some contemporary music books also include drawings, another aspect of the accomplishments: one Austen album includes a sketch of a woman's head at the opening of a sonata movement, and a drawing of a horse in the inside back cover (fig. 2.8). The high rag content of contemporary paper meant that even needlework skills might be brought to bear on musical materials: the Austens' battered copy of the Winchester College song 'Dulce domum' in the family scrapbook developed a tear across the middle of the song sheet that was neatly sewn up by an early user (fig. 2.9).

Cipran delt   Strongthair

LONDON   Sold by Longman & Brodcrip N.º 26, Cheapside & N.º 13 Hay Market.

Ouverture des Pretendus

146 *Feuille de Terpsichore*, Prix 1.ᵗᵗ 4.ˢ A Paris Chez Cousineau rue des Poulie

Ouverture des Prétendus. Musique de M. Le Moine.

Allegro. Arrangée par M. Blattman avec accomp.ᵗ de Violon.

5ᵉ Année
N.º 37.
Harpe

Allegretto
Andantino
mez. forte
forte
mez. for.
forte
forte
fine
piano
Da Capo

The handmade aspect of manuscript copies contributed to their significance for early owners. Sharing in the sentimental attachments of handcrafted decorative objects in this period, manuscripts had the additional dimension of preserving the personal material trace of the copyist in their handwriting. As the volume of print material exploded in the second half of the eighteenth century, manuscripts began to acquire new meanings that included enhanced affective associations. That Austen and her family viewed manuscripts in this way is suggested not only by the careful curation of her teenage writings, but also by the preservation of her two music copybooks, which she kept even when her piano and many other music books were sold in 1801.[19] Similarly, loose manuscripts were kept and bound by later Austen family members, perhaps as much for a memento of the music-making of their copyists as to bring the music together for new users. The worth accorded to domestic music manuscripts by early owners is at odds with the significance granted to such manuscripts today. As copies of existing print sources rather than products of compositional process, they do not fit into the conventional scholarly protocols for the manuscripts of significant composers; and as evidence of the circulation of music, they do not fit neatly into narratives about the gradual ascendancy of print. Like the activity of domestic music making itself, the fabrication of manuscript music books can easily become entangled in debates over ornament and accomplishment; so that the crafting of musical material by women at home becomes unhelpfully tarred with the brush of 'neither useful, nor really art' that has dogged assessments of women's handicrafts and decorative arts in the period.[20]

If manuscript copying can be read as related to the culture of domestic craft, sheet music has more often been seen as a commodity.[21] The explosion of the music printing trade in the late eighteenth century was accompanied by new marketing strategies, many targeted at female buyers. Women's engagement with sheet music is thus easily dismissed as part of a feminine culture of consumption, similar to the acquisition of fans, ribbons or hats in being driven by fashion rather than artistic imperatives. Women's practices of buying and binding sheet music have thus often been understood as a trivial form of accumulation rather than arising from collector mentalities based on intellectual principles, and in consequence they do not figure in the history of collection in the same way as masculine acquisition of books. Recent scholarship on gender and material culture in the eighteenth century provides a more complex picture of women's purchasing habits and their meaning, however.[22] Understanding that all consumption (including men's book and art collection) has social and relational aspects, and that women's acquisition of goods cannot be simply reduced to the decorative, allows for more nuanced understanding of the meanings attached to the collection of printed sheet music.

Although provincial buyers could obtain music from local music shops, London was the centre of the music publishing trade, and most vocal music in particular was

opposite **Figure 2.8** Marginal drawing in a copy of an unidentified keyboard sonata in a binder's volume of items copied by various Austen family members, including Jane Austen. © Richard Jenkyns. Image by the University of Southampton Digitisation Unit.

DOMUM.

Con - ci - na - mus O So - da - les! E - ja! qu - id fi - - le - mus?

No - bi - le can - ti - cum, Dulce me - los, Domum. Dul - ce Do - mum re - - fo - ne - mus.

Chorus.

Do - mum, Do - mum, Dul - ce Do - mum, Do - mum, Do - mum, Dul - ce Do - mum,

Dul - ce, Dul - ce, Dul - ce, Do - mum, Dul - ce Do - mum re - - fo - ne - mus.

2

Appropinquat ecce! felex
Hora gaudiorum:
Poft grave tædium
Advenit omnium
Meta petita laborum.
Domum, &c.

3

Mufa! libros mitte, feffa;
Mitte penfa dura:
Mitte negotium;
Jam datur otium:
Me mea mittito cura!
Domum, &c.

4

Ridet annus, prata rident:
Nofque rideamus.
Jam repetit Domum
Daulias advena:
Nofque Domum repetamus.
Domum, &c.

Heus! Rogere! fer caballos:
Eja! nunc eamus;
Limen amabile,
Matris et ofcula,
Suaviter et repetamus.
Domum, &c.

6

Concinamus ad Penates;
Vox et audiatur:
Phofphore! quid jubar,
Segnius emicans,
Gaudia noftra moratur?
Domum, &c.

linked with London pleasure gardens, concerts or shows. The music publishers whose prints dominate the Austen albums – Bland, Preston, Dale and Birchall, for example – had addresses in fashionable shopping streets, where purchasers could acquire the latest music as part of the shopping expeditions that formed an important part of the period's respectable sociability.[23] Writing to Cassandra on 16 September 1813 (letter 88), Jane Austen described a day's shopping that involved the purchase of a dinner set from Wedgwood, the acquisition of lace, stockings and netting from other purveyors in the area around Leicester Square, and a stop at Robert Birchall's shop in New Bond Street to buy music, including a set of pieces that had been requested by family friend Martha Lloyd. This kind of 'proxy shopping', in which a friend or family member obtained items for someone else, was an important aspect of contemporary social glue.[24] The folds still evident on some sheet music, and the addresses sometimes written on the outside blank covers, suggest that it was posted to performers in the provinces by friends or relatives in urban centres. Eleanor Jackson's songbook includes several examples of pieces with folds or addresses suggesting they were sent by post, and in a letter of 21 February 1817 (letter 151), Jane Austen thanked Fanny Knight for sending a set of quadrilles.

Buyers often signed their sheet music on purchase, and sometimes added the date: this is the case for Elizabeth Bridges' music acquired before her marriage. Composer or publisher signatures on the copies began to become fashionable in the 1790s, assuring the buyer of the authenticity and accuracy of the musical content. Eleanor Jackson's songbook contains enough such signatures that it begins to look like an autograph collection. As in other aspects of sheet music consumption, music publishers soon began to capitalize on the trend by including engraved composer signatures on their title pages, mimicking the look of the handwritten autographs and commodifying the 'inner circle' air of personal connection they implied.

Owners left sheet music unbound for varying amounts of time but, most commonly, binder's volumes include items purchased within one to five years. Collections from before 1790 have diverse binding styles, and their contents are equally varied in size, quality of printing and print layout, with little standardization of, for example, the format of songs. These could appear in score, or with keyboard accompaniment; with figured bass or a written-out realization; with vocal text underlaid to the right hand, or vocal line on a separate stave. Some volumes in the Austen family collection reflect this variability, and they are also modestly bound. From the 1790s onward, buyers increasingly had sheet music bound into folio albums of a more uniform style, featuring half-calf bindings and covers of marbled paper over board. The spines usually feature some blind stamping or tooling, and the covers may include a gilt-stamped leather label with the owner's name or a content description. For example, Elizabeth Bridges' volume of keyboard music includes a front label in Italian, 'Cembalo' (harpsichord), and one of Jane Austen's books of vocal music is labelled 'Songs' (fig. 2.10). As the bindings began to show more conformity, music printers facilitated compilation by producing more

Figure 2.9 Sewn repairs to the Winchester College song 'Domum' in the 'scrapbook' album. © Jane Austen's House Museum. Image by the University of Southampton Digitisation Unit.

highly polished products – with more uniform sizes, more elegant engraving and more elaborate title pages – that looked better in such albums than the often rougher-looking sheet music of earlier times.

On purchase, sheet music entered the buyer's performance repertory, at least as long as the items remained unbound. Continuation of use after binding is less clear. Some owners seem to have bound up sheet music only when it was no longer in current use, in volumes too thick and tightly bound for music stands or keyboard instrument desks, and without any index or pagination permitting location of a particular item. For these volumes, the act of binding the sheet music up seems to signal the end of its usefulness as performance material and its move into a different realm of social significance. In other binder's volumes, manuscript annotations, such as new continuous pagination and tables of contents, made access to the individual items more efficient after binding. Most of the volumes in the Austen collections fall into this category: they are generally well indexed, usually include continuous pagination and most are slim enough to use comfortably at an instrument, suggesting that the music continued to serve for performance.

Compiling indices and adding continuous pagination were part of individualizing the music album, a process that began with the choice of repertoire and continued through the annotation of individual items, to the arrangement of content and selection of binding style. These elements of personalization provide connections between binder's volumes and manuscript copybooks, suggesting that the line between the fabrication of a personalized music book via the assembly of printed sheet music items and the construction of a personal collection through copying is less sharp than might first appear. This is even more clearly the case for volumes that bring together items copied on separate sheets of manuscript paper (rather than being written into a pre-assembled manuscript copybook) or that contain a mix of manuscript and printed items. A particularly fascinating example is the Austens' 'scrapbook', a volume that contains twenty manuscript items interspersed among nearly thirty printed pieces. Here, stubs in the binding enable the removal and addition of different items, which were glued into the stubs rather than being bound into the spine as they were in standard binder's volumes. The dates of individual items indicate that contents continued to be added over a long period, beginning *c*.1775 and continuing to *c*.1810. Austen herself seems to have compiled the manuscript index to this book; she certainly signed the title page and copied some of the manuscript items inserted between the older printed music items, which were probably acquired by an older relative who may have begun the book. This album may have started as a conventional binder's volume, but the flexibility of its subsequent use is more reminiscent of a scrapbook or manuscript miscellany.[25]

Several aspects of the circulation of music within gentry families have impeded its serious assessment as a contribution to intellectual life: the concept of accomplishments as trivial attainments; disregard for the feminine culture of domestic craft; the characterization of sheet music for the domestic market as commodity inimical to art. Yet closer study reveals many links between the making of music books and the practices associated with commonplacing, the compilation of manuscript miscellanies and other forms of creating and assembling texts, all of which were central to Georgian literary culture.[26] Scholars have emphasized the importance of these practices to the reading, writing and transmission of texts, in particular but not exclusively for women; and recent work on manuscript culture underlines the durability of these activities even as their meaning slowly shifted in the age of print.[27] Like commonplace books, music compilations provided their makers with opportunities to operate individual choices about musical repertories and styles, and to comment upon them through placement, juxtaposition and annotation; the act of making manuscript copies of printed music provided scribes with an insider's view on musical notation, form and style. Vocal music offered the further possibility of entry into broad-reaching textual networks, creating a route for the transmission of poetry in English and other languages.[28]

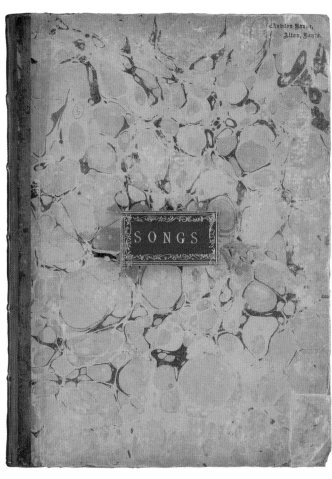

Austen's characters rarely buy or copy music. But nor do we see them copying poetry or annotating their reading, though we can imagine these practices behind the scenes of reading aloud and talking about books that are such a constant feature of Austen's fiction. The knowledge displayed by musical characters such as Jane Fairfax and Frank Churchill in *Emma*, Marianne Dashwood and John Willoughby in *Sense and Sensibility*, Mary Crawford in *Mansfield Park*, Anne Elliot in *Persuasion* and virtually every character in *Pride and Prejudice*, would have been obtained by engagement with the material stuff of music, just as it was by Austen herself. It is significant that intelligent conversation in Austen's novels – between Elizabeth Bennet and Fitzwilliam Darcy, for example, or Anne Elliot and Captain Harville – very often involves both music and books. Books of music like those Austen and her family owned and used were a significant part of the exchange of objects and ideas that for Austen is the basis of human social interaction and a central focus of her fiction.

Figure 2.10 Front cover of Jane Austen's volume of canzonet and Scots song prints. © Jane Austen's House Museum. Image by the University of Southampton Digitisation Unit.

1 See, for example, Patrick Piggott, *The Innocent Diversion: A Study of Music in the Life and Writings of Jane Austen*, Douglas Cleverdon, London, 1979; David Selwyn, *Jane Austen and Leisure*, Hambledon, London, 1999; Mollie Sandock, "'I burn with contempt for my foes": Jane Austen's Music Collection and Women's Lives in Regency England', *Persuasions*, vol. 23, 2001, pp. 105–17; Kathryn L. Libin, 'Daily Practice, Musical Accomplishment, and the Example of Jane Austen', in Natasha Duquette and Elizabeth Lenckos (eds), *Jane Austen and the Arts: Elegance, Propriety, Harmony*, Lehigh University Press, Bethlehem, PA, 2013, pp. 3–20.

2 Jeanice Brooks, 'Les collections féminines d'albums de partitions dans l'Angleterre au début du XIXe siècle', in Christine Ballman and Valérie Dufour (eds), *'La la la Maistre Henri': Mélanges de musicologie offerts à Henri Vanhulst*, Brepols, Turnhout, 2009, pp. 351–65; Jeanice Brooks, 'Musical Monuments for the Country House: Music, Collection and Display at Tatton Park', *Music & Letters*, vol. 91, 2010, pp. 513–35.

3 The books are available as digital facsimiles at *The Austen Family Music Books*, <https://archive.org/details/austenfamilymusicbooks>. The discussion below identifies the books using the shelfmarks employed in this digital facsimile edition. See also Samantha Carrasco, 'The Austen Family Music Books and Hampshire Music Culture, 1770–1820', PhD thesis, University of Southampton, 2013.

4 Deirdre Le Faye, *Jane Austen's 'Outlandish Cousin': The Life and Letters of Eliza de Feuillide*, British Library, London, 2002; Adrian Rose, 'Jane Austen's Cousin, Eliza de Feuillide, and Music in Paris c.1780–90', *The Consort*, vol. 69, 2013, pp. 71–86.

5 Elizabeth attended the Misses Stevenson's school in Bloomsbury in the 1780s (Deirdre Le Faye, *Jane Austen: A Family Record*, Cambridge University Press, Cambridge, 2004, p. 70). On opera's elite associations, see Jennifer Hall-Witt, *Fashionable Acts: Opera and Elite Culture in London*, 1780–1880, University of New England Press, Lebanon, NH, 2007.

6 In a letter of 5 September 1796 (letter 5) to her sister Cassandra, Jane Austen describes an informal ball with the Bridges family during which Anne Finch played for the dancing.

7 On the St Albans and Killerton collections, see Brooks, 'Les collections féminines'.

8 On music in educational debates, see Leslie Ritchie, *Women Writing Music in Late Eighteenth-Century England: Social Harmony in Literature and Performance*, Ashgate, Aldershot, 2008, pp. 36–56.

9 See, for example, Richard Leppert, *Music and Image: Domesticity, Ideology and Socio-Cultural Formation in Eighteenth-Century England*, Cambridge University Press, Cambridge, 1988, pp. 28–50. On the tendency for modern scholarship to frame the eighteenth-century home as prison, see Amanda Vickery, *Behind Closed Doors: At Home in Georgian England*, Yale University Press, New Haven, CT, 2009, p. 3.

10 Jenkins 01 features her signature, and CHWJA/19/1 was mainly copied by the same scribe. On Mrs Cawley, see Elizabeth Boardman, 'Mrs Cawley and Brasenose College', *Collected Reports of the Jane Austen Society* 2001–2005, Jane Austen Society, Winchester, 2005, pp. 201–8.

11 Le Faye, *Family Record*, p. 57.

12 Austen's niece Anna Lefroy remembered a music master coming to Steventon (Austen-Leigh, *Memoir*, ed. Sutherland, p. 183). Austen mentions Chard in a letter of 1 September 1796 (letter 4).

13 On the dressing room, see Deirdre Le Faye, *Jane Austen: The World of Her Novels*, Frances Lincoln, London, 2002, p. 140. Anna Lefroy remembered 'Aunt Jane's Pianoforte' in the room; Anna was born in 1793, so the memory probably dates from the late 1790s.

14 See Pierre Dubois, *Music in the Georgian Novel*, Cambridge University Press, Cambridge, 2015, p. 276.

15 Brooks, 'Musical Monuments', pp. 517–19.

16 Manchester, Central Library, MS f 823.894C1.

17 In her response, Austen congratulates Fanny on the ruse: 'Your sending the Music was an admirable device, it made everything easy, & I do not know how I could have accounted for the parcel otherwise; for tho' your dear Papa most conscientiously hunted about till he found me alone in the Din⁹-parlour, Your Aunt C. had seen that he *had* a parcel to deliver.—As it was however, I do not think anything was suspected' (18 November 1814, letter 109).

18 Austen-Leigh, *Memoir*, ed. Sutherland, p. 171.

19 The *Reading Mercury* notice of the Steventon parsonage sale included 'a piano forte in a handsome case (by Ganer) [and] a large collection of music by the most celebrated composers'. See <http://www.victoriacountyhistory. ac.uk/explore/sites/explore/files/explore_assets/2013/03/09/steventon_parsonage_sale_transcript.pdf>.

20 Vickery, *Behind Closed Doors*, p. 231.

21 James Davies, 'Julia's Gift: The Social Life of Scores, c.1830', *Journal of the Royal Musical Association*, vol. 131, 2006, pp. 287–309.

22 John Styles and Amanda Vickery (eds), *Gender, Taste, and Material Culture in Britain and North America*, 1700–1830, Yale University Press, New Haven, CT and London, 2006, pp. 12–13.

23 For addresses, see Charles Humphries and William C. Smith, *Music Publishing in the British Isles from the Beginning Until the Middle of the Nineteenth Century*, 2nd edition, Blackwell, Oxford, 1970.

24 Claire Walsh, 'Shops, Shopping, and the Art of Decision Making in Eighteenth-Century England', in Styles and Vickery (eds), *Gender, Taste, and Material Culture*, pp. 151–77.

25 Robert K. Wallace, 'Jane Austen's Neglected Song Book', *Collected Reports of the Jane Austen Society* 1976–1985, Jane Austen Society, Chippenham, 1989, pp. 121–5.

26 See Candace Bailey, 'Binder's Volumes as Musical Commonplace Books: The Transmission of Cultural Codes in the Antebellum South', *Journal of the Society for American Music*, vol. 10, no. 4, 2016, pp. 446–69.

27 See, for example, Margaret J.M. Ezell, *Social Authorship and the Advent of Print*, Johns Hopkins University Press, Baltimore, MD, 1999; David Allan, *Commonplace Books and Reading in Georgian England*, Cambridge University Press, Cambridge, 2010.

28 Jeanice Brooks, 'In Search of Austen's "Missing Songs"', *Review of English Studies*, n.s. vol. 67, 2016, pp. 914–45.

3

Jane Austen's Pelisse-Coat

Hilary Davidson

Somewhere around 1813 Jane Austen may have acquired a silk pelisse. It could not have been before 1812; it may have been in 1814. A pelisse is a kind of coat-dress, made popular after women's clothing lost bulky skirts and became columnar in the late 1790s. This one is made of an expensive silk, patterned with falling oak leaves, lined in white silk, and adorned with more silk cord (fig. 3.1). Austen had only three or four short years to wear it before her untimely death in 1817. The barely worn material, reminder of a beloved aunt, stayed in the family, now with one member and now another, until it came to Hampshire County Museums and Archive Service in 1993. By that point, no one could quite remember if it had really been Jane Austen's; but her fame had grown so extraordinarily in the intervening years that even the possibility it had belonged to her was enough to make the pelisse an important object. Today, most of the known Austen 'relics' are jewellery and accessories: a turquoise ring, a bracelet, a topaz cross, a muslin scarf.[1] Clothing is different. It envelops and reflects the body, especially the body it was made for in the early nineteenth century before mass-manufacture and the sewing machine. A garment is where style and consumer cultures of an age manifest themselves, demonstrating how the wearer may have negotiated those cultures to reflect her own taste and situation in life. It also leaves a template for what her body may have been. I shall use this pelisse, the only known garment with a strong Austen connection, to explore the world of Regency dress production and fashion consumption as Jane Austen would have known it and as she extended it to the worlds of her fictional characters.

How did a woman obtain clothing in the 1810s? It was not a simple business, as Austen complained as early as 24 December 1798: 'I cannot determine what to do about my new Gown; I wish such things were to be bought ready made' (letter 15). Women made small linen items such as caps and shifts at home for themselves and shirts for their menfolk. In larger gentry families, a seamstress might be brought in for days or

Opposite and overleaf

Figure 3.1 Jane Austen's pelisse: front and back views. © Hampshire County Council. Provided by the Hampshire Cultural Trust.

a week at a time to do bulk manufacture of such essentials. These intimate linen garments were a Regency woman's first layer of clothing. Over the shift she wore stays (a corset). Although softer, less heavily boned and more body-shaped than the mono-bosomed contraptions of the late eighteenth century, short or long stays were still required to mould the finished outer figure. Bought from professional, usually male, staymakers, they were an infrequent investment for the gentry shopper.[2] Then came petticoats, less like underwear than underskirts that were sometimes visible. There was a hierarchy of petticoats from plain white linen or, increasingly, cotton lining garments, to skirts of finer quality, meant to be seen and made of livelier textiles. Old gowns that had become too shabby to wear were recycled as visible petticoats. Jane Austen confided in the same early letter (24 December 1798) to her sister Cassandra: 'I will not be much longer libelled by the possession of my coarse spot[ted muslin], I shall turn it into a petticoat very soon.' Such is the kind Elizabeth Bennet reveals to be 'six inches deep in mud' in *Pride & Prejudice* (ch. 8) as the result of prudently tucking up her better outer skirt. In winter or damp climes, a wool flannel petticoat was an essential if unglamorous addition.

So far, so reasonably straightforward. It is the provision of outer clothing that taxed and engaged Austen and her contemporaries. Women wore a dress, usually called a gown, as their main garment, complemented by a variety of outerwear, from the high-waisted, short spencer jacket to the ubiquitous pelisse, cape and cloaks, in endless combination (fig. 3.2a and 3.2b). To get a gown, first the fabric must be purchased. The length of uncut cloth required for the purpose was also called a gown, as it had been in the eighteenth century and as Austen makes explicit in a letter of 20 May 1813: 'I shall take the opportunity of getting my Mother's gown—; so, by 3 o'clock in the afternoon she may consider herself the owner of 7 yds of B[lac]k Sarsenet' (letter 84). The garment and its material are synonymous. But where and how to make this purchase? Villages and small towns had their shops selling textiles, like the indispensable Ford's in *Emma*'s Highbury, 'the principal woollen-draper, linen-draper, and haberdasher's shop united; the shop first in size and fashion in the place' (ch. 21). Austen and her family too sought textiles in their various local towns of Alton, Basingstoke and Southampton in Hampshire. Major purchases, however, were if possible executed in the metropolises of London and to a lesser extent Bath. The silk for this pelisse would have constituted a major purchase. It is made of a twilled, figured silk sarcenet (also spelled sarsnet or sarsenet), of a brown ground with a pattern of oak leaves in pale gold silk. Given the date and the wartime banning of French imports, it was almost certainly woven in England. Although genuine Indian muslins could compete in price, silk, the 'queen of textiles', maintained its centuries-old status as the most luxurious fabric in the hierarchy of fashionable cloths. The more complicated the weave, the more labour involved, and so the more it cost. A decorative silk, such as the sarcenet, would have represented a considerable outlay for Austen. Unfortunately, only one of her letters survives from late 1812 when it is most likely the fabric was bought, and we have no record of any purchase by her that matches this cloth.

Despite this, research into other contemporary women's account-keeping reveals what such a textile might have cost. Barbara Johnson (1738–1825) indefatigably kept a record throughout her life of all her clothing fabric purchases, together with a swatch of the material, in a large account book. This unique record is now in the Victoria & Albert Museum (V&A). Johnson purchased a number of plain and twilled and figured sarcenets in the early nineteenth century. One, from 1809, is a very close match in colour, weave and design to the Austen pelisse silk. It cost nine shillings and sixpence per yard (fig. 3.3). A similarly scaled small-leaf-patterned sarcenet is used in an 1807 pelisse now in the collection of the Fashion Museum, Bath.[3] After undertaking a detailed replication of the Austen pelisse, I calculated it would take 7.5 yards of silk to make the garment.[4] Silk fabrics had much narrower widths than cotton, linen and wool cloths, running from half a yard (18 inches) wide to around 22 inches. Accordingly, silk not only cost more per yard, the purchaser also needed more of those yards to make into clothing. A plain brown sarcenet for a pelisse cost Barbara Johnson six shillings a yard in 1811 and, for a gown, the same amount in 1814. A twilled sarcenet cost her nearly the same, at 5s.9d. a yard in 1812.

Sarcenet was one of the most popular clothing fabrics. It appears frequently in accounts for outer fabrics and for linings. Initially, I thought the white, plain-weave silk lining of the pelisse was also a sarcenet, of the sort bought by London-based widow Mrs Mary Topham (1752–1825) in 1812 to line a white satin garment.[5] However, the lining's softness, its light weight, slight shine and translucency have since made me revise the identification to persian, an even commoner fabric, popular for its relative cheapness. In December 1814, Austen delighted in a letter from her niece Anna Lefroy describing a shopping expedition for persian: 'I was particularly amused with your picture of Grafton House; —it is just so. –How much I should like finding you there one day, seated on your high stool, with 15 rolls of persian before you' (letter 116). Almost twenty years earlier, on 9 January 1796, she

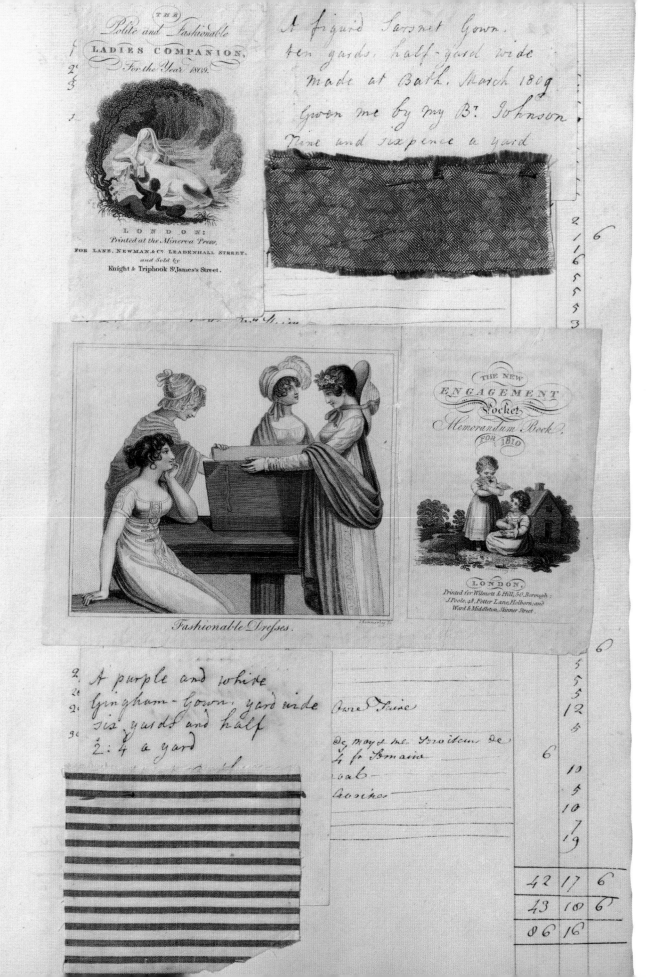

A figured Sarsnet Gown.
ten yards, half-yard wide
made at Bath. March 1809
Given me by my B⁰ Johnson.
Nine and sixpence a yard

2 | 16 5 5 3

Fashionable Dresses.

A purple and white
Gingham-Gown, yard wide
six yards and half
2:4 a yard

6

5 5 5 12 5

6

10 5 10 7 19

42	17	6
43	10	6
86	16	

Bought of B. M. Nias & Company,
N.⁴ Charles Street, Middlesex Hospital,
WHOLESALE AND RETAIL LINEN DRAPERS,
and Importers of Turkey Carpets, &c.

pp. 60–61

Figure 3.2a Fashion plate from Ackermann's *Repository* showing a fur-trimmed pelisse, November 1811. Wikimedia Commons.

Figure 3.2b Fashion plate from *La Belle Assemblée*, April 1814. Oxford, Bodleian Library, Per. 2474 d.188, before p. 181.

opposite **Figure 3.3** A page from Barbara Johnson's album showing a sample of sarcenet (1809). © Victoria and Albert Museum, London.

above **Figure 3.4** Bill heading showing an illustration of a draper's window. Oxford, Bodleian Library, John Johnson Collection, Bill Headings 22 (71).

herself had admitted to spending all her money on 'white gloves and pink persian' (letter 1). Persian was around half the price of sarcenet.[6] This economy would have suited Austen's always straitened purse more comfortably.

Grafton House, on the corner of Grafton Street and New Bond Street in fashionable Mayfair, was one of the major London drapery 'warehouses' – large retail and wholesale emporia – and one the Austen family patronized when they were in town (fig. 3.4). When, in *Pride and Prejudice*, Mrs Bennet panics about Lydia's wedding clothes and stirs herself to write to her sister Gardiner about the business (ch. 49), it is because the girl, lacking her female relatives' expertise in shopping, 'does not know which are the best warehouses'. This small detail raises two important points about the process of buying clothes in Regency England. First, it relied on shoppers' prior experience and knowledge of the products they purchased. Regency shoppers dealt intimately with cloth every day of their lives; the difference between a 'true Indian muslin' and an as-yet inferior British product would have been apparent immediately (as discussed in *Northanger Abbey*, ch. 3). With a growing number of retailers to choose from, all tempting the unwary shopper, understanding what would wash and wear well, what would fray, which dyes might be fast and what was a bargain depended on a near-intuitive haptic sense, residing in the hands and eyes of the would-be purchaser at the counter fingering the cloth to determine its qualities. Lydia Bennet, in particular, shows herself as insensible in her spending as in everything else. The 'ugly' bonnet she carelessly buys (ch. 39) while waiting for her sisters would have cost around a guinea, no small outlay for a girl spending a limited allowance from her father. It is more than even Mrs Bennet's over-fond maternal pride can countenance that Lydia should be let loose choosing 'all the particulars of calico, muslin, and cambric' (ch. 49) without an older woman to share her long experience in evaluating the textiles on offer.

The second point to note here is the communal nature of Regency shopping. New purchases often involved a number of people in a network of family and friends extending around the country. The gown we hear Austen buying for her mother in London in 1813 is the expression of a practice known as proxy shopping, where purchases were made by people in a relationship network for other people in that network, its bonds formed of trust and intimacy. Claire Walsh and Miles Lambert both explore the practice of 'familial commissioning' with its reliance 'on the informal personal or commercial networks that had long assisted in transferring material goods to the most rural locations in Britain'.[7] Proxies were not only economic agents, they were equally important as aesthetic agents, a responsibility requiring a degree of trust equal to the monetary one, but of more nebulous character. It is an anxious task to find a textile another person will agree is a 'pretty' cambric or a 'quality' muslin. The proxy shopper must 'think herself or himself into the skin of the person commissioning a purchase, intimately understanding that person's likes, dislikes and requirements'.[8] Family members made good proxy shoppers because of their implicitly shared understandings. The Austens constantly shopped on behalf of each other and close friends. Proxy shopping also crossed genders. Jane's brother Charles bought her silk stockings, for example, and although male proxy shopping tended towards handkerchiefs, bonnets and other smaller accessories, men seemed not 'to have been any less efficient at shopping or less interested in it than women'.[9] The pelisse sarcenet was so expensive Austen would have bought it herself, though she and Cassandra trusted each other with other textile purchases. Jane shopping in London on 18 April 1811 merrily admitted to 'spending all my Money; & what is worse for *you*, I have been spending yours too' on purchases including 10 yards of muslin, on the chance of her sister liking it as she knew the texture 'was just what we prefer', 'but at the same time if it sh^d not suit you, you must not think yourself at all obliged to take it; it is only 3/6 p^r y^d, & I sh^d not in the least mind keeping the whole' (letter 70).

So significant an investment as the pelisse would have run the gauntlet of family opinion. The Austen family network expected consumption to be shared and discussed collectively. When Jane bought even a pair of bargain gloves, she knew everybody at home would 'be hoping & predicting that they cannot be good for anything' (20 May 1813, letter 84). In the same vein, she disapproved of her niece Anna's purple pelisse, not so much for its surprising colour, but for suspecting 'nothing worse than its' being got in secret, & not owned to anybody' (30 November 1814, letter 114). Anna had trespassed against the family etiquette of discussion. Contrast this with the opinions freely expressed about Austen's new gown, recorded in a letter of 20 November 1800: 'Charles does not like it, but my father & Mary do; my Mother is very much reconciled to it, & as for James, he gives it the preference over every thing of the kind he ever saw' (letter 27). These fleeting comments expose the tangled webs of familial approval as well as the social and cultural obligations surrounding the getting of new clothes.

Austen's sarcenet purchase may have held further significance within her family in 1813. The figured pattern identified as oak leaves had strong associations with Britain's naval prowess during the sustained Napoleonic conflicts of the early nineteenth century, a navy in which two of her six brothers served.[10] From the official Royal Navy march 'Heart of Oak' (1760) to the profusion of oak-tree-laden mourning memorabilia produced for Nelson's funeral (1806), the oak leaf and acorn motifs expressed a patriotic Britishness invested in the navy. The design was popular enough at the time to appear also as a printed cotton cambric. The repeated use of a pattern in different fabrics was so unusual that I have not so far discovered another instance (fig. 3.5).

In the complicated business of getting new clothes in Regency England, the picture is a little less clear when it comes to having the fabric sewn up. This is a topic that would benefit from closer scholarly attention to how decisions about clothing styles were formed and new ideas transmitted. Austen never mentions how prevailing taste and 'fashion' at any particular moment connected with her own preferences and together shaped the form of the garment arriving from the maker. The moments of fabrics' transformation *into* dress are clouded, and her fiction matches this relative silence. Professional dressmaking is mentioned only in *Northanger Abbey* and *Persuasion*; in the latter, the reference to Mrs Croft's dress- or mantua-maker is introduced and abandoned in the discarded draft chapters of the novel's original ending.

Those who constructed women's clothing were known as mantua-makers, after the open-fronted women's gown popular since the late seventeenth century. 'Dressmaker' gradually replaced the older term beginning in about 1800 (fig. 3.6). Maria Edgeworth addressed the new phrase with a certain asperity in 1813: 'I have half an hour before the cursed mantuamaker, I beg her pardon *dressmakers* appointment.'[11] Mainly female, these professionals ranged from those with formal apprenticeship training, to an experienced maker, to women setting themselves up to make money from their sewing abilities in a reasonably respectable trade. Austen mentions an actual cost for manufacture only once, when during a stay in London she had pelisses sewn for herself and Cassandra by a 'young woman in this Neighbourhood' (18 April 1811, letter 70).[12] The maker charged 'only' eight shillings which Austen considered reasonable. In fact, seven to eight shillings is the remarkably consistent cost, with no increase for inflation, for the making of a dress across surviving accounts so far examined from the period *c.*1800– 20.[13] It is the extras, such as the value of the main fabric, the cost of the body lining, thread, ribbons and trimmings, which contributed most to final costs, from around a pound to as much as eight pounds, for women's garments amongst the gentry and middling sorts. When eight shillings is translated into its equivalent of £20–30 sterling in 2016, it is difficult to see how dress- and mantua-makers made a profit.[14] Although I am a quick and experienced hand-sewer, it still took me thirty hours of labour to produce the Austen pelisse replica. How long did it take those accustomed only to hand-sewing, to rhythms smoothed into automation by countless hours of repetition? And did they compensate for a labour-to-income shortfall through judicious mark-ups on the extras?

Could Jane Austen have made this pelisse herself? She was an excellent sewer. Her skills are best documented in letters where she records making shirts for her brothers, a common practice among women in a family who would make shirts by the half dozen or dozen.[15] Besides Austen's own high estimation of her skills, her nephew remembered in 1869 that

> Her needlework both plain and ornamental was excellent, and might almost have put a sewing machine to shame. She was considered especially great in satin stitch [possibly seen in the muslin shawl in Jane Austen's House Museum]. She spent much time in these occupations, and some of her merriest talk was over clothes which she and her companions were making, sometimes for themselves, and sometimes for the poor.[16]

'Clothes' in this context is a deceptive word since small frocks, shirts, aprons and other lap-sized garments are a different matter from full dresses. As dress historian Janet Arnold explains, 'It must have been a temptation for the amateur to run up a dress when they were as simple as those of the early 1800s. However they did need fitting— and probably a lot of muslin dresses made at home were worn for mornings, while the dressmaker… would have been called in to tackle the ones worn on more public occasions.'[17] Among gentry women it appears that even those in poorer circumstances availed themselves of mantua-makers for gowns and other long body garments.[18] Given the absence of references to making gowns in her letters, the necessary expertise in stitching and cutting, and the tendency for women not to make these outer items, especially in an expensive silk that required careful handling, the Austen pelisse fits perfectly and materially into the category of professionally made clothing.

Figure 3.5 Figured cambric from Ackermann's *Repository*, May 1812. © Hilary Davidson.

In support, the Austen pelisse reveals its professional origins in the complex cut of the sleeve, which must derive from an expert pattern-drafter. It cannot, however, be the pelisse made in London, and described in the letter of 18 April 1811 as having expensive buttons, since this pelisse has no buttons and can be dated stylistically to between 1812 and 1814. Dating a garment relies on subtle points of observation and differentiation. Here, the amount and positioning of pleating and fullness in the sleeve head are the best date indicators. The high neck, puffed decoration and small amount of increase in the lower skirt also tally with garments and engraved fashion plates included in magazines from this date. The decoration is restrained for a garment of the 1810s. Mantua-makers' bills itemized separately the making-up costs from the 'body lining', thread and any trimmings and decoration, all of which contributed to the final style and could be expensive outlays. Mrs Topham's accounts give a fuller idea of the costs and components involved in a pelisse. On 23 April 1814 she bought '8 yards of Twilled Sarcenet 8/6 for Pelisse', total £3.8s. Then she bought an extra half-yard, and two bottles of 'Green tincture', which may have been for dying the silk, since on 3 May she added 7 yards and a half of 'Green Trimming' for the pelisse (15s.) with two frogs (10d.) – a knotted braid fastening – and 2 yards of cord (1s.6d.).[19] Cord also features on the Austen pelisse. The additional expenses itemized above were for embellishing Mrs Topham's pelisse after it was made up and suggest that the Austen cord could have been bought and applied separately, though, since the thread and the stitching hand are the same as the rest of the construction, it was sewn on when the gown was made. The total documented cost of Mrs Topham's 1814 pelisse was £4.15s.1d., excluding thread and making.

Even using cheaper sarcenet, like Barbara Johnson's at around 2s.6d. a yard less, the financial investment in materials for such an item emphasizes the quality and importance as an article of clothing of the Austen pelisse. I estimate it to have cost somewhere around £5.11s.6d. total, including the labour of the dress- or mantua-maker, who may well have been based in London. How and why the various decisions over detail and trimming were made to achieve its final appearance are still obscure. If it did belong to Austen, the pelisse might be the garment mentioned in a letter of 24 August 1814 from London: 'I must provide for the possibility, by troubling you to send up my Silk Pelisse by Collier on Saturday.—I feel it would be necessary on such an occasion' (letter 105). The 'possibility' referred to is a plan to call on family friends on her return journey to Chawton from London.[20] Her identification of the pelisse by no other descriptor than 'silk' suggests that Austen had only one such expensive garment at the time of writing, suitable for an 'occasion', though she had one or more other pelisses: a trimmed one is mentioned on 30 April 1811 (letter 72). If she had more than one silk pelisse, other qualifying adjectives would have been needed. Costly silk was not a stranger to Austen's wardrobe as by 1813 she owned gowns of 'China Crape' and lilac sarcenet.[21] Her other pelisses might be less ornamental and more practically protective, the kind Captain Wentworth evokes in *Persuasion*:

Figure 3.6 Illustration to the entry 'The Ladies' Dress-maker' from John Souter, *The Book of English Trades: And Library of the Useful Arts: With Seventy Engravings*, 7th edition (John Souter, London, 1818). Oxford, Bodleian Library, 1773 f.25, after p. 222.

'I had no more discoveries to make, than you would have as to the fashion and strength of any old pelisse, which you had seen lent about among half your acquaintance, ever since you could remember, and which at last, on some very wet day, is lent to yourself.' (ch. 8)

Women wore such plain woollen-cloth pelisses for walking and riding.

Garments generally had a high net value for their Regency wearers. They were a considerable and infrequent investment for gentry consumers of Austen's social level, who planned, discussed and collaborated upon new clothing with relatives, acquaintances and professionals. Once the gown structure existed it might be refashioned for as long as the fabric endured. Many surviving garments in museum collections show evidence of careful alterations to improve or update the style. By contrast, the Austen pelisse is as it came from its maker and shows very little wear (fig. 3.7). If it was hers, she had no more than five years' use, including a year of illness when a fine pelisse would have been socially superfluous. The only alteration is the probably accidental loss of a belt that was once stitched on at the central back seam and fastened under the bust at the front. The belt on the reconstruction (fig. 3.8) takes its pattern from a similar pelisse in the V&A.[22] The inch-wide white silk waist ribbon that secured the pelisse inside has also been torn from its place.

A silk ribbon and the cord on front and cuffs may seem minor elements when compared to the whole pelisse, but they are worth examining more closely because such details of applied haberdashery represented a significant vehicle for Regency women's appropriation of style and expression of individual taste. The trimmings on the Austen pelisse are unusual in showing no evidence of alterations, reflecting either its value or the short time of its use. Jane and Cassandra were otherwise constant amenders of their wardrobes, a normal practice for the time but one leant upon more frequently to refresh clothing in households, like that of the Austen women, where money was never abundant. The point of alterations was not only to extend the life of a garment and presumably prevent the wearer from becoming bored with her limited wardrobe, but also to keep up with the tides of fashion. Haberdashery applied in inventive, novel ways was an easier, cheaper way to achieve freshness and fashion when investment in a new garment was a significant financial outlay. The importance of trimmings to the Regency dresser cannot be overestimated.

Mrs Topham's accounts show that extras such as lace, flowers, ribbons, pins, fringing, shoe binding and roses, gimp and galloon (types of braid), cord, tape, wadding and buttons formed 47 per cent of the quantity of textiles and clothing-related items bought by her between 1811 and 1815, although fabrics constitute the greater cost. Ribbons in particular form the overwhelming majority of purchases at around 42 per cent of the haberdashery, or around 20 per cent of the total number of textile items, bought in every colour, width and quality on a weekly basis throughout the accounting

Figure 3.7 Detail of Jane Austen's pelisse. © Hilary Davidson.

period of 1810–25. Austen again gives us an insight into how women might utilize these frequent ribbon purchases to renew their look:

> I have determined to trim my lilac sarsenet with black sattin ribbon just as my China Crape is, 6ᴰ width at the bottom, 3ᴰ or 4ᴰ at top.—Ribbon trimmings are all the fashion at Bath, & I dare say the fashions of the two places are alike enough in that point to content *me*. (5–8 March 1814, letter 98)

Ribbons are specified by their cost, which relates to their width and the quality of their weave; they were available to those with even the most meagre budget. They could be sarcenet, taffeta, embossed or the type with a 'perl edge' that Austen, in the same letter, describes herself as trying 'to draw … up into kind of Roses, instead of putting it [the ribbon] in plain double plaits [pleats]'. She reveals here how the inventive sewer used ribbons and other trimmings as changeable demonstrations of taste, like those on a gown from the 1810s (fig. 3.9).

Another key question for this period, then, is how did women get information about changes in style that might inspire a new neckline of ribbon roses, or remain '*au fait* as to the newest modes of being trifling and silly' (*Persuasion*, ch. 17)? An accepted narrative is that the explosion of print media, in the form of magazines aimed at ladies and containing an engraved and tinted image plate or two of the latest fashions every month (like the kind in figs 3.2a and 3.2b), became a key source of style information.[23] This idea retrospectively applies a practice documented for the later nineteenth century. However, to date I have yet to find any primary evidence supporting its use in the Regency period. What is notable about the dress dissemination practices Austen records for her lifetime is the absence of the *represented* body as a medium for new fashion information. Instead, people watched other people and observed what they wore. Everything came through the *living* body. Someone had seen it or touched it for themselves and told another person they already knew, verbally or in writing, or they had bought goods for their community – practices abundantly recorded in her letters. Austen's works contain not one mention of fashion plates or other artistic, flat representations of a dressed body involved in creating dress, an absence backed up by many other primary sources. Instead, where personal acquaintance ran out, her 'neighbourhood of voluntary spies' (*Northanger Abbey*, ch. 24) simply used their eyes to furnish them with particulars. Mrs Smith in *Persuasion* links into the Bath servants'

Figure 3.8 A replica of the pelisse with belt. © Hilary Davidson.

gossip network through her nurse, Mrs Rooke, to relish reports of 'lace and finery' passed on about 'pretty, silly, expensive, fashionable' Mrs Wallis (*Persuasion*, ch. 17). Too ill to see for herself, Mrs Smith can participate in communal dress through her proxy eyes. With the same knowledgeable ability on which proxy shopping relied, people watching dress could apply economic as well as style evaluations, what Kathryn Sutherland describes as 'social judgement'.[24] The wonderful monster Mrs Elton assumes her dress will be assessed through public scrutiny at the Highbury ball, while she assesses others and happily allocates herself top place in village fashion and style (*Emma*, ch. 38). Austen, too, recorded on 8 January 1801 how she enjoyed the 'satisfaction of estimating [the] Lace & … Muslin' of the 'expensively & nakedly dress'd' Mrs Powlett (letter 30). However the decisions that came to create its final appearance were made, Austen in wearing this pelisse would have experienced the scrutiny of family, friends and strangers, all applying an instinctive assessment of the gown through summarizing all its comprising elements, as detailed above, a summary we in the twenty-first century must labour extensively to reconstruct.

The great question around the pelisse is, of course, was it really Jane Austen's? The short answer is that we will probably never certainly know. The longer answer is that nothing about its qualities, construction and especially its size contradicts the story that she did indeed wear it. The evidence in its favour is strong. My more technical article on reconstructing the pelisse outlines its many congruencies with what we know of Austen's bodily shape.[25] In particular, the pelisse matches closely descriptions of her long, spare figure, which range from an unkind neighbour's 'a thin upright piece of wood or iron' to a 'tall, thin *spare* person with very high cheekbones', 'tall and slight, but not drooping', and the more complimentary 'slight and elegant'.[26] Austen herself considered that she was 'a tall woman'.[27] The woman who wore this pelisse was also tall and thin with long arms and a round chest. Her vital statistics were approximately thus: 31- to 33-inch bust, 24-inch waist, 33- to 34-inch hips; she was between 5 feet 6 inches and 5 feet 8 inches tall, which is categorically tall for a woman in the early nineteenth century. The best body double I have yet found to fit the replica pelisse is Juniper Bedwell-Wilson, a tall, thinly figured girl to whom all the comments on Austen equally apply (fig. 3.8). Her measurements are: 30-inch bust, 24-inch waist, 30-inch hips.[28] Juniper gives us an idea of how the pelisse looked when worn and, perhaps, of the elegant figure of Austen herself.

Figure 3.9 Ribbon trimming. © Hilary Davidson.

Dress was for Jane Austen, her family, her milieu and by extension her fictional characters, a negotiation based upon personal networks of taste and possibilities for consumption. The importance of these networks as disseminators of new ideas about dress and the material means of creating it is central to Regency fashion. For gentry dressers, those of Austen's own rank, the eyes and hands of family and of social and professional acquaintance were still the primary mediators of novelty, quality, change and fashion in dress and its constituent parts. Her letters demonstrate her own personal and lively interest in dress, no matter how discreet she is on the matter of her fictional characters' clothes (never does she describe what her heroine is wearing). Unpicking and reassembling is the critic's way of taking a text apart and putting it back together, word by word, noticing as she goes rhythms, secrets and perspectives not available any other way. This pelisse is a material text as richly explicit as any of Austen's literary constructions. It, too, can be 'read' in the same way, through the process of unpicking and remaking to reveal a whole world of experience around the business of getting fashionably dressed. Thoroughly examining the qualities and contexts of the pelisse, which quite probably belonged to Jane Austen, is a new way of scrutinizing the life and times of this already powerfully scrutinized author, who will, nonetheless, never be as examined as she is beloved.

1   All in the collection of Jane Austen's House Museum, Chawton, Hampshire.

2   See Lynn Sorge-English, *Stays and Body Image in London: The Staymaking Trade, 1680–1810*, Pickering & Chatto, London, 2011 for further details of the staymaking trade.

3   Bath, Fashion Museum, BATMC I.06.1232.

4   Hilary Davidson, 'Reconstructing Jane Austen's Silk Pelisse Coat, *c.*1812–14', *Costume*, vol. 49, 2015, pp. 198–223. DOI: <http://dx.doi.org/10.1179/0590887615Z.00000000076>.

5   Sarcenet lining cost 5s.3d. and 5s.6d. per yard in 1810. Mary Topham, 'Lady's Account Book' 1810–25, Chawton House Library, Chawton, Hampshire, MS. 6641.

6   Persian is recorded as costing 2s.6d. per yard in 1812 and 1813, 2s.4d. and 2s.9d. in 1817. Topham, 'Lady's Account Book'.

7   Miles Lambert, 'Sent from Town: Commissioning Clothing in Britain during the Long Eighteenth Century', *Costume*, vol. 43, 2009, pp. 68–84, p. 82 and passim.

8   Claire Walsh, 'Shops, Shopping and the Art of Decision Making in Eighteenth-Century England', in John Styles and Amanda Vickery (eds), *Gender, Taste and Material Culture in Britain and North America, 1700–1830*, Yale University Press, New Haven, CT and London, 2006, p. 163.

9   Walsh, 'Shops, Shopping and the Art of Decision Making', p. 170.

10   Charles and Frank Austen were both midshipmen at the time. Frank eventually rose to become Admiral of the Fleet. See Chapter 5, this volume.

11   16 May 1813, *Maria Edgeworth. Letters from England 1813–1844*, ed. Christina Colvin, Clarendon Press, Oxford, 1971, p. 59.

12   18–20 April 1811, letter 70.

13   See Topham, 'Lady's Account Book', and Eliza Jervoise, *Eliza Jervoise's Account Book*, 1812–19, Winchester, Hampshire Record Office, MS 44M69/E13/13/12.

14   A range taken from calculations on the National Archives Currency Converter for the year 1810, <http://www.nationalarchives.gov.uk/currency/defaulto.asp#mid> (adjusted for inflation from 2005 through *Office for National Statistics Consumer Price Indices – CPI indices:* 1988 *to* 2014, <http://www.ons.gov.uk/ons/datasets-and-tables/data-selector.html?cdid=D7BT&dataset=mm23&table-id=1.1>) and *Historical UK Inflation and Price Conversion*, <http://safalra.com/other/historical-uk-inflation-price-conversion/>, which is based on Jim O'Donoghue, Louise Goulding and Grahame Allen, 'Consumer Price Inflation Since 1750', *Economic Trends*, No. 604, 2004, pp. 38–46.

15   'We are very busy making Edward's shirts, and I am proud to say that I am the neatest worker of the party.' 1 September 1796, letter 7.

16   Austen-Leigh, *Memoir*, ed. Sutherland, pp. 77–9.

17   Janet Arnold, 'The Dressmaker's Craft', *Costume*, vol. 7, supplement 1, January 1973, pp. 29–40. DOI: http://dx.doi.org/10.1179/cos.1973.7.s1.29.

18   Male tailors usually made cloth pelisses and riding habits.

19   Topham, 'Lady's Account Book'.

20   Deirdre Le Faye, *A Chronology of Jane Austen and Her Family:* 1600–2000, Cambridge University Press, Cambridge, 2006, p. 487.

21   6–7 November 1813, letter 96, and 5–8 March 1814, letter 98.

22   V&A Museum, Accession number T.24-1946, *c.*1809, <http://collections.vam.ac.uk/item/O13824/pelisse-unknown/>.

23   For example, the assertion that 'While the fashion magazine is, for the historian, a fairly reliable source, we must not overlook the influence it exerted on contemporary taste. It gave readers all over the country descriptions of standard fashions, and was therefore instrumental in persuading a much more general adoption of current modes. It helped to establish uniformity at least throughout those classes who habitually accepted it as a guide', in C. Willett and Phillis Cunnington, *The History of Underclothes*, Dover Publications Inc., New York, 1992, p. 157. Though fashion plates may not yet have been a source of dressmaking information, this does not contradict the suggestion (made in Chapter 8, this volume) that they could offer aesthetic guidance in depictions of dress.

24   Kathryn Sutherland, 'Jane Austen and Social Judgement', British Library, *Discovering Literature: Romantics and Victorians: The Novel* 1780–1832, <http://www.bl.uk/romantics-and-victorians/articles/jane-austen-and-social-judgement>, accessed 26 February 2016.

25   Davidson, 'Reconstructing Jane Austen's Silk Pelisse Coat', pp. 218–20.

26   Cited in Claire Tomalin, *Jane Austen: A Life*, Viking, London, 1997, pp. 108 and 111.

27   25 January 1801, letter 33.

28   My thanks to Juniper Bedwell-Wilson and her family for their generous participation in the pelisse reconstruction project.

4

The Art of the Letter

Deidre Lynch

One hundred and sixty-one letters written by Jane Austen have survived (fig. 4.1).
The earliest in the group, from the writer's twenty-first year, opens a window onto an
everyday life in which the memorable events are shopping (the purchase of white gloves
and pink silk), the latest thing in late-eighteenth-century crafting (the trimming of some
'old paper hats' of her mother's manufacture) and party-going above all: at the ball held
the night before, Austen reports to her sister, she engaged 'in everything most profligate
and shocking in the way of dancing and sitting down' with a young man from the
neighbourhood. The tone of mock horror Austen uses here to frame her latest doings in
the marriage market – and to burlesque the moralizing publications of her day – would
have augmented this letter's entertainment value when Austen sent it off as a birthday
greeting to Cassandra on 10 January 1796 (letter 1). One indication that it did, so that
Cassandra might thereafter have demanded more of the same, is that this jokey tone
persists in other letters Austen dispatched that year, when the family visits that would
claim one or the other of the sisters throughout their adult lives separated the pair once
again. 'Here I am once more in this Scene of Dissipation & vice', Austen writes, for
instance, on 23 August 1796 (letter 3), reporting her arrival in London, 'and I begin
already to find my Morals corrupted.'

   The pleasures that Austen's letters have for the modern readers who encounter them
in a printed book or on the Web derive from additional sources. They come from the
sense of listening in on this author at a moment when we know more than she does,
knowing as we do and as she cannot, that she is already en route to literary fame. In
theory, at least, these pleasures also derive from the mildly transgressive thrill involved
in intruding on others' privacy and reading words intended for others' eyes. Those
pleasures were, in fact, frequently discussed in the literary culture of Austen's day.
'We please ourselves with beholding the writer in a situation which allows him to be
at his ease', wrote the Reverend Hugh Blair in 1773 as he explained in his *Lectures on*

Figure 4.1 Jane Austen's
writing desk. © British Library
Board.

Rhetoric why collections of authors' letters to family members and friends or the period's new life-and-letters biographies were becoming an especially lucrative sector of the British book market. Authors' letters, Blair suggests, are valuable publications precisely because they are not addressed, as published writings must be, to impersonal posterity but instead to intimates. Once collected and put into print, however, those unstudied, unbuttoned productions grant posterity the means to discover, Blair states, the 'real character' of their writer.[1]

Austen, widely read, would certainly have known the pleasures Blair describes. In her published work and her manuscript letters alike, she alludes to the celebrated epistolary collections of the day, especially the letters exchanged between Samuel Johnson and his friend Hester Thrale Piozzi, published by the latter in 1788. But the process of reading for a hidden, private personality that Blair endorses in his overview of this new publishing phenomenon is of limited purchase when it comes to the archive of family correspondence that the Austens began sharing with the world shortly after the novelist's death.

There are indications, to be sure, that the family itself would have disagreed with this proposition. When, in 1884, the novelist's great-nephew, Lord Brabourne, published the first book-length collection of Austen's letters (then numbering ninety-four in all), he justified his enterprise – and his attempt to steal some thunder from his second cousin James Edward Austen-Leigh, who had published his *Memoir of Jane Austen* fourteen years earlier – by claiming in his preface that the letters could give a picture of the novelist's real life 'as no history written by another person could give'.[2] (Audible in that statement is Brabourne's boasting about how his branch of the family had contrived both to preserve and to inherit more of the novelist's letters than the other branches had; in the 1840s Cassandra Austen had arranged for her niece and Brabourne's mother, Fanny Knight, later Lady Knatchbull, to inherit most of the letters that Cassandra had received from her sister, probably in recognition of the fact that so many of them had either been written or received at the Knights' estate in Kent.)[3] The letters Brabourne is printing contain, he promises, 'the confidential outpourings of Jane Austen's soul to her beloved sister, interspersed with many family and personal details, which, doubtless, she would have told to no other human being'.[4] Though other passages characterize the reading situation differently, here Brabourne affirms to his readership that they have been positioned to occupy Cassandra's place. With these printed pages, he says, you can revive that intimate *tête-à-tête*.

Brabourne's description is at odds with many readers' experience of Austen's correspondence. Those letters are in many ways less aptly construed as writings *about* the individual than they are writings operating to acknowledge and fortify links attaching this individual to others.[5] To read the letters aright requires doing justice to precisely the dimensions of a female familiar correspondence that Brabourne's description slights (dimensions as crucial to Austen's letters as to those exchanged by the many eighteenth- and early nineteenth-century women who did not become famous for their publications). We must recall that generally such letters were in the first instance written to fulfil daughterly and sisterly duty, and that they were often written simply to confirm that the channels of communication remained open and that relations remained reciprocal. Such letters are more aptly construed as semi-public documents of sociability than as diaristic expressions of private sentiment.

Despite Brabourne's picture of his great-aunt pouring out her 'soul' on paper, Austen's letters are also generally less soulful than materialistic. They deal in physical things more often than ineffable feelings. White gloves and paper hats, for instance; the furniture at Godmersham, which (in a letter to Cassandra from 8–9 November 1800 (letter 25)) is in the process of being rearranged; spruce beer (currently being brewed *again*, reports another letter to Cassandra on 9 December 1808 (letter 62)) – all these objects claim space on Austen's paper.

Austen's writing matter itself often provides her with subject matter. To read one of these letters in a book or on a computer screen means, in fact, missing out when one gets to the droll passages in which Austen contrives for the physical materials with which she writes, the paper and ink, to loom into her correspondent's view, as something beyond mere supports for her message's meaning. In a declaration that makes writing as her process converge with writing as her subject, Austen comments to Cassandra on 28 October 1798 (letter 10), 'I am quite angry at myself for not writing closer; why is my alphabet so much more sprawly than Yours?' The question jolts us into awareness of the medium – with its uniform lettering and regular spacing – that defines *our* experience of this letter and separates it from Cassandra's.

En masse the letters represent some of the most exuberant writing we have inherited from the early nineteenth century, and that is a reason to read and reread them. Even so, there are good reasons why in that reading we might feel haunted by a sense of loss. One reason is that the very technological processes that have brought the letters before us, converting them into printed text, also reinforce our irrefragable distance from them.

Flame and scissors

Indeed, viewed with a cold eye, the archive of this correspondence might appear a somewhat disappointing and patchy thing. There are, as noted, 161 letters. In the Oxford University Press edition that R.W. Chapman prepared in 1932, the manuscript caches that had been passed down along three separate family lines – with a set bequeathed to Fanny Knight, another set bequeathed to another niece, Caroline Austen, and then a third set handed down by the descendants of Jane and Cassandra's younger brother, Charles – were belatedly united. That total of 161 encompasses those three sets, along with a few additional letters that had come onto the market in time for Chapman to include them and then nine more that came to light after his death.

This total represents, it must be confessed, a mediocre survival rate: Chapman's successor as editor, Deirdre Le Faye, calculates that the novelist must have written three thousand letters during her lifetime. From the outset, then, obstacles confront the reader who seeks in the letters the quasi-diary that will yield knowledge of the author's real character. Gaps – encompassing entire years (1797; 1802–3) – mar the record. Another problem is readers' lack of access to the letters to which Austen responded: the reading experience can be like hearing only one side of a telephone conversation. 'You are indeed the finest comic writer of the present age', Austen wrote to Cassandra on 1 September 1796 (letter 4), but Cassandra's half of the conversation that the pair continue over the following two decades is wholly inaudible.

Of course, modern audiences in the main know Austen's sister *not* as a comic genius, but rather as the spoilsport who, in destroying part of her sister's papers, cheated us of letters we would have wished to read – letters whose content is the more alluring precisely because it is inaccessible. For almost as long as Austen's letters have been in print, so has the story of how, some time in the 1840s, Cassandra, while putting her family papers in order, burnt the greater part of the letters and also snipped away portions of several that remained. As a consequence of this famous pruning of the epistolary archive, the letters that are *not* there have long been sensed hovering, spectrally, over readers' encounter with those that are.

When he apologizes for the scantiness of the manuscript materials he had to hand when preparing *A Memoir of Jane Austen* (1870), Cassandra's nephew J.E. Austen-Leigh seems to refer to this pruning. In the half-century since Jane Austen's death, Austen-Leigh sighs, her 'nearest relatives, far from making provision [for a memoir], had actually destroyed many of the letters and papers by which it might have been facilitated'.[6] The next generation after Austen-Leigh's in fact took to explaining away the lack of feeling that some commentators criticized in Austen's letters by scapegoating Cassandra: the consequence of Cassandra's overzealous guarding of her sister's privacy was, they suggested, that she had transmitted to posterity a distorted, unflattering picture of her sister. Hence, a great-great-niece, Mary Augusta Austen-Leigh's rather florid statement from 1920: the letters are 'but "a gleaning of grapes when the vintage is done"—when all that was precious had been safely gathered up . . . in Cassandra's faithful memory, and nothing had been left behind excepting that which even she deemed to be altogether negligible'.[7]

Yet Kathryn Sutherland responds shrewdly to this Austen family legend, one founded upon scanty evidence, by reminding us that it is entirely possible there never were any confidential letters to be held back.[8] In fact, Cassandra may have destroyed relatively little. And, of course, long before some of them were subjected to flame and scissors at Cassandra's hands, many of Austen's letters (those to individuals outside the kin network, for example) seem already to have disappeared. Many might have been discarded even before her death.

Learning the details about provenance and transmission that form the backstory of the letters clarifies how multiple causes colluded to make this archive a diminished thing. Consider the case of the first of the letters that the family published, a letter Austen composed in her sick room in Winchester in May 1817 (letter 161), two months before her death. It appeared in print in partial form later in 1817 in the 'Biographical Notice' that accompanied the posthumous edition of *Northanger Abbey* and *Persuasion*, where Henry Austen, his sister's executor, used it to demonstrate, as he stated, the facility with which, even on her deathbed, she could 'turn from complaint to cheerfulness'.[9] One would think that the final or near-final production from Austen's pen would be deemed especially valuable, but this epistle was in fact misplaced following Henry's partial transcription.

The manuscript of that 'first' letter from 1796 that reports on shocking ways of dancing and sitting down has likewise gone missing, so that at present the sole authority documenting its existence is Brabourne's collection. It numbered among the fourteen manuscript letters that disappeared following their appearance in print in that collection, when Brabourne decided to consign to the auction rooms the manuscript materials on which his book had been founded. At that point, those fourteen missing manuscripts became the casualties, it seems, of shoddy record-keeping by the auctioneers and of the carelessness of the private collectors who were their clientele. In the meantime, other members of the Austen family compounded these losses through their over-ready compliance with the demands of Victorian autograph hunters. In several cases, portions of the letters – the signature lines especially – that those family members had either retained or received as their share of Cassandra's bequest have been cut away.

Scraps and patches

In some ways, even when left intact, a letter to Cassandra might strike the reader as a tissue of discontinuities – a patchwork. Carol Houlihan Flynn puts it well: as one of Austen's bulletins on her daily doings wanders mercurially from topic to topic, it piles up 'disjointed fragments of everyday social exchange'.[10] The 'little matters' – yet 'highly important' – treated in the Austen letter from 9 December 1808 (letter 62) that reports on spruce beer, are thoroughly, jarringly jumbled together, the dashes enabling the writer to segue from one 'little' topic to the next also serving as graphic marks of these topics' disconnection. Beyond news of the brewing, one hears of the whereabouts of a Miss Curling, then the whereabouts of some bracelets, then some recent visitors, and so on, until finally Austen runs out of paper and calls on Cassandra 'to distribute the affectionate love of a heart not so tired as the right hand that belongs to it'.

In an essay from 1910 the pioneering sociologist George Simmel made such a style the hallmark of sociability in its purest form: 'it … inheres in the nature of sociable conversation that its object matter can change lightly and quickly; for, since the matter is only the means, it has an entirely interchangeable and accidental character.'[11] Simmel's account of talk as an end in itself, of talk for talk's sake, unlocks some qualities of the letters' disjointed style. Austen's expectation in December 1808 that her sister will be able to follow the abrupt zigzags of her line of thought might also be construed as a marker of the intensely private nature of this correspondence. Such a letter relegates outsiders to 'the surface of things'.[12] Vivien Jones compares Austen's epistolary exchanges with Cassandra to the texts we fire off on our smartphones to keep our nearest and dearest informed of our social activities or progress on domestic chores. In a paradoxical way, these letters, Jones notes, combine this intense intimacy (who else but our intimates would care about those chores?) with an anti-confessional stance.[13] The confessions that we do get in the letters to Cassandra – as when, in January 1796, Austen owns up to her 'profligate and shocking' ballroom interactions with Tom Lefroy – generally turn out to be mock confessions. With the hyperbole, Austen, in what might well be a self-protective strategy for a dowerless young woman, disavows any emotional investment in what went on the night before; her idiom actively diminishes the possibility that anything serious could have been afoot in the ballroom.

In the *Memoir* Austen-Leigh apologizes for the trifling nature of his aunt's letters. The few he has seen resemble, he says, 'the nest which some little bird builds of the materials nearest at hand, of the twigs and mosses supplied by the tree in which it is placed; curiously constructed out of the simplest matters'.[14] Modern commentators often deplore the condescension audible in this passage, faulting Austen-Leigh for playing up Austen's narrow horizons and for evoking a cosiness at odds with the waspish wit filling her writings. Perhaps Austen-Leigh's analogy better represents how it feels to us to read the letters than how it felt to write them. Arguably the 'little' creature piecing together scraps more appropriately emblematizes the novelist's readership than it does the novelist: some of those Victorian autograph collectors, after all, pasted samples of Austen's handwriting into their scrapbooks or used them to extra-illustrate their printed books (an edition of *Emma* in one case that we know of, a copy of the American anthology *A Gallery of Distinguished English and American Female Poets* in another). Those Victorian scrapbookers engaged in practices that brought literary culture into an awkwardly intimate relation with the humbler world of household handicraft.

To an extent, though, that commentators have tended to underestimate, a letter-writer like Austen would already have understood those worlds as being in proximity. When, on 31 May 1811 (letter 74), she asks Cassandra, 'Have you remembered to collect pieces for the Patchwork?', the question might as easily be probing her interlocutor's readiness to send off a letter as her preparations for their current sewing project (fig. 4.2).

At this early nineteenth-century moment, when technologies for making paper from wood pulp were a half-century in the future and when paper continued to be

Figure 4.2 The patchwork quilt made by the Austen women in the early 19th century. © Jane Austen's House Museum.

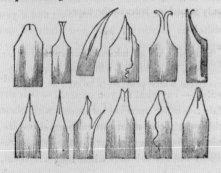

Figure 4.3 'The Miseries of Writing': illustration showing worn-out quill pen nibs from James Beresford, *The Miseries of Human Life*, 10th edition, 2 vols (P. Wright and sons, London, 1825), vol. 1, p. 193. Oxford, Bodleian Library, 247126 f.47.

manufactured, at great expense, from cloth rags exclusively, women of Austen's social class, required to spend so many waking hours on needlework, would perhaps have aligned quite readily duties involving cloth and thread and epistolary duties involving paper and ink. (Indeed, the eighteenth-century novelist Samuel Richardson had had one of his heroines commend the use of the pen as the most proper pastime for her sex, 'next to the Needle'.)[15] Moreover, several of the period's popular handicrafts for women – activities appearing in Austen's correspondence when, for instance, she mentions, in January 1796 (letter 1), Mrs Austen's paper hats and, in September 1813 (letter 89), the paper screen on which Fanny Cage, a Knight family connection, has been working – involved treating paper as though it *were* cloth. During this era the former was, like the latter, a 'robust, useful, expensive material' that could be folded and pleated, and even sewed and embroidered.[16] The costliness of paper – during the eighteenth century it accounted for more than half the production costs involved in publishing a book – itself heightened the sensitivity with which book-writers and letter-writers alike regarded their material medium. This is the heightening registered in those moments when Austen calls on her correspondent to stop *reading* and instead *look* at the texture and dimensions of the paper that is the carrier for this reading matter. Such paper consciousness is sometimes doubled by a comparable self-awareness about the state of the writer's tools – the consistency of the ink, say, or the sharpness or dullness of the end of the quill pen that forms the letters on the page. Prior to the era of the ballpoint pen, writing required considerable manual dexterity on the part of the penwoman. Quill pens could, for instance, be terribly user-unfriendly, requiring repeated mending and surviving a mere week when wielded by an energetic writer (fig. 4.3).

There were many reasons, in short, why early nineteenth-century people would remember what we forget when reading the books that turn their manuscripts into print – which is that the letters they sent and received were physical objects, not bodiless texts. They were things belonging to the material world, wrought through physical labour. Austen's workmanlike attitude to the labours of the pen is conspicuous in particular in the multitude of paper-saving techniques she appears to have honed as a penwoman. Her thrifty reluctance to use more than a single sheet is evident every time she appropriates what might well have been left as white space and uses it to squeeze in more words – writing those extra sentences (upside down) onto the space above the date at the top of the first page or between the lines of that page, or doubling her page's capacity by crossing her letters – by, that is, writing at a right angle across her first swathe of writing (fig. 4.4). In Austen's *Emma* Jane Fairfax is presented as especially proficient at such 'chequer-work', as Miss Bates notes in describing the letters her niece sends off weekly to Highbury from London: 'in general she fills the whole paper and crosses half' (*Emma*, ch. 19).

The Regency lady, states a magazine essay from 1883 with considerable nostalgia, was not like us. She 'wrote with the honest determination to give her friend "the worth of her money" in filling her paper up to the tiniest corner with a regular chronicle which she had been thinking over for many days'.[17] As this Victorian commentator, beneficiary of a nation-wide penny post instituted in 1840, is aware, postal rates (assessed by weight and distance) were never higher than during Austen's lifetime. Thanks to repeated price hikes, the cost, for example, of sending a letter of a single sheet from London to Edinburgh rose from seven pence in 1797 to one shilling and two pence by 1812.[18] That cost was a key factor determining the appearance of letters: it mandated the paper consciousness and paper-saving techniques referred to above. This expense was borne by the recipient of a letter, not its sender: eighteenth-century and Regency postmen collected postage due at the moment of delivery (fig. 4.5). Hence, on 12 November 1800 (letter 26), Austen's acknowledgement to her friend Martha Lloyd that the letter of hers that Martha is currently reading will have cut into Martha's pocket money and diminished by the value of three pence 'the Elegance of your new Dress for the Hurstbourn Ball'.

'The real subject matter of letter-writing', historian Roger Chartier states, 'is the writing of the letters.'[19] During Austen's era one way that this recursiveness is manifested is that a letter often opens with a balance sheet of sorts, the writer deploying the language of credit and debt as she keeps tabs on who owes whom and on the discrepancy in the word counts occasioning that debt.[20] Austen's show of shame in October 1798 about how 'sprawly' her 'alphabet' is compared with Cassandra's closely written lines gets re-enacted frequently, in fact, over the two decades of the correspondence. Her sister, and also her friends, Austen suggests, generally give better value for money: 'I will endeavour to make this letter more worthy your acceptance than my last, which was so shabby a one that I think Mr. Marshall could never charge you with postage' (21–23 January 1799 (letter 18)); 'I thank you for writing so much; you must really have sent me the value of two letters in one' (7–8 January 1807 (letter 49)); 'I shall take care not to count the lines of your last Letter; You have obliged me to eat humble-pie' (29–30 November 1812 (letter 77) to Martha Lloyd).

Women's work

'Every body allows that the talent of writing agreeable letters is peculiarly female', says Henry Tilney to Catherine Morland in *Northanger Abbey* (ch. 3). His gallantry is founded on a long-standing association of women with the letter form – an association forged

pp. 86–7 **Figure 4.4** Jane Austen, letter to Cassandra, 26–27 May 1801, unfolded. © Jane Austen's House Museum.

Paragon — Tuesday May 2 —

My dear Cassandra,

For your letter from Kintbury & for all
the compliments on my writing which it contained, I now
return you my best thanks. — I am very glad that Martha
goes to Chilton; a very essential temporary comfort her
presence must afford to Mrs Craven, and I hope she
will endeavour to make it a lasting one by exerting
those kind offices in favour of the young man, from
which you were both with-held in the case of the
Harrison family by the mistaken tenderness of one
part of ours. — The Endymion came into Portsmouth
on Sunday, & I have sent Charles a short letter by
this day's post. — My adventures since I wrote to
you three days ago have been such as the time would
easily contain; I walked yesterday morning with
Mrs Chamberlayne to Lyncombe & Widcombe, and
in the evening I drank tea with the Holders. Mrs
Chamberlayne's pace was not quite so magnificent
on this second trial as in the first; it was nothing
more than I could keep up with, without effort; &
for many, many yards together on a raised narrow
foot-path I led the way. — The walk was very beauti

most of the Story because it came in to advantage, but in fact he only asked me whether I were to be at Sidney Gardens in the evening or not. — There is now something like an engagement between us & the Phaeton; which to confess my frailty I have a great desire to go out in; — whether it will come to anything must remain with him. — I really believe he is very harmless; people do not seem afraid of him here, and he gets Groundsel for his birds & all that. — My Aunt

Aug 26th 1801

Miss Austen
The Rev.d J. C. Fowle
Kintbury
Newbury

will never be easy till she visits them; — She has been repeatedly trying to fancy a necessity, for it now on our ac: :counts, but she meets with no encouragement. — She ought to be particularly scrupulous in such matters, & she says so herself — but nevertheless — — — — well — I am come home from Mrs Lysons as yellow as I went; — You cannot like your yellow gown half so well as I do, nor a quarter neither Mr Rice & Lucy are to be married, one on the 9th & the other on the 10th of July. — Yrs affec: J A.

by the feminocentrism of the epistolary novel, a fictional genre staffed by beleaguered scribbling heroines who struggle simultaneously to preserve their virtue and their paper supply (fig. 4.6), and by the praise conventionally bestowed on real rather than fictional female letter-writers like Madame de Sévigné, the seventeenth-century aristocrat whose letters were applauded by Blair (fig. 4.7). The association was buttressed as well by venerable stereotypes about female volubility. Letters, after all, were not writing as that was usually understood; they lay on the borders of literacy as elite male preserve. As many authors of the period's letter manuals insisted, driving home the paradoxical point that the epistolary art that they needed to teach their readers should nonetheless appear as though it came naturally, the elegant phrases for which one had studied were out of place in letters (fig. 4.8). 'When you write to a friend … the thoughts should appear naked, and not dressed in the borrowed robes of rhetoric, for a friend will be more pleased with that part of a letter which flows from the heart than that which is the product of the mind', states H.W. Dilworth in *The Complete Letter-Writer* of 1783.[21] Letters, Hester Piozzi observed, prefacing her collection of Johnson's correspondence, are 'familiar chat spread upon paper for the advantage or entertainment of a distant friend' – a definition that would lead her readers to anticipate something more tame and feminized than the *talking for victory* for which Dr Johnson was celebrated.[22]

But Henry Tilney actually dissents from his era's commonplaces about women's natural affinity for letter-writing. Even Catherine Morland, slow on the uptake, realizes how hollow his gallantry is, once he observes that the specimens of female epistolary art that he has seen have been flawless 'except in three particulars': 'A general deficiency of subject, a total inattention to stops, and a very frequent ignorance of grammar.' The lack within a humdrum, restricted, eventless everyday life of any topic on which to write – Henry's 'deficiency of subject' – was indeed *the* handicap defining the art of the female familiar letter. Austen frequently acknowledges that dilemma as she opens or closes a letter: 'Where shall I begin? Which of all my important nothings shall I tell you first?' (15 June 1808 (letter 52)); 'There, I flatter myself I have constructed you a Smartish Letter, considering my Want of Materials' (9 February 1807 (letter 50)). The letters are in this respect continuous with the novels, whose realism depends on the premise that, because lives without incident may yet be highly important, a dearth of materials is no true obstacle for narrative art. (Indeed, the narrator of *Northanger Abbey*, who sometimes protests the Morland family members' tendency to behave in ways 'consistent with the common feelings of common life' (ch. 2) rather than in the splashier fashion of other people's characters, shows herself to be rather adept at crafting narrative out of next to nothing.) Female letter-writers, as Austen realized, were often obliged to assemble many letters, to many correspondents, out of mere scraps of news: another reason that the art of scrimping, of making do with less, to the fore when the Austen women sewed their patchwork quilt at Chawton Cottage (see fig. 4.2), pertained to the culture of female letter-writing.

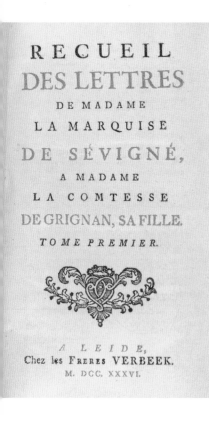

RECUEIL
DES LETTRES
DE MADAME
LA MARQUISE
DE SÉVIGNÉ,
A MADAME
LA COMTESSE
DE GRIGNAN, SA FILLE.
TOME PREMIER.

A LEIDE,
Chez les FRERES VERBEEK.
M. DCC. XXXVI.

above **Figure 4.7**
Frontispiece and title page of
*Recueil des lettres de Madame
La Marquise de Sévigné*
(Frères Verbeek. Leiden,
1736), Oxford, Taylor Institute
Library, VET. FR. II.A.69 (t.1).

opposite **Figure 4.8**
Frontispiece from *The
Universal Letter Writer
or Whole Art of Polite
Correspondence* (1808).
Oxford, Bodleian Library,
Vet. A5 f.4092.

Late in life, another early nineteenth-century woman who had made a living by her pen, the novelist Amelia Opie, declared that, had she not early on determined to conceive of that obligation as a delight rather than a burden, 'It might have been inserted in the bills of mortality, dead of letter writing'.[23] Part of the burden was precisely that letters had to get written regardless of whether or not there was news to write about – and not only to keep epistolary accounts balanced. Overwhelmingly in this era it was women's work – the duty of the daughters of the house in particular – to keep the far-flung members of a family in contact and so confirm the pact that linked them. *Plus ça change*: in 1987, the anthropologist Micaela di Leonardo noticed how much time and skill contemporary American women were expected to expend on 'kin work' – 'the conception, maintenance, and ritual celebration of cross-household kin ties, including visits, letters, telephone calls, presents, and cards'.[24]

According to the Austen scholar Deborah Kaplan, letters in which women do that networking – fulfilling, for instance, the daughterly duty to pass on to one's brother one's father's message about the price of sheep (as in a November 1798 letter (11) Austen addressed to Cassandra at their brother Edward's house in Kent) – are most aptly seen as 'corporate productions'. Women often took on male kin's interests as their own; in a female familiar letter, 'I' may very quickly metamorphose into 'we'.[25]

If, then, the letters Austen sent to members of her family circle are not straightforward vehicles for self-expression and confession, if in this forum Austen does not really appear to speak, as Hugh Blair might propose, in her 'real character', the reason is in part that a female letter-writer of Austen's day was frequently expected to speak on behalf of others. From time to time, Austen cedes space on her writing paper to her young nephews and nieces, enabling these small fry to leave their marks. Non-human actors on occasion prove similarly importunate. In a letter dated 8–9 November 1800 (letter 25), Cassandra in Kent thus learns from her sister back in Hampshire that the new tables have arrived, 'are both covered with green baize & send their best Love'. From a similarly droll letter dated 24 August 1805 (letter 45), Cassandra learns that her white mittens have been found: 'they were folded up within my clean night cap, & send their duty to you'.

In all probability those voluble tables and mittens sent their duty to many: for 'letters were the communal possessions of certain circles … and a letter to one was seen as a letter to all'.[26] During that discussion over Miss Bates's tea table of Jane Fairfax's letters, Emma is positioned to make her feeble compliment about 'the excellence of Miss Fairfax's handwriting' – evidently discernible despite the 'chequer-work' (*Emma*, ch. 19) – precisely because Jane's aunt inevitably hands these communications round to all her acquaintance. To similar effect earlier in *Emma*, the congratulatory missive that Frank Churchill sends off to his new stepmother on the occasion of the latter's marriage to his father almost automatically becomes, like Mr Churchill himself, 'one of the boasts of Highbury': 'For a few days every morning visit in Highbury included some mention of

the handsome letter Mrs. Weston had received ... It was, indeed, a highly-prized letter' (*Emma*, ch. 2). Through the prolonged circulation that sent them beyond their original addressee and into the hands of additional readers, letters helped define the limits of a community (a community eager to identify material for conversation in the letters passed on to them and skilled at turning that chat mediated by paper back into chat of the face-to-face variety). This, too, was letters' function. Letters went visiting from family to family, Austen's contemporary Mary Russell Mitford suggested, 'much in the same way as the country newspaper visits in rotation every house in a country village'. Thus it came to pass, as Mitford explains in this same 1811 letter, that one of the letters she herself had been sending off to a Miss R— in London was 'actually returned to me here by the hand of a mutual friend to whom she had lent it'.[27]

Mitford's anecdote delivers, in tandem with *Emma*, an account of epistolary practice interestingly distinct from the familiar story about the imperfect privacy of a private correspondence that was so often recounted in the epistolary novels she and Austen would have read in their youth. In those, tragedy is in the offing whenever letters are diverted from their addressee (as they almost invariably are) and into the wrong hands. Austen's *Sense and Sensibility*, for instance, replays this eighteenth-century plot in the section in which the letters that Marianne dispatches through the local penny post to Willoughby after her arrival in London are with mortifying consequences intercepted by the heiress to whom Willoughby has become engaged since his arrival in town.

The story of Austen's own letters, however, better resembles the one that Mitford recounts than the one that *Sense and Sensibility* does. Much is lost en route when letters continue their travels and traverse the passage between manuscript and print, but even so the story of Austen's correspondence teaches us a considerable amount, for instance, about the ease with which female familiar letters could be readdressed and appropriated by a widening circle of readers. This story teaches us something, too, about the readiness of those letters' authors to consider themselves the nodes within a network.

1   Hugh Blair, *Lectures on Rhetoric and Belles Lettres*, 4th edition, Strahan, Cadell and Creech, London, 1790, vol. 3, p. 67.

2   'Preface', *Letters of Jane Austen*, ed. Edward, Lord Brabourne, 2 vols, Richard Bentley, London, 1884, vol. 1, p. xiii.

3   On the letters' transmission as family heirlooms, see Kathryn Sutherland, 'Jane Austen's Life and Letters', in Claudia L. Johnson and Clara Tuite (eds), *A Companion to Jane Austen*, Blackwell, Oxford, 2009, pp. 13–30.

4   'Preface', Brabourne, *Letters of Jane Austen*, vol. 1, p. xii.

5   Compare Lindsay O' Neill, *The Opened Letter: Networking in the Early Modern British World*, University of Pennsylvania Press, Philadelphia, 2015, p. 4.

6   Austen-Leigh, *Memoir*, ed. Sutherland, p. 132.

7   Mary Augusta Austen-Leigh, *Personal Aspects of Jane Austen*, John Murray, London, 1920, p. 49.

8   Kathryn Sutherland, *Jane Austen's Textual Lives*, Oxford University Press, Oxford, 2005, p. 80. See also Jo Modert, 'Introduction', in *Jane Austen's Manuscript Letters in Facsimile*, Southern Illinois University Press, Carbondale, 1990, p. xxvi.

9   Henry Austen, 'Biographical Notice of the Author', in Austen-Leigh, *Memoir*, ed. Sutherland, p. 142.

10   Carol Houilhan Flynn, 'The Letters', in Edward Copeland and Juliet McMaster (eds), *The Cambridge Companion to Jane Austen*, 2nd edition, Cambridge University Press, Cambridge, 2011, pp. 97–110 (p. 98).

11   Georg Simmel, 'The Sociology of Sociability', *American Journal of Sociology*, vol. 55, no. 3, 1949, pp. 254–61 (p. 259).

12   Flynn, 'The Letters', p. 100.

13   Vivien Jones, 'Introduction', in Jane Austen, *Selected Letters*, ed. Vivien Jones, Oxford University Press, Oxford, 2004, pp. xiv, xi.

14   Austen-Leigh, *Memoir*, ed. Sutherland, p. 51.

15   Samuel Richardson, *Clarissa*, 4 vols, Dent, London, 1932, vol. 4, p. 495.

16   Talia Schaffer, *Novel Craft: Victorian Domestic Handicraft and Nineteenth-Century Fiction*, Oxford University Press, Oxford, 2011, p. 17.

17   'Letters and Letter Writers', *Work and Leisure: The Englishwoman's Advertiser, Reporter, and Gazette*, vol. 8, 1883, p. 242.

18   Duncan Campbell-Smith, *Masters of the Post: The Authorized History of the Royal Mail*, Allen Lane, London, 2011, p. 106.

19   Roger Chartier, 'Introduction', in Roger Chartier, Alain Boureau and Cécile Dauphin (eds), *Correspondence: Models of Letter Writing from the Middle Ages to the Nineteenth Century*, Princeton University Press, Princeton, NJ, 1997, p. 19.

20   As O' Neill notes, 'the strict accounting of letters grew, especially as [following Royal Mail improvements] the excuses for not sending a letter decreased' (*The Opened Letter*, p. 121).

21   W.H. Dilworth, 'Introduction', in *The Complete Letter Writer; Or Young Secretary's Instructor*, Glasgow, 1783, p. 3.

22   *Letters to and from the Late Samuel Johnson*, ed. Hester Thrale Piozzi, 2 vols, Strahan and Cadell, London, 1788, vol. 1, p. iv.

23   Cecilia Lucy Brightwell, *Memorials of the Life of Amelia Opie*, Fletcher and Alexander, Norwich, 1854, p. 334.

24   Micaela di Leonardo, 'The Female World of Cards and Holidays: Women, Families, and the Work of Kinship', *Signs*, vol. 12, no. 3, 1987, pp. 440–53 (p. 442).

25   Deborah Kaplan, *Jane Austen Among Women*, Johns Hopkins University Press, Baltimore, MD, 1992, pp. 47–8.

26   O' Neill, *The Opened Letter*, p. 42.

27   *The Life of Mary Russell Mitford, Told by Herself and in Letters to her Friends*, ed. A.G.K. L'Estrange, 2 vols, Harper, New York, 1870, vol. 1, p. 123.

Novelist
in the World

which is certainly gives you joy, my dear —— ——
can ever express the Thankfulness of my heart for the sight
Belov'd A——g——s in the most perfect Health & Spirits. and I
Mr. W—— enjoys the same, and added to your happiness in
Him, by appearing even better than when he went, as read
Son does. pray make my congratulations and best complime
With those of the Nuns, acceptable to him, and accept the
from them yourself. The frightfull Paragraph which app
in the Papers too on Saterday of the Guards being order'd to
West Indies, I hope & trust is totally groundless — it made
almost sick at the Idea — the Agent in Town has said to da
(May 18th) that he does not in the least beleive it. I figu
Myself, my dear freind, the Meeting of Mr W. with Yourself a
little ones — and truly participate in your joy — wishing it l
To last, and daily to encrease. I fear the Situation of you
Father will renew Those difficulties Mr W. before experien
and that in this respect Your present Comfort will be interrup
Mr W. Situation on Every account must render it most dan
For him to be known in visiting Mr P. — your all may d
On this, my dear, and too much Caution cannot be us'd
Pray does S——y take up her abode in N—— with Mr P
Or only come to him of days? — tell me, is he not y
Sick of France and French Madness? —
I had a letter a few days ago from Barbados, date apri
With particular accounts of the dreadfull Scenes which h
Been acting in Grenada & St Vincents — by the Charibs
Aigated by the french — their Massacring Men, women &

5

Women Writing in Time of War

Kathryn Sutherland

From his wartime posting in the eastern Mediterranean Rupert Brooke wrote home to England in April 1915:

> I cannot write you any description of my life. It is entirely featureless. It would need Miss Austen to make anything of it. We glide to & fro on an azure sea & forget the war – I must go & censor my platoon's letters.[1]

In 2017, we are at the same historical distance from the Great War of 1914–18 as those men and women then alive were from Britain's long campaign against Revolutionary and Napoleonic France – a war that raged for twenty-two years, from 1793 to 1815, with only a brief respite in 1802–3. It was a war that spanned almost the whole of Jane Austen's adult life. Through the nineteenth century, that war, too, had come to be known as the 'Great War' and was fought across the same ground that would be contested a hundred years later: France, Italy and Spain, the Low Countries, Central Europe and the Middle East. The Great War of 1795–1815 was a world war, extending to America in the west and India in the east. In 1914–18 soldiers in the trenches were reading the writers of that earlier conflict – Wordsworth, Byron and Austen. In his classic study, *The Great War and Modern Memory*, Paul Fussell examined the literary frames that gave meaning to the British experience of the 1914–18 war. He identified a particular phenomenon, 'the Curious Literariness of Real Life', that those in the trenches affirmed in a variety of ways: novels, volumes of poetry, the latest issue of *Punch* and *Country Life*, and antiquarian catalogues were routinely delivered to the dug outs of Ypres and the Somme by the Field Post Office;[2] British soldiers at Ypres wrote, printed and circulated their own paper, the *Wipers Times*; Robert Chapman, in civilian life the Assistant Secretary at the Clarendon Press, Oxford, now an artillery officer, planned and executed schools' editions of *Mansfield Park* and *Emma* from his posting in

Opposite detail of Figure 5.4

Figure 5.1 Two crosses bought with naval prize money for Jane and Cassandra by their brother Charles in 1801. © Jane Austen's House Museum.

Figure 5.2 Entry recording the death of Admiral Nelson at Trafalgar from logbook of HMS *Canopus* for October 1805, kept by Frank Austen as Captain. National Maritime Museum MS. AUS/2B. © National Maritime Museum, Greenwich.

the Balkans. Even the caustic revision of traditional genres and themes – love, nature and religion – by trench poets Wilfred Owen, Edmund Blunden and Edgell Richword, may better be seen as testing rather than refuting the relationship between literature and life and, in the process, refiguring the comforting and familiar to exorcize and repair a damaged world. Looking back from 2017 upon this time of close reading and counter-reading, of reading for life and against the grain, what appear remarkable are the missed readings – missed because lodged in plain sight; and among them, the evident engagement of Jane Austen's wartime vision.

Austen's social vision gained new significance in 1914–18 because, seemingly insulated from war, it represented an England worth fighting for: England imagined as the immemorial village clustered round the great house and the church. So argued Reginald Farrer in a centenary tribute in July 1917:

> all the vast anguish of her time is non-existent to Jane Austen, when once she has got pen in hand, to make us a new kingdom of refuge from the toils and frets of life. Her kingdoms are hermetically sealed, in fact, and here lies the strength of their impregnable immortality; it is not without hope or comfort for us nowadays, to remember that 'Mansfield Park' appeared the year before Waterloo, and 'Emma' the year after.[3]

Austen's popular and critical reception through much of the twentieth century was built on her seeming ignorance of public events, well described by Marilyn Butler as her 'discreet' approach to ideas. Such ignorance has even worked in her favour: while contemporary women writers, like Mary Wollstonecraft and Maria Edgeworth, might campaign in fiction for female education and economic emancipation, Austen's 'ladylike avoidance of "themes" has always been received as proof of her artistry'.[4] No novelist of 'themes' in her own day when political partisanship shaped the arts, to her readers in 1917, searching anxiously for safe harbour, she did not appear even to have been conscious that she was a wartime writer.

How could this be? Turbulent public events touched closely the private lives of several members of the Austen family. Living in Paris in the 1780s, Jane's glamorous cousin Eliza Hancock met and married the self-styled Comte de Feuillide, a captain in the Queen's Regiment of Dragoons. A frequent visitor to her Austen cousins at Steventon, Eliza was in England only days before the storming of the Bastille on 14 July 1789. Though she escaped the excesses of the Revolution, her husband was guillotined in 1794. During the brief cessation of war in 1802, and now married to Jane's brother Henry, Eliza made an unsuccessful trip to France to recover the comte's confiscated property. Settled in London, Henry's and Eliza's lives remained closely entwined with those of the exiled French community. Moving in émigré society on her regular visits there, Jane Austen attended their benefit concerts, heard of their misfortunes and

81. 69

81. 69½

The Weazle made Telegraph Signal, "Enemy defeated, but our Fleet off Cadiz in want of Assistance."

¼ past Noon Capt? Parker of the Weazle came on board, and brought the information as follows;— "On Monday the 21st Instant at 11 A.M. the British Fleet under the command of Vice Admiral Lord Viscount Nelson (consisting of 27 Ships of the Line) brought the combined Fleets of France and Spain (consisting of 33 Ships of the Line) to close Action, which after an arduous contest of 5 hours, termina-ted in a complete Victory on the part of the Former, the Enemy having lost 17 Ships captured & one burnt; amongst the former were two Spanish first rates and the French Commander in chiefs' Ship.— Our loss though not accurately as-certained was known to be great in Men; and unfortunately for his

72. 69

Country which can never sufficiently lament his loss, or too highly honor his memory, at the head of the list stands the name of the gallant Nelson."— Great and important as must be the victory, it is alas! dearly purchased at the price paid for it.— Never could England boast a naval Commander so eminently qualified for maintaining her superiority on the seas, as was her Nelson.— To the soundest judgement he united the most prompt decision and active energy, and possessed the happy talent of conciliating the

89. 68½

regards of all ranks of Officers and Men under his command, without losing sight of what was due to the service— Witness the exertions, till that mo-ment unknown, made at different times by his Squadron to complete their water and prepare for sea in a shorter period than could have been supposed possible.— His Memory will long be embalmed in the hearts

90. 68½

of a grateful Nation;— May those he has left behind him in the service strive to imitate so bright an example!!!

declared herself amused 'to see the ways of a French circle'.[5] Over the years, her letters make frequent mention of Henry and Eliza's émigrée housekeeper, Mme Bigeon, to whom she left £50 (the same amount as to Henry) in her will.

Jane Austen's adult life ran in parallel to Napoleon's rise and fall. They were very near contemporaries: her dates 1775–1817; his dates 1769–1821. Two of her brothers, Frank and Charles, were sailors who saw service in the Revolutionary and Napoleonic wars and the American War of 1812. They sent home gifts – 'Gold chains & Topaze Crosses', bought with prize money, realized by the capture of enemy ships (fig. 5.1) – and letters, from the East and West Indies, the Middle East and Mediterranean, the North Sea, the Baltic and North American waters; and Jane and Cassandra Austen posted replies: from Chawton to 'Captn Austen, HMS Elephant, Baltic', and to China.[6] Frank Austen, flag captain of HMS *Canopus*, one of six ships-of-the-line told off by Nelson to re-provision, wrote to his fiancée, Mary Gibson, on 27 October 1805, of his great disappointment at missing the action at Trafalgar six days before:

> As a national benefit, I cannot but rejoice that our arms have been once again successful, but at the same time I cannot help feeling how very unfortunate we have been to be away at such a moment, and by a fatal combination of unfortunate though unavoidable events to lose all share in the glory of a day which surpasses all which ever went before, is what I cannot think of with any degree of patience.[7]

His sister repaired the record in *Persuasion* (ch. 3), when she allowed Admiral Croft, rear admiral of the White (there was also a Red and a Blue), a share in Nelson's victory, while his brother-in-law, Frederick Wentworth, attains his captaincy after the action off St Domingo in the Caribbean in February 1806 (ch. 4), where Frank Austen commanded the *Canopus*. In *Mansfield Park* Austen paid tribute to four of her brothers' ships, the *Canopus*, the *Endymion*, the *Cleopatra* and the *Elephant*, modelling Fanny Price's sailor brother William on her own little brother, Charles.[8] And in a letter of 12 October 1813, she joked: 'Southey's Life of Nelson;—I am tired of Lives of Nelson, being that I never read any. I will read this however, if Frank is mentioned in it' (fig. 5.2).[9]

Austen's wartime vision is neither detached nor limited; what conspires to conceal her response in plain sight is her commitment to record events from the perspective of everyday reality – the daily routines of women (and men) who are waiting at home for letters from brothers or husbands campaigning overseas, who are reading the Army and Navy Lists for notice of men killed and officers promoted, and scanning the papers for news. *The Times* established a foreign news office during the Revolutionary War, and in 1799 the *Naval Chronicle* began publishing. A monthly journal of current record, lists of ships lost, destroyed and captured, naval poetry and biographies of famous sailors – a mix, in other words, of practical information, news and literature – the *Naval Chronicle*'s

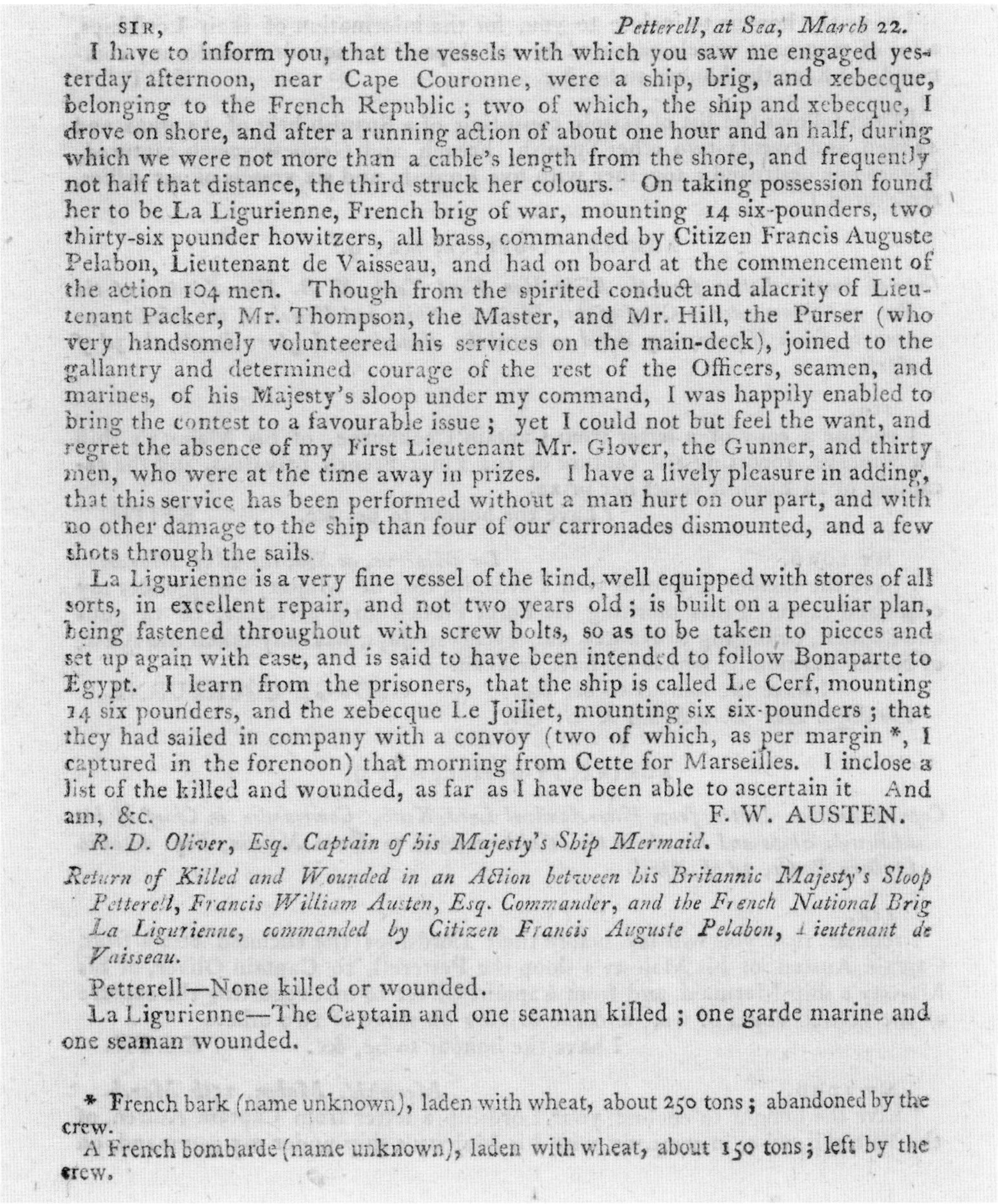

SIR, *Petterell, at Sea, March 22.*

I have to inform you, that the vessels with which you saw me engaged yesterday afternoon, near Cape Couronne, were a ship, brig, and xebecque, belonging to the French Republic; two of which, the ship and xebecque, I drove on shore, and after a running action of about one hour and an half, during which we were not more than a cable's length from the shore, and frequently not half that distance, the third struck her colours. On taking possession found her to be La Ligurienne, French brig of war, mounting 14 six-pounders, two thirty-six pounder howitzers, all brass, commanded by Citizen Francis Auguste Pelabon, Lieutenant de Vaisseau, and had on board at the commencement of the action 104 men. Though from the spirited conduct and alacrity of Lieutenant Packer, Mr. Thompson, the Master, and Mr. Hill, the Purser (who very handsomely volunteered his services on the main-deck), joined to the gallantry and determined courage of the rest of the Officers, seamen, and marines, of his Majesty's sloop under my command, I was happily enabled to bring the contest to a favourable issue; yet I could not but feel the want, and regret the absence of my First Lieutenant Mr. Glover, the Gunner, and thirty men, who were at the time away in prizes. I have a lively pleasure in adding, that this service has been performed without a man hurt on our part, and with no other damage to the ship than four of our carronades dismounted, and a few shots through the sails.

La Ligurienne is a very fine vessel of the kind, well equipped with stores of all sorts, in excellent repair, and not two years old; is built on a peculiar plan, being fastened throughout with screw bolts, so as to be taken to pieces and set up again with ease, and is said to have been intended to follow Bonaparte to Egypt. I learn from the prisoners, that the ship is called Le Cerf, mounting 14 six pounders, and the xebecque Le Joiliet, mounting six six-pounders; that they had sailed in company with a convoy (two of which, as per margin *, I captured in the forenoon) that morning from Cette for Marseilles. I inclose a list of the killed and wounded, as far as I have been able to ascertain it. And am, &c. F. W. AUSTEN.

R. D. Oliver, Esq. Captain of his Majesty's Ship Mermaid.

Return of Killed and Wounded in an Action between his Britannic Majesty's Sloop Petterell, Francis William Austen, Esq. Commander, and the French National Brig La Ligurienne, commanded by Citizen Francis Auguste Pelabon, Lieutenant de Vaisseau.

Petterell—None killed or wounded.

La Ligurienne—The Captain and one seaman killed; one garde marine and one seaman wounded.

* French bark (name unknown), laden with wheat, about 250 tons; abandoned by the crew.

A French bombarde (name unknown), laden with wheat, about 150 tons; left by the crew.

Figure 5.3 *Naval Chronicle*, 3 (1800), p. 410, a letter from Captain F.W. (Frank) Austen of HMS *Petterell*, written 22 March 1800, describing his pursuit and capture of the French ship *La Ligurienne*. Oxford, Bodleian Library, Hope adds. 480.

stated intention was to unite a readership of sailors with the general public (fig. 5.3). Written and printed war correspondence brought far-flung campaigns to London, Edinburgh and Hampshire villages, even as the movement of news and information homewards exposed the ignorance, one of another, of each separate theatre of war. In a global war, where is the front? Home (in this case, England) was the place where intelligence was funnelled and whence it circulated. The domestic reader could not know the immediacy of war, but with official despatches, war journalism and an efficient postal service she had the means to be better informed than ever before, 'could claim greater knowledge of the war than could any one individual actively participating in the war'.[10] Of course, there were long gaps without news and between events and their reporting: the Navy List could only tell you your brother or husband was alive a month ago; and when the *Times* of London announced on 2 October 1798 'the news' of Nelson's victory at Aboukir Bay and the destruction of the French fleet, the event was already three months old.[11] There was then no telegraph as in 1914, no communications satellites as in the Iraq war of 2003; but some features that we can recognize as modern in the second-hand, home-centred experience of war were emerging.

Penelope Maitland, wife of General Sir Alexander Maitland, wrote from Totteridge, north London, on 9 September 1799 to her young correspondent Charlotte West, then living at 44 Hans Place, Kensington, London, with the latest news of a son and a husband serving with the British troops in Holland:

> My Dear M[rs] West,
>
> Within this half hour a Letter has arrived from My Dear August[s] written on the 4th and tho' some letters of Particular consequence are pressing for answers, I cannot delay the pleasing information he desires me to convey to you of Captain West's good health …
> What you & I have both suffer'd my dear Madam, has Been truly inexpressible—and alas! What we still feel! But May God make us unfeignedly thankfull for his Unspeakable Mercies hitherto! *Our Freinds* in Holland Have (with the British Troops) gain'd immortal honor, & I humbly hope & trust may be brought to us with their Dearly purchas'd Laurels—sure they may be so call'd, for never was greater fatigue than they have undergone, and their Lying 3 nights on the *Sand* (which my Augus[s] Says, '*was rather Cool*') has, as it might be expected, brought on a Diarrhoea among soldiers & officers. My son Said he had a Slight touch of it, which makes me very Uneasy, but he adds that as they were now in Villages, he Hop'd it Might cease.[12]

Her next letter, postmarked 30 September 1799, supplied further information:

> My Dear M[rs] West,
>
> I yesterday had the joy of a letter from my Son in Holland, the date, Petten, 13th inst. But had not the same Post brought ^ to the Gen[l]^ another of a later date, viz: the 20th, the day after the last sad Engagement, I had still been Under much disquietude. he was Exceedingly considerate & kind to write in so much hurry and So Fatigu'd to assure us he was well—I cannot be sufficiently

of which I sincerely give you joy, my Dear Charlotte — No words
can ever express the Thankfulness of my heart for the sight of my
Belov'd A—g—s in the most perfect Health & Spirits, and I hope
Mr W— enjoys the same, and added to your happiness in seeing
Him, by appearing even better than when he went, as really my
Son does. pray make my congratulations and best compliments
with those of the Nuns, acceptable to him, and accept the same
from them yourself. The frightfull Paragraph which appear'd
in the Papers ~~too~~ on Saterday of the Guards being order'd to the
West Indies, I hope & trust is totally groundless — it made me
almost sick at the Idea — the Agent in Town has said to day
(May 18_th) that he does not in the least beleive it. I figure to
Myself, my dear freind, the Meeting of Mr W. with Yourself and
Little ones — and truly participate in your joy — wishing it long,
To last, and daily to Increase. I fear the Situation of your
Father will renew those difficulties Mr W. before experienc'd,
and that in this respect Your present Comfort or it be interrupted.
Mr W. situation on Every account must render it most dangerous
For him to be known in visiting Mr P. — your all may depend
On this, my dear, and too much Caution cannot be us'd.
Pray does S—y take up her abode in N— with Mr P—
Or only come to him of days? — tell me, is he not yet
Sick of France and French Madness? —
I had a letter a few days ago from Barbados, date April 4_th
With particular accounts of the dreadfull Scenes which have
Been Acting in Grenada & St Vincents — by the Charibs ins=
tigated by the french — their Massacring Men, women & children
Tearing infants from the Breast, holding them up by a Leg with one
hand,

at He may
Love him
to us.
prefer this
arts!
you have
thize to my
ther in such
be his
uld induce
obnoxious
reasons;
d by the
t he was
d his ex=
d that was
im having
l after a
hang'd in
n New
dreadfull
situation
he will
an Equal
e and
iously
our dear
Continent.

thankfull to God for his preservation now in 3 engagements!—he Had not had his Cloaths off in a Fortnight – but there is no Cessation from terror. there seems a necessity to fight every inch of the Way, exactly contrary to the first expectation—plainly it Evinces the deception the *great People* here were under, in fancying the *easy admittance* into Holland. Augustus commission'd me To tell you, my dear Freind, Capt West was perfectly well, and not ^ to all appearance^ in any ^respect^ the worse for all he had undergone. in my answer, which Went yesterday, I with much pleasure Sent the good account I had Had *of* & *from* you.

The two women had been corresponding since 1783, when Charlotte was still Miss Perry. In 1795 her father, the radical newspaper proprietor Sampson Perry,[13] had been imprisoned in Newgate for his liberal Revolutionary sympathies, much to the public embarrassment of his daughter, now married to an army officer, Captain Charles West; and Perry was still incarcerated in 1799. In their letters the women recast war in intimate and familial terms; it is brought home, shared and commented on, become a cause for mutual sympathy or congratulation. They wait for the post-boy, they scrutinize dates and postmarks, they weigh the truth of reports in the papers – 'The frightfull Paragraph which appear'd in the Papers on Saturday of the Guards being order'd to the West Indies, I hope & trust is totally groundless' (4 May 1795) – they criticize military policy and read between the lines. Their prejudices are as combat-sharpened as any soldier's: 'I am truly alarm'd at the Idea of Bringing a number of *Irish* Troops to this Country, and sending 8000 soldiery to that horrid Dissaffected Nation' (29 October 1803). For Penelope Maitland domestic life is shaped by war and Charlotte is 'My Dear Military Freind' (fig. 5.4).

Austen's surviving correspondence allows similar glimpses into the unpredictable and circuitous networks by which news travelled to and from war zones:

> [Wednesday 11 February 1801] a letter from Charles to myself.—It was written last Saturday from off the Start [a headland on the Devon coast], & conveyed to Popham Lane [a stagecoach stop in Hampshire] by Cap^tn^ Boyle ... he came from Lisbon in the Endymion, & I will copy Charles' account of his conjectures about Frank.—'He has not seen my brother lately, nor does he expect to find him arrived, as he met Capt: Inglis at Rhodes going up to take command of the Petterel as he was coming down, but supposes he will arrive in less than a fortnight from this time, in some ship which is expected to reach England about that time with dispatches from Sir Ralph Abercrombie.'

On Wednesday 10 April 1805, she wrote to Charles 'in consequence of my Mother's having seen in the papers that the Urania was waiting at Portsmouth for the Convoy for Halifax [Nova Scotia]', where he was then based; and on 25 April 1811, she relayed to

Figure 5.5 Thomas Rowlandson, *Female Politicians*, 1809. Oxford, Bodleian Library, Curzon b.4 (3).

Chawton indirect news, again of Charles, once more in North American waters, picked up at one of Eliza Austen's parties in Sloane Street, London:

> Capt. Simpson told us, on the authority of some other Capt[n] just arrived
> from Halifax, that Charles was bringing the Cleopatra home, & that she was
> probably by this time in the Channel—but as Capt. S. was certainly in liquor,
> we must not quite depend on it.—It must give one a sort of expectation however,
> & will prevent my writing to him any more.—I would rather he sh[d] not reach
> England till I am at home …[14]

In war, any distinction between public and private news quickly breaks down: public reports are scoured for private information, while personal communications carry public intelligence and disclosures to be shared (fig. 5.5). Nor do hand-written letter and print differ as much as we might imagine in their timeliness or trustworthiness, as we see in *Mansfield Park*, where the newspaper 'esteemed to have the earliest naval intelligence' and Midshipman William Price's letter to his sister, despatched as his ship 'came up Channel', arrive on the same day (ch. 24). In *Emma*, it is given to Jane Fairfax, a war orphan, whose infantry officer father died 'in action abroad' (ch. 20), to extol the marvels of the post office:

> 'The post-office is a wonderful establishment!' said [Jane Fairfax].—'The regularity and dispatch of it! If one thinks of all that it has to do, and all that it does so well, it is really astonishing!' (ch. 34)

Jane Austen is the first English novelist to explore the effect of contemporary war on the home front. We might say that she was war-conditioned – wartime was the ordinary, everyday time of her adult life. It may not be coincidental that her first publisher, Thomas Egerton, specialized in military and political works from his shop on the east side of Whitehall, just across from the Admiralty Office. He had run his 'Military Library' for two decades when he accepted *Sense and Sensibility*, in 1810 or 1811.[15] We know from *Pride and Prejudice*, Austen's second novel, that by 1813 the south of England resembled a military camp: in 1793 there were only seventeen permanent infantry barracks; within twelve years there were 168.[16] Her brother Henry served in the Oxfordshire militia, rising to the rank of captain before resigning his commission in 1801. Remarkably, given the likelihood of infiltration by foreign spies, camps were open to the public, who were invited in to admire military manoeuvres: 'What the people saw at the camps was war mediated as spectacle, extravaganzas of movement, sound, and colour which imitated the theatre of battle' (fig. 5.6).[17] Such 'theatre' provides the perfect backdrop in *Pride and Prejudice* for silly Lydia Bennet's seduction and elopement. Living in Southampton in 1807–9, Austen would have seen naval preparations at close quarters. Chawton is now a sleepy Hampshire village, but when she moved there in July 1809 it lay at a vital junction on the roads to Winchester, Gosport and London. Making land on the south coast, Napoleon might well have marched with his army past Jane Austen's door on his way to London.

War provides the rhythm to which all Austen's novels unfold: the way they turn on misinformation, plans delayed or disrupted, unexpected mediations, the anxious wait for a letter or for something to happen. For characters within and readers of Austen's novels, the absence of event is the precondition for an invasion of the ordinary by the extraordinary and for the extraction and minute inspection of meaning from the day's slightest crease. By the 1810s, when Austen was publishing, the big ideas for change that had driven the novel in the early 1790s appeared hopelessly tarnished. Now writers of every political persuasion manifested a widespread counter-revolutionary conservatism, in light of French subjugation of much of Europe and after almost two decades of war.

Figure 5.6 *Dr Syntax at a Review*, from *The Tour of Doctor Syntax In Search of the Picturesque*, a poem by William Combe, illustrated by Thomas Rowlandson (1812). Oxford, Bodleian Library, 13 θ 147, plate 13.

This is the context for Austen's own famous quietism.

Quietism is most evident in the two great mature novels, *Mansfield Park* and *Emma*, written between February 1811 and the end of March 1815, during the late phase of the protracted Napoleonic Wars. Austen's earliest writings, by contrast, suggest a more pliant response to changes signalled by events in Revolutionary France. 'Kitty, or the Bower', dedicated to her sister Cassandra in August 1792, carries in the person of its heroine, Kitty Peterson, a strong challenge to the meanness of female opportunities that chimes with more overtly polemical texts, like the 'Preface' that Charlotte Smith affixed to *Desmond. A Novel*, and dated 'June 20, 1792':

> But women it is said have no business with politics—Why not?—have they no interest in the scenes that are acting around them, in which they have fathers, brothers, husbands, sons, or friends engaged?—Even in the commonest course of female education, they are expected to acquire some knowledge of history; and yet, if they are to have no opinion of what *is* passing; it avails little that they should be informed of what *has passed*…[18]

In numerous ways, Austen's apprentice novella is alert to the libertarian politics of its day: from Kitty's championship of female independence and economic rights – 'do you call it lucky, for a Girl of Genius & Feeling … to be married to a Man of whose Disposition she has no opportunity of judging till her Judgement is of no use to her, who may be a Tyrant, or a Fool or both' – to her aunt's comically exaggerated anti-Jacobin fears for imminent social and moral collapse, summed up in her frequent recourse to the comment that 'every thing is going to sixes & sevens and all order will soon be at an end throughout the Kingdom'.[19] Written before the execution of Louis XVI on 21 January 1793 precipitated Britain into war with France, the story witnesses a surprising political daring in the teenage Austen. In fact, Austen's writing career follows more closely than we might expect fluctuations in the British response to the contemporary situation – from the social and sexual assertion and freer spirit of her early work through the defensive conservatism of her middle period and on to a late (post-Waterloo) celebration of risk.

The events of *Mansfield Park* are precisely contemporary with their date of writing – the narrative unfolding in the shadow of the Anglo–American War of 1812, the blockade of the Atlantic and continuing conflict with France. Austen's sailor brother, Frank, newly promoted to captain and on duty in the Azores and the Baltic in 1812 and 1813, was a major influence on the book's moral landscape and may have directed her rather unusual choice of reading during its composition, *Essay on the Military Policy and Institutions of the British Empire* (1810), by Charles Pasley, Captain in the Royal Engineers: 'a book which I protested against at first, but which upon trial I find delightfully written & highly entertaining.'[20] Pasley writes with a soldier's

Figure 5.7 *The Glorious Pursuit of Ten against Seventeen*, Nelson's pursuit of the French fleet in July 1805 prior to Trafalgar. Oxford, Bodleian Library, Curzon b.4 (1).

common sense and exasperation at the inadequate preparations and half-measures of the British government in the face of Napoleon's brutal fighting machine. His experiences in the Spanish Peninsula campaign underlie his call for better strategy, a more efficient deployment of forces and a more professional army. Austen must have relished his plain style, dry wit and irony, not to mention his unreserved praise for the British navy – explanation enough for her comment that he is '[t]he first soldier I ever sighed for' (fig. 5.7). Pasley writes:

> nothing but the greatest unanimity and firmness on the part of the nation, nothing but the wisest measures on the part of the government, can save us, and with us the rest of the civilized world, from swelling the triumph of the haughty conqueror … nothing but our naval superiority has saved us from being at this moment a province of France.
>
> … But how are we to improve the deficiencies of our military system, and to acquire greater skill in the art of war? Not, certainly, by remaining inactive, by never venturing to attack our enemy; by running away from every country, in which we know that he can attack us; and by even running away from some countries, without waiting to ascertain whether it be possible for him to get at us or not; lest we should, by any accident, risk the lives of our valuable soldiers.
>
> It is remarkable, that we have had no canting about valuable lives ever urged as a reason for neglecting any opportunity, however hazardous, of destroying the enemy's ships; and yet life is fully as dear to the mariner as to the soldier.[21]

Mansfield Park is a wartime mediation on the place of family in the defence of the nation. From this springs the ideological freight of apparently personal conversations and the symbolic placing of its major characters: the newly ordained clergyman Edmund Bertram; the energetic midshipman William Price, who has seen 'every variety of danger, which sea and war together could offer' (ch. 24); and introspective Fanny Price, self-dedicated to nurturing the family's moral welfare. The novel's present time is divided between the spacious, well-proportioned Northamptonshire estate of Mansfield Park and the cramped conditions of naval Portsmouth, but its backdrop is global, comprising Sir Thomas Bertram's voyage to Antigua and William Price's past campaigns in the Mediterranean and West Indies, with North America and the Netherlands in prospect. An English Channel port of great strategic significance, Portsmouth was, at the time, the most regularly fortified town in England, with evidence everywhere of a city dedicated to war. During visits to the dockyards (with its new blocking machinery, to the design of the French engineer Marc Isambard Brunel), during walks on the city's ramparts and saluting battery, and at worship in the Garrison Chapel, the sophisticated rake Henry Crawford makes his unsuccessful assault on Fanny Price's heart (fig. 5.8).

> ### THE CAMPUS NAUTICA,
> ### A GRAND NAVAL EXHIBITION,
>
> CONTINUES open at the Great Room, Spring-Gardens, Charing-crofs, every day, from Ten o'clock till Five in the afternoon.
>
> The fubject, a VIEW OF THE FLEET AT SPITHEAD, on the 1ft of May, 1795, in the act of getting under fail, to avoid danger from the BOYNE, of 98 guns, which had unfortunately taken fire; diverfified with innumerable groups of figures and boats, an extenfive View of the Ifle of Wight, &c.
>
> ——— " O, do but think
> You ftand upon the rivage, and behold
> A city on th' inconftant billows dancing;
> For fo appears this Fleet majeftical!"
>   Shakefpear's Henry V.
>   Admiffion One Shilling.
>   *₊* A fire is in the Room.

In *Mansfield Park*, family fortunes offer a microcosm of the nation at war. In war, the family's chief shield is religion – religion directed outwards to serve a social or public interest. Austen, the daughter and sister of clergymen, considered her own faith at this time of war as bound up in the reforms spearheaded by the Evangelical wing of the Anglican Church, by abolitionists like William Wilberforce and Zacharay Macaulay, and members of the so-called Clapham Sect, who emphasized the importance of moral rearmament and of setting a good example. The Austen brothers and sisters were part of this socially conservative early nineteenth-century movement for improvement. Cassandra read and recommended to Jane Evangelical works directed at women by Thomas Gisborne and the redoubtable Hannah More. Frank Austen, whose patron Admiral Gambier was a noted Evangelical, attracted attention for his piety as 'the officer who knelt in church'. It was during Frank's 1805 and 1806 tours of duty in the West Indies that he formed a hostile view of the treatment of slaves. In 1816 Henry Austen, one-time militia officer and Army agent, became 'an earnest preacher of the evangelical school'.[22] A letter of 2 September 1814 to her friend Martha Lloyd makes clear Jane Austen's own ardent opinion that Britain's share in military victory is bound up with the nation's religious health. There was reason for optimism: Napoleon had abdicated only months before, in April 1814, and was packed off to exile on Elba. But the prospect of further war with America was cause for alarm:

Figure 5.8 'Campus Nautica', news cutting describing 'A Grand Naval Exhibition' at the Great Room, Spring Gardens, Charing Cross, London, February 1796. The exhibit is a painting of the British fleet at Spithead, Portsmouth. Oxford, Bodleian Library, John Johnson Collection, Dioramas 5 (30f).

The [?Americans] cannot be conquered, & we shall only be teaching them the skill in War which they may now want. We are to make them good Sailors & Soldiers, & [?gain] nothing ourselves. – If we *are* to be ruined, it cannot be helped – but I place my hope of better things on a claim to the protection of Heaven, as a Religious Nation, a Nation inspite of much Evil improving in Religion, which I cannot believe the Americans to possess. (letter 106)

War is history, as Catherine Morland, the heroine of *Northanger Abbey*, confidently understands.[23] But how will war be described and how many histories might war tell? This is the challenge Austen set herself in *Persuasion*, her last completed novel, issued posthumously in 1818 and thus, by chance, lent a personal-historical perspective from which to view her own too short life. *Persuasion* is Austen's most time-stamped novel – a tale of mourning and loss (lost youth, lost beauty, lost happiness, lost estates), in which the little non-events of Anne Elliot's private history do duty for years of separation and war. *Persuasion* is also Austen's most auspiciously dated novel. Begun on 8 August 1815, a day on which the *Times* carried news of Napoleon's departure for St Helena, its action is set precisely one year earlier 'at this present time, (the summer of 1814)' (ch. 1). The significance of this slight fictional time lag is worth pondering: written *after* Waterloo, its events unfold *before* Waterloo, during the brief respite from war following the Treaty of Paris (June 1814) that ended abruptly with Napoleon's escape from Elba in February 1815. In the real and fictional summer of 1814 that peace looked secure; with it, naval officers returned home, among them Captain Frederick Wentworth, who, after eight years of fighting and promotion, and flush with prize money, is a different prospect from the penniless young sailor Anne had been persuaded to reject (fig. 5.9). 'It was now his object to marry. He was rich, and being turned on shore, fully intended to settle as soon as he could be properly tempted' (ch. 7). While he has spent the intervening years since they last met hazarding his life and advancing his fortunes, Anne has found consolation for her diminished existence in public accounts of war – 'She had only navy lists and newspapers' (ch. 4) – her secret store of naval information supplying the timeline that charts her own empty years. Will Wentworth's homecoming offer the chance to recover what was lost? The emotional, even erotic, tension that builds through the novel is witness to how keenly lives are balanced between loss and hope, past and future, in times of crisis. The narrative moves from autumn to spring; hope recovers; at the same time, the far-sighted reader's slight dislocation from events ensures the poignant understanding that, like peace, happiness is fragile and not without risk. The resumption of conflict, and with it the threat of loss, lie just beyond the novel's frame. In *Persuasion*, and through Anne Elliot's quiet characterization, Austen offers her most subtle domestic mediation on war's cost.

In *Sanditon*, the novel begun in January 1817 and laid aside after only twelve chapters, we sense a world opening up to change after eighteen months of European peace. Like *Persuasion, Sanditon* turns a satirical focus upon the landed gentry who no longer wisely maintain their estates and who, in consequence, no longer guarantee the nation's stability. In *Persuasion* Austen aligned herself with the values of the rising professional classes, men like her sailor brothers, whose advancement is by virtue of merit and risk – much as her own progress was as a professional novelist.[24] But in the post-war climate of boom and bust, the sailor's meritorious risk has been replaced by the sheer recklessness of landed men like Mr Parker, who abandons his family estate for property speculation in a new seaside resort. Mr Parker, too, is a type of modern man made restless, dislocated, by years of war and wishing to turn events to advantage:

> 'Ah!'—said Mr. Parker.—'This is my old house—the house of my forefathers—the house where I and all my brothers and sisters were born and bred—and where my own three eldest children were born … You will not think I have made a bad exchange, when we reach Trafalgar House—which, by the bye, I almost wish I had not named Trafalgar—for Waterloo is more the thing now. However, Waterloo is in reserve—and if we have encouragement enough this year for a little Crescent to be ventured on— (as I trust we shall) then we shall be able to call it Waterloo Crescent—and the name joined to the form of the building, which always takes, will give us the command of lodgers—. In a good season we should have more applications than we could attend to.'— (ch. 4)[25]

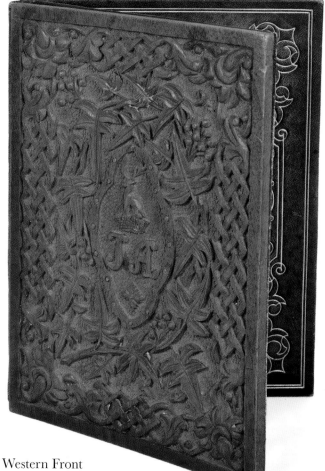

Figure 5.9 A wooden letter case, carved by Frank Austen on one of his many long sea voyages. © Jane Austen's House Museum.

In 1916, in a macabre imposition of normality, soldiers on the Western Front named their trenches after London streets – Piccadilly, Regent Street, the Strand. After any war, buildings patriotically named to honour victories both commemorate and cleanse the action they displace, turning it into history. The end of war in 1815 mobilized holidaymakers – tourists replacing troops. If, in 1817, the full lodging houses of Waterloo Crescent were still in prospect, the battlefield at Waterloo had already been systematically picked over by curious visitors seeking trophies. Within weeks of the battle, fought on 18 June 1815, war tourists had arrived in Belgium; among the first was Walter Scott, who set out in August. Even earlier, on the scene within days, was Charlotte Anne Waldie, whose unflinching account, styled 'Circumstantial Details …

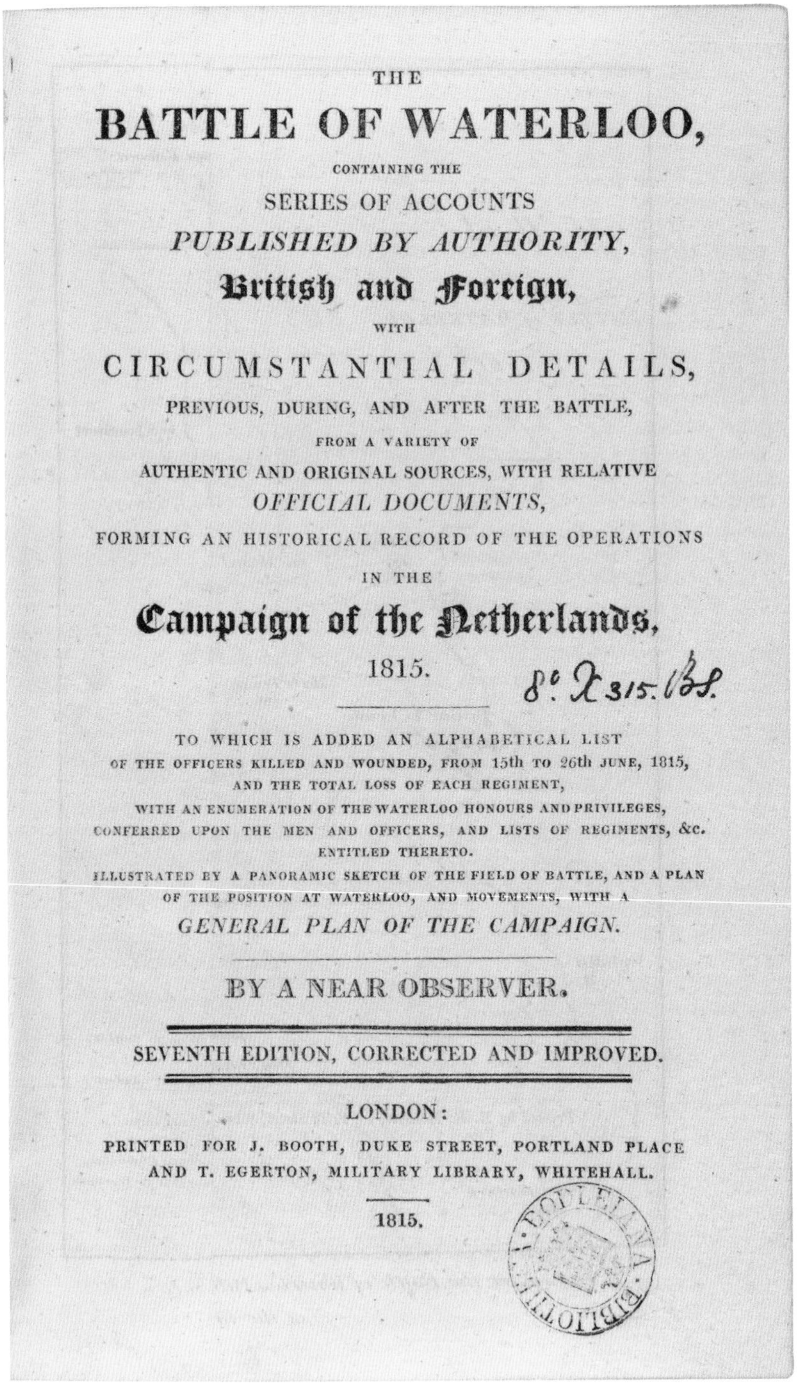

THE

BATTLE OF WATERLOO,

CONTAINING THE

SERIES OF ACCOUNTS

PUBLISHED BY AUTHORITY,

𝔅𝔯𝔦𝔱𝔦𝔰𝔥 𝔞𝔫𝔡 𝔉𝔬𝔯𝔢𝔦𝔤𝔫,

WITH

CIRCUMSTANTIAL DETAILS,

PREVIOUS, DURING, AND AFTER THE BATTLE,

FROM A VARIETY OF

AUTHENTIC AND ORIGINAL SOURCES, WITH RELATIVE

OFFICIAL DOCUMENTS,

FORMING AN HISTORICAL RECORD OF THE OPERATIONS

IN THE

𝔆𝔞𝔪𝔭𝔞𝔦𝔤𝔫 𝔬𝔣 𝔱𝔥𝔢 𝔑𝔢𝔱𝔥𝔢𝔯𝔩𝔞𝔫𝔡𝔰,

1815.

TO WHICH IS ADDED AN ALPHABETICAL LIST
OF THE OFFICERS KILLED AND WOUNDED, FROM 15th TO 26th JUNE, 1815,
AND THE TOTAL LOSS OF EACH REGIMENT,
WITH AN ENUMERATION OF THE WATERLOO HONOURS AND PRIVILEGES,
CONFERRED UPON THE MEN AND OFFICERS, AND LISTS OF REGIMENTS, &c.
ENTITLED THERETO.
ILLUSTRATED BY A PANORAMIC SKETCH OF THE FIELD OF BATTLE, AND A PLAN
OF THE POSITION AT WATERLOO, AND MOVEMENTS, WITH A
GENERAL PLAN OF THE CAMPAIGN.

BY A NEAR OBSERVER.

SEVENTH EDITION, CORRECTED AND IMPROVED.

LONDON:

PRINTED FOR J. BOOTH, DUKE STREET, PORTLAND PLACE
AND T. EGERTON, MILITARY LIBRARY, WHITEHALL.

1815.

Figure 5.10 Title page of
*The Battle of Waterloo … with
Circumstantial Details* (1815).
Oxford, Bodleian Library,
8° X 315 BS.

by a Near Observer' (fig. 5.10), of the sights and smells of Waterloo went through seven editions before the end of the year:

> soldiers' caps pierced with many a ball, and trodden under foot—eagles that had ornamented them—badges of the legion of honour—cuirasses—fragments of broken arms, belts and scabbards innumerable—shreds of tattered cloth, shoes, cartridge boxes, gloves, highland bonnets, feathers steeped in mud and gore … innumerable papers of every description, that had been thrown out of the pockets of the dead, by those who had pillaged them. French love-letters, and letters from mothers to their sons, and from children to their parents, were scattered about in every direction. … we found only one English letter. It was from a soldier's wife to her husband.[26]

In an expanded edition of 1817, retitled *A Few Days Residence in Belgium*, Waldie has rewritten that final detail: 'The quantities of letters and of blank sheets of dirty writing paper were so great that they literally whitened the surface of the earth.'[27] The image of the battlefield bleached by paper multiplies as it anonymizes the letters sent by mothers, wives and children to their soldier sons, husbands and fathers. But the effect is no less shocking in its reminder that domestic and military, home and war, cannot be held apart.

1   *The Letters of Rupert Brooke*, ed. Geoffrey Keynes, Faber & Faber, London, 1968, pp. 680–1.

2   Paul Fussell, *The Great War and Modern Memory*, Oxford University Press, New York and London, 1975, pp. ix and 66–7: 'The postal service brought the troops their usual magazines: one simply indicated a change of address and the subscription continued uninterrupted.'

3   Reginald Farrer, 'Jane Austen, *ob.* July 18, 1817', *Quarterly Review* (July 1917), in Brian Southam (ed.), *Jane Austen: The Critical Heritage*, vol. 2, Routledge & Kegan Paul, London, 1987, p. 249.

4   Marilyn Butler, 'History, Politics, and Religion', in J. David Grey (ed.), *The Jane Austen Handbook*, Athlone Press, London, 1986, p. 194.

5   Jane Austen, 18–20 April 1811, letter 70; and see Deirdre Le Faye, *Jane Austen's 'Outlandish Cousin': The Life and Letters of Eliza de Feuillide*, British Library, London, 2002.

6   Jane Austen, 26–27 May 1801, letter 38; 3–6 July 1813, letter 86; and 26 July 1809, letter 69.

7   Quoted in John H. and Edith C. Hubback, *Jane Austen's Sailor Brothers: Being the Adventures of Sir Francis Austen, G. C. B., Admiral of the Fleet, and Rear-Admiral Charles Austen*, John Lane, London, 1906, p. 156. Frank's long serial letter, begun 15 October and finished three weeks later, is only known from a transcript; it is quoted in more detail in Brian Southam, *Jane Austen and the Navy*, 2nd edition, National Maritime Museum Publishing, Greenwich, London, 2005, pp. 98ff.

8   All four are recorded in *Mansfield Park*, ch. 38; Frank served on the *Canopus* and the *Elephant*, and Charles on the *Endymion* and the *Cleopatra*. See 6 July 1813, letter 86, to Frank: 'I have something in hand – which I hope on the credit of P.&P. will sell well, tho' not half so entertaining. And by the bye – shall you object to my mentioning the Elephant in it, & two or three other of your old Ships? – I *have* done it, but it shall not stay, to make you angry. – They are only just mentioned.'

9   Letter 91.

10 Mary A. Favret, 'War Correspondence: Reading Romantic War', *Prose Studies*, vol. 19, 1996, pp. 173–85 (p. 177).

11 Mary A. Favret, *War at a Distance: Romanticism and the Making of Modern Wartime*, Princeton University Press, Princeton, NJ and Oxford, 2010, p. 73.

12 Bodleian Library, Oxford, Maitland Correspondence (uncatalogued).

13 Oxford Dictionary of National Biography, Sampson Perry (1747–1823). Perry wrote and published from Newgate Prison *An Historical Sketch of the French Revolution* (2 vols, 1796). <http://www.oxforddnb.com/view/article/21998>, accessed 10 June 2016.

14 Letters 34, 43 and 71.

15 See Kathryn Sutherland, 'Jane Austen's Dealings with John Murray and His Firm', *Review of English Studies*, n.s. vol. 64, 2012, pp. 105–26 (pp. 106–7).

16 Jenny Uglow, *In These Times: Living in Britain Through Napoleon's Wars* 1793–1815, Faber & Faber, London, 2014, p. 36.

17 Gillian Russell, *The Theatres of War: Performance, Politics, and Society*, 1793–1815, Clarendon Press, Oxford, 1995, p. 34.

18 Charlotte Smith, *Desmond. A Novel*, 3 vols, G.G.J. and J. Robinson, London, 1792, vol. 1, pp. iii–iv.

19 'Kitty or the Bower', *Volume the Third*, in Jane Austen, *Teenage Writings*, ed. Kathryn Sutherland and Freya Johnston, Oxford University Press, Oxford, 2017.

20 Letter 78, 24 January 1813, to Cassandra Austen.

21 C.W. Pasley, *Essay on the Military Policy and Institutions of the British Empire*, 3rd edition, Edmund Lloyd, London, 1811, pp. 1–2, 321–2. The work was reissued in 1914.

22 For Cassandra Austen's Evangelical reading, see 30 August 1805, letter 47, and 24 January 1809, letter 66; Hubback and Hubback, *Jane Austen's Sailor Brothers*, p. 114, records Frank's piety; Henry Austen's Evangelicalism is already evident in his 1817 'Biographical Notice' of his sister, written as a preface to *Northanger Abbey*; see, too, Deirdre Le Faye, *Jane Austen: A Family Record*, Cambridge University Press, Cambridge, 2004, p. 262.

23 '... history, real solemn history, I cannot be interested in ... wars or pestilences, in every page; the men all so good for nothing, and hardly any women at all', *Northanger Abbey*, ch. 14.

24 Writing of his failure to see action at Trafalgar (see note 7 above), Frank Austen pointed out to his fiancée exactly what this meant for his prospects: 'I shall have to lament our absence on such an occasion on a double account, the loss of pecuniary advantage as well as professional credit.'

25 The Strand Bridge in London, begun in 1811, was renamed Waterloo Bridge in 1816.

26 *The Battle of Waterloo, containing the series of accounts published by authority ... with Circumstantial Details ... by a Near Observer*, 7th edition, J. Booth and T. Egerton, London, 1815, pp. 41–2.

27 [Charlotte Anne Waldie] *Narrative of a Residence in Belgium during the campaign of 1815; and of a visit to the field of Waterloo, by an Englishwoman*, London, 1817, p. 281.

6

Making Books: How Jane Austen Wrote

Kathryn Sutherland

Jane Austen's spectacles, an empty inkwell, her writing desk and a scattering of manuscripts survive to help us piece together a story of how she wrote. In a letter her contemporary, the poet John Keats, invited his correspondents, his brother George and sister-in-law Georgiana, to imagine his scene of writing on Friday 12 March 1819:

> the candles are burnt down and I am using the wax taper–which has a long snuff on it–the fire is at its last click–I am sitting with my back to it with one foot rather askew upon the rug and the other with the heel a little elevated from the carpet–I am writing this on the Maid's tragedy which I have read since tea with Great pleasure–Besides this volume of Beaumont & Fletcher–there are on the tabl[e] two volumes of chaucer and a new work of Tom Moores call'd 'Tom Cribb's memorial to Congress'–nothing in it–These are trifles–but I require nothing so much of you as that you will give me a like description of yourselves, however it may be when you are writing to me–Could I see the same thing done of any great Man long since dead it would be a great delight: as to know in what position Shakespeare sat when he began 'To be or not to be'–such thing[s] become interesting from distance of time or place [fig. 6.1a and 6.1b].[1]

It is evening; candles and fire burn low; Keats rests the letter he writes (this very letter we now read) upon a book, opened at a named text – a play he has been reading. His 'heel a little elevated from the carpet', the foot taking the pressure on its ball, suggests the poise and concentration of a body absorbed in the act of writing – perhaps his foot helps support the weight of the book, which may lie on his knee, rather than the table, covered with other books, near which he sits. These details are 'trifles' that matter because, carried across time and place inside the letter, they reanimate its written trace, restoring the connection between the marks on paper and the hand that wrote them.

opposite: Figure 6.7 detail

Punk of Quality. The great and powerful (whom you
call wise and good) do not like to have the privacy
of their self love started by the obtrusive and unma-
nageable claims of Literature and Philosophy, except
through the intervention of people like you, whom; if
they have common penetration, they soon find out
to be without any superiority of intellect; or if they
do not whom they can despise for their meanness
of soul. You "have the office opposite to saint Peter"
that "keep a corner in the public mind, for foul
prejudice and the corrupt power to knot and
gender in." You volunteer your services to people
of quality to ease scruples of mind and qualms of
conscience; you lay the flattering unction of usual
morals and cunnel'd sense to their souls — You persuade
them that there is neither purity of morals, nor depth
of understanding, except in themselves and their
hangers on; and would prevent the unhallowed
names of liberty and humanity from ever being
whispered in ears polite! You, sir, do you not
all this? I cry you mercy then: I took you for
the Editor of the Quarterly Review." This is the
sort of feu de joie he keeps up — there is another
extract or two — one especially which I will copy
tomorrow — for the candles are burnt down and
I am using the wax taper — which has a long
snuff on it — the fire is at its last click — I am
sitting with my back to it with one foot rather
as it were upon the rug and the other with the heel
a little elevated from the carpet — I am writing
this on the Maids tragedy which I have read since
tea with great pleasure — Besides this volume

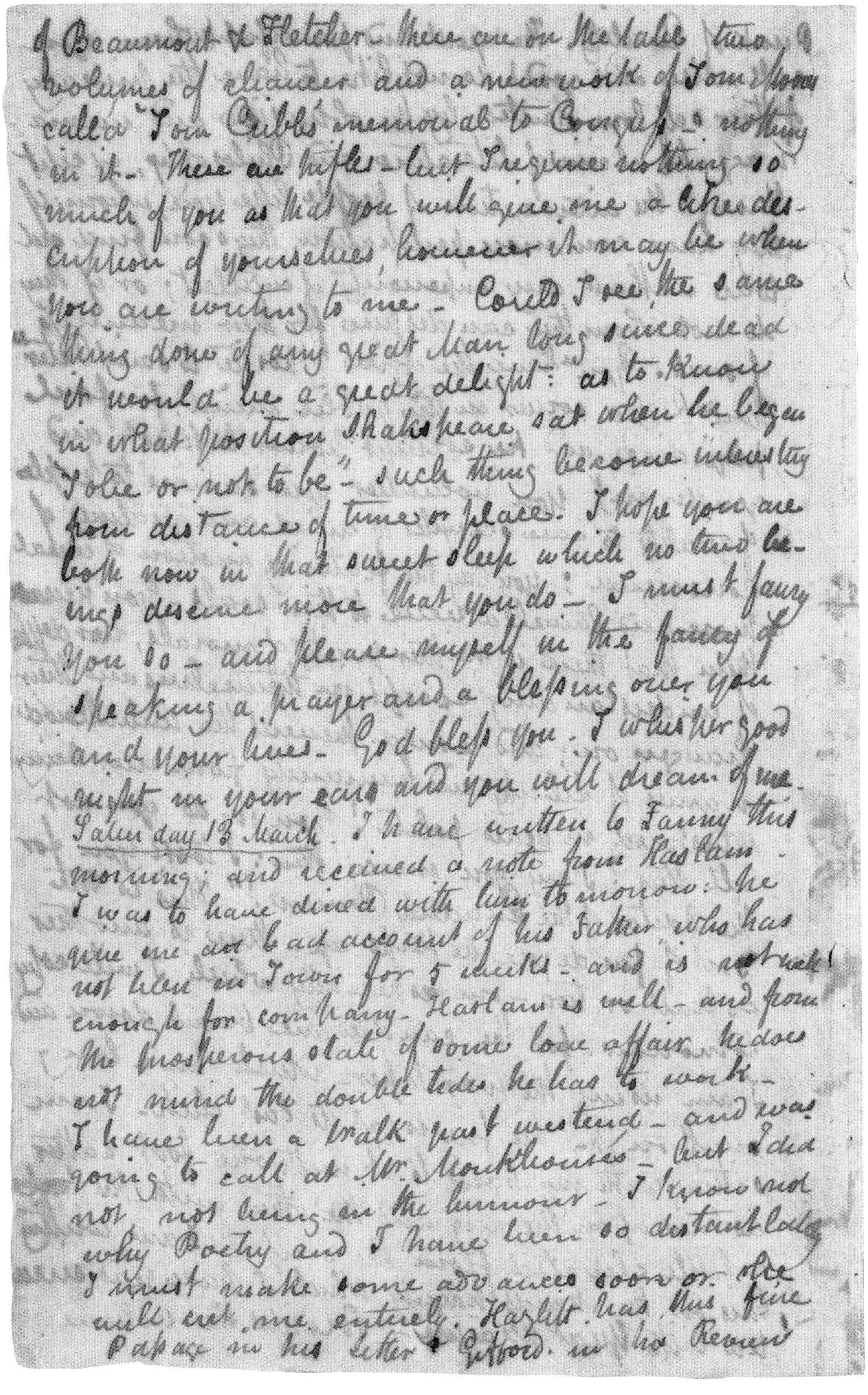

of Beaumont & Fletcher— there are on the table two
volumes of chaucer and a new work of Tom Moore
call'd "Tom Crib's memorial to Congress"— nothing
in it— These are trifles— but I require nothing so
much of you as that you will give me a fine description of yourselves, however it may be when
you are writing to me— Could I see the same
thing done of any great Man long since dead
it would be a great delight: as to know
in what position Shakspeare sat when he began
"To be or not to be"— such things become interesting
from distance of time or place. I hope you are
both now in that sweet sleep which no two be-
ings deserve more that you do— I must fancy
you so— and please myself in the fancy of
speaking a prayer and a blessing over you
and your lives— God bless you— I whisper good
night in your ears and you will dream of me.

Saturday 13 March— I have written to Fanny this
morning; and received a note from Haslam—
I was to have dined with him to morrow: he
give me not bad account of his Father who has
not been in Town for 5 weeks— and is not well
enough for company— Haslam is well— and from
the prosperous state of some love affair he does
not mind the double tides he has to work—
I have been a walk past west end— and was
going to call at Mr Monkhouses— but I did
not not being in the humour— I know not
why Poetry and I have been so distant lately
I must make some advances soon or else I
will cut me entirely. Hazlitt has this fine
Passage in his Letter— Gifford. in his Review

Figure 6.1 From a letter of
John Keats to George and
Georgiana Keats, 12 March
1819. Harvard University,
Houghton Library, MS. Keats
1.53, seq. 223–4.

A L Barbauld

Someone, who held his body in a particular way at a particular moment in a particular place, wrote this.

As Keats says, such trifles rarely survive. But, surprisingly, we have something similar for Jane Austen. In her case, it is a memory of a scene of writing recollected many years later by two of her nieces, Marianne and Louisa Knight, who probably recalled Austen's visit to their home at Godmersham, Kent, in autumn 1813 when they were young girls:

> Aunt Jane would sit quietly working [sewing] beside the fire in the library, saying nothing for a good while, and then would suddenly burst out laughing, jump up and run across the room to a table where pens and paper were lying, write something down, and then come back to the fire and go on quietly working as before.

> She was very absent indeed. She would sit silent a while, then rub her hands, laugh to herself and run up to her room.[2]

Their accounts lack the particularity of Keats's and they conflict slightly – did Aunt Jane remain in the room with the rest of the company? or did she seek a space apart to record her thoughts? But they share details, too: her withdrawal into herself, her private delight and the sudden dart to capture something (but what?) on paper. Where Keats is his own observer, we do not know what Austen committed to paper under her nieces' noticing eyes: *Mansfield Park* is reported as 'Finished soon after June 1813' and *Emma* 'begun Jany 21st 1814'.[3]

Keats and Austen lived at a time when handwriting and, in particular, the signatures or autographs of historical figures and celebrated authors, confirmed the link with personality and biography, as the collector Isaac Disraeli argued:

> Assuredly Nature would prompt every individual to have a distinct sort of writing, as she has given a peculiar countenance–a voice–and a manner. The flexibility of the muscles differs with every individual, and the hand will follow the direction of the thoughts, and the emotions and the habits of the writers. The phlegmatic will portray his words, while the playful haste of the volatile will scarcely sketch them; the slovenly will blot and efface and scrawl, while the neat and orderly minded will view themselves in the paper before their eyes.

And he concluded: 'the vital principle must be true, that the hand-writing bears an analogy to the character of the writer.'[4] This widespread view encouraged the inclusion of signatures as well as portraits as frontispieces to published volumes and an amateur enthusiasm for autograph collecting (fig. 6.2). It fed more slowly into a concern to preserve and value authors' literary remains.

Figure 6.2 Frontispiece to *The Works of Anna Laetitia Barbauld*, edited by Lucy Aikin (2 vols, Longman, Hurst, Rees, Orme, Brown and Green, London, 1825). Oxford, Bodleian Library, 25.318, vol. 1.

Thirteen of the novel manuscripts of the greatest author of the age, Sir Walter Scott, went on sale at Evans's rooms, 93, Pall Mall, London, on 19 August 1831, to considerable fanfare. Scott was a household name; his literary achievement was remarkable, as the descriptive notes to Evans's *Catalogue of the Original Manuscripts of the Waverley Novels* made clear: 'The Annals of Literature scarcely afford a similar instance of facility of Composition. The Public will be astonished to perceive the few erasures, alterations or additions, which occur from the first conceptions of of [*sic*] the Author, to their final transmission to the Press.'[5] Even so, the actual sale brought in far less than expected; in retrospect, it has come to be seen as the moment when the market for modern literary papers was first tested with the draft compositions of a living author.[6]

Jane Austen's contemporary fame was, by comparison, modest, and if Scott's carefully preserved manuscripts found little commercial value, hers were not considered worth keeping once set in type. Once the novels were published, their manuscripts were so much waste paper. There is no manuscript evidence for the six novels printed during and immediately after her short life as a published author (only seven years, from 1811 to 1818): no manuscript for *Pride and Prejudice* or *Emma*. The only exception is two cancelled chapters from *Persuasion*, a novel published six months after her death, which may have survived simply because they were substituted at a late stage with a different ending and thus not used for print. Of the 1,100 pages of fiction manuscripts extant in Austen's hand, all represent works which, for one reason or another, remained unpublished in her lifetime. Some are fair-copy manuscripts, like the three notebooks of teenage writings, labelled by her 'Volume the First', 'Volume the Second' and 'Volume the Third', and the slightly later novella in letters, *Lady Susan*; others are frustrated and messy drafts of beginnings to novels never finished – *The Watsons* and *Sanditon* – and that discarded ending to *Persuasion*. In Austen's case, then, we have a stark separation between works that remained in manuscript and works that were printed, with no obvious overlap between the two.

This distinction lends her manuscripts a particular fascination – as experiments, apprentice works, false starts, false endings and the enigmatic opening chapters of the last novel. In the manuscripts we discover another Jane Austen; their subject matter remains even today less familiar than that of the famous six novels. At the same time, they contextualize that brief publishing career with evidence that witnesses to a thirty-year-long writing career, from Austen's earliest exuberant entries, aged 11 or 12, into *Volume the First* (in 1786 or 1787) to the final words of *Sanditon*, beneath which, aged only 41, she wrote 'March 18' (that is, 18 March 1817). Whether the hand is carefully copying a finished passage onto a clean page or scratching out and reworking a stubborn phrase on a much-corrected draft, the manuscripts' appearance implies a narrative about their writing, a first-hand knowledge unavailable from print, bound up, as Keats suggests, with the intimacy of performance and a sense of the presence of the author.

Why were Austen's manuscripts kept? The simple answer is that her immediate family cherished them as precious mementos. Cassandra Austen, the executor and chief

Figure 6.3 *The Watsons* booklets displayed. Oxford, Bodleian Library, MS. Eng. e. 3764.

was an old quaintance.——"So late, my dear; what
are you talking of; cried the husband with sturdy
pleasantry. We are always at home before
midnight: they would laugh at Osborne Castle
to hear you call that late; they are but just
rising from dinner at midnight."——"That is
nothing to the purpose.——retorted the Lady calmly.
The Osbornes are to be no rule for us.
You had much better meet every night, & break up
two hours sooner."——so far, the subject was very
often carried; but Mr. & Mrs. Edwards were wise
as never to pass that point, & Mr. Edwards
now turned to something else;——he had lived
sufficiently long in the Idleness of a Town to
become a little of a Gossip, & having some
curiosity to know more of the
circumstances of his young guest
than had yet reached him, he began
with "I think Miss Emma, I remember your aunt very well about 30 years ago;
I am
pretty sure I danced with her in the old
rooms at Bath, the year before I married.
She was a very fine woman then——but like
other people I suppose she is grown somewhat
older since that time.——I hope she is likely
to be happy in her second choice."

beneficiary of her sister's will, lived until 1845, keeping fiction manuscripts and letters together. Evidence of wear to their physical structures – rubbed and creased bindings, frayed paper edges and Indian ink blots – bears out family stories that during these years (1817–45) the manuscripts were read and perhaps copied within the extended family circle. Cassandra made a copy of *Sanditon* that survives, and their brother Frank's daughters, Fanny Sophia Austen and the novelist Catherine Hubback, later recalled Aunt Cassandra reading aloud from two manuscripts, *The Watsons* and *Sanditon*, at family parties. On these occasions reading turned into a kind of conversation 'expressed quite naturally in terms of [Aunt Jane's] novels'.[7] After Cassandra's death, the manuscripts were divided among surviving brothers, nieces and nephews. From the late nineteenth century, they found their way into auction houses and thence into public and private collections. The latest of the fiction manuscripts to appear on the market was the larger portion of *The Watsons*, bought at auction by the Bodleian Library, Oxford, in July 2011. Only sixty-eight small pages of handwritten text, it sold for one million pounds.[8]

The unfinished novel *The Watsons* is a good place to begin to think about what her manuscripts suggest of how Jane Austen wrote. The earliest surviving draft of a novel by the adult Austen, it was probably composed in Bath in 1804–5 when she was 28 or 29, and after drafts of the novels eventually published, several years later, as *Sense and Sensibility*, *Pride and Prejudice* and *Northanger Abbey*. This makes it her fourth novel. As recently as 1803, she had sold the manuscript of *Susan* for £10 to Crosby and Co. Crosby asserted his right not to publish, and it was bought back much later, perhaps in 1816, and only finally published in 1818, after her death, as *Northanger Abbey*. But in 1804 this was an unknown future, and we can assume that the successful sale of her first novel gave Austen confidence to begin another. After a tentative opening written onto a single folded leaf of four pages, *The Watsons* takes shape as eleven small homemade booklets of eight pages each. It is a work in progress, with its first and second thoughts, its deletions and revision, all on display. We literally see it growing, from page to page, and from booklet to booklet beneath the writer's hand (fig. 6.3). A narrative of around 17,500 words, about one-sixth the length of a completed Austen novel, it appears to progress with confidence, until it breaks off abruptly. It has no title, no chapter divisions and no pagination, though each booklet is numbered in the top right-hand corner. We call it *The Watsons* after Austen's nephew and early biographer, James Edward Austen-Leigh, who gave it that descriptive title in 1871, from the name of the manuscript's central family and, as he put it, 'for the sake of having a title by which to designate it'.[9]

In the months following her death, Austen's brother Henry had spun some of the most stubborn fictions about her artless way of writing – 'in composition she was equally rapid and correct'; 'Every thing came finished from her pen'[10] – inventions that simply do not stand up once we look inside these little booklets with their crossings out, squeezed insertions and multiple signs of the sheer struggle to create. His reluctance to concede his sister's hard work, its inevitable imperfections and her professionalism was curious

Figure 6.4 'Of Emma I have nothing but *good* to say. I was sure of the writer before you mentioned her. The m.s. though plainly written has yet some indeed, many little omissions, & an expression may now & then be mended in passing through the press … I will readily undertake the revision.' A letter from his editor William Gifford to John Murray, encouraging him to publish *Emma* and offering to correct the author's faulty punctuation. © National Library of Scotland, John Murray Archive, MS. 42248.

James to Sep 29 – 1815

My dear Sir

The wanderings of my letter
are to be repelled because that it contained some answers to questions
which I am not sure that I now remember. Not to waste time however
I will proceed with what I recollect. Of Emma I have nothing but
good to say. I was sure of the
wonder before you mentioned them.
The m.s. though plainly written has
yet some carelessness, & an expression
evidently done too little
may now & then be mended in passing
through the press. If you print it
which I think you will do (though
I can say nothing as to its price)
I will readily undertake the revision. If its folio is with your views
I should prefer Roworth as the
printer, your little man, Dove, is
apt to give one rather too much
trouble — but this, as you like.

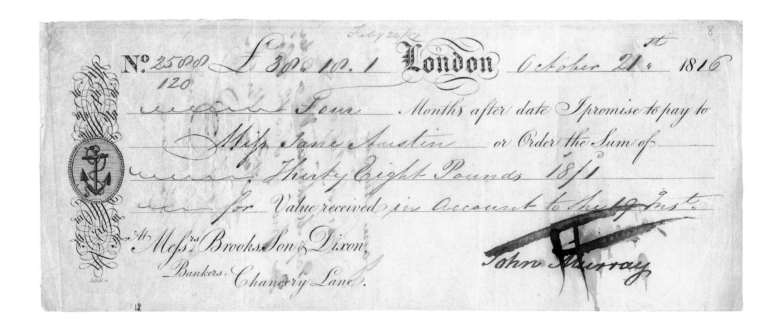

since, as her informal agent, he was well placed to observe how determined was her ambition and how thoroughly she involved herself in every aspect of the novel business: from negotiations with publishers and attention to production values (to be on hand for proofing, she stayed in London throughout the printing of her novels) to the careful accounts she kept of her profits. Rather, his hagiographic obituary style – 'Neither the hope of fame nor profit mixed with her early motives' – has obscured a woman who proudly declared: 'I have now therefore written myself into £250.—which only makes me long for more' and 'tho' I like praise as well as anybody, I like … *Pewter* too' (figs 6.4 and 6.5).[11]

Through the nineteenth century the myths accumulated. Some decades after his aunt's death Austen-Leigh, by now an elderly, stuffy Victorian clergyman, excused female authorship by confounding the work of writing with more orthodox domestic pastimes, comparing her 'clear strong handwriting' to her neat sewing, the care with which she sealed a letter and her skill at family games of spilikins.[12] The associations sound absurd to us in their attempt to explain away an activity as downright unfeminine as prolonged literary composition. Already in 1866, *The Englishwoman's Domestic Magazine* expressed its frustration at the idea that Jane Austen, a serious woman writer, should be reduced to such pious platitudes, remarking 'now we can think of her as nothing less than an angel writing novels with a quill plucked from one of her own wings'.[13] It was not until 1926 that R.W. Chapman's *Two Chapters of Persuasion* made available a collotype facsimile of one of Austen's draft manuscripts for the general reader to examine and decide for themselves.

Unlike Austen-Leigh, Jane Austen was not proud of her handwriting; she regularly laments in letters its untidiness and its general lack of grace: 'You are very amiable & very clever to write such long Letters; every page of yours has more lines than this, & every line more words than the average of mine. I am quite ashamed', she teasingly complains to Cassandra, in a letter of 20 June 1808 (letter 53); and to brother Frank, on 25 September 1813 (letter 90): 'you write so even, so clear both in style & Penmanship … it is enough to kill one.' Yet the first thing the modern reader notices is the controlled penmanship and extreme economy of *The Watsons* manuscript: how closely written over its small pages are, every one filled to the very edges, with no margins or white space left for revision or expansion (fig. 6.6). Like most people at the time, Austen wrote with a goose quill pen using iron gall ink. In three places the writing spills over onto separate leaves, which bear the marks of having been patched onto the booklets and held in place with straight steel pins. Tailored precisely to the spaces they fill, like patches that mend a shirt or gown, all three show Austen repairing and strengthening her story at that particular point.[14]

Working manuscripts look different from print; they look other. With correction and revision exposed, they require us to consider how meaning is made. Their rawness, too, is more than artistic; it hints at the life of the writer. Manuscripts, we sense, are touched by life – quite literally, since they have borne the impress of the writer's hand: her quirks of spelling, how she formed her letters, how she filled her page are all clues to how she worked and therefore to who she was. The *Watsons* booklets are home-made and their pages are small (19 x 12 cm; 7.5 x 4.75 inches), fashioned by cutting and

Figure 6.5 Cheque from John Murray to Jane Austen following the publication of *Emma*. © National Library of Scotland, John Murray Archive. MS. 4 2001, fol. 8r–v.

folding larger sheets of writing paper and nestling their leaves one inside the other (fig. 6.7). The thicker booklets of the *Persuasion* and *Sanditon* manuscripts were constructed in similar fashion, suggesting this was a preferred surface – writers, then and now, as we know, can be creatures of extreme, even obsessive, habit – making it likely that the lost manuscripts of *Pride and Prejudice*, *Mansfield Park* and *Emma* were also formed of multiple little booklets.

Why little booklets? Again, Austen-Leigh, in myth-making mood, tells us something of his aunt's way of working at Chawton, which became her home in July 1809. From here all her novels were dispatched for publication. She wrote in the family sitting-room, which also served as a space for entertaining visitors. We learn of the 'small sheets of paper which could easily be put away, or covered with a piece of blotting paper', of the 'swing door which creaked' but was never oiled because it gave notice of someone approaching, and of the pen 'busy at the little mahogany writing-desk'.[15] The mahogany writing-desk survives; it may have been a nineteenth-birthday present from her father. The little booklets might easily elude prying eyes. But we can deduce more: each one modest, when they are piled together these little booklets also simulate in size and shape, gathering by gathering, the appearance of an emerging novel.[16] Writing into booklets (rather than onto single leaves or an assortment of paper structures like so many of her contemporaries – William Godwin and Frances Burney, for example) encouraged Austen from the earliest moment of putting pen to paper to associate drafting a manuscript with bookmaking (fig. 6.8). Perhaps practices already in evidence in her teenage mock books, *Volume the First*, *Volume the Second* and *Volume the Third*, developed over time into a professional preference for building a story; perhaps they were even a necessary composition ritual.

A particular material surface may promote a particular way of working. The draft booklets of *The Watsons*, *Persuasion* and *Sanditon* provide repeated evidence for the writing challenge that Austen set herself. Her booklets do not just ghost the emerging novel; as draft surfaces they are fraught with risk. Combined with the density that characterizes the way she fills her paper from the outset, the booklet represents a near tyrannical structure, one that closes off options and leaves the writer dangerously exposed: get it right the first time, for there are few opportunities for extensive reworking of description and dialogue, for turning back or reordering the story line. The booklet challenges the writer to keep moving forward. Of course, material can still be deleted and new matter inserted – the three patches in *The Watsons* and a small pasted panel in *Persuasion* show that – but flexibility is limited; there are few options within a closely filled booklet for generating new material in an alternative order and sequence (fig. 6.9). Booklets, then, suggest a writer confident in her intentions and purpose. Do the fatter booklets of the late manuscripts, of *Persuasion* (32 pages) and *Sanditon* (formed of three booklets of 32, 40 and 80 pages), indicate mounting self-belief and a willingness to take even greater risks?

Figure 6.6 An opening from *The Watsons* showing how densely Jane Austen filled her pages. Oxford, Bodleian Library, MS. Eng. e. 3764, booklet 4, pp. 2–3.

engaged this week, cried the boy, "we are to dance down every couple." — On the other side of Emma, Miss Osborne, Miss Carr, & a party of young men were standing in very lively consultation — & soon afterwards she saw the smartest officer of the sett, walking off to the Orchestra to order the dance, while Miss Osborne passing before her, to her little expecting Partner hastily said — "Charles, I beg your pardon for not keeping my engagement, but I am going to dance these two dances with Col.ⁿˢ Beresford. I know you will excuse me, & I will certainly dance with you after Tea." And without staying for an answer, she turned again to Miss Carr, & in another minute was led by Col. Beresford to begin the Sett.

If the poor little boy's face had been interesting in its happiness to Emma, it was infinitely more so in his sudden reverse; — he stood the picture of disappointment, with crimson'd cheeks, quivering lips, & eyes bent on the floor. His mother, stifling her own mortification, tried to soothe his, with the prospect of Miss Osborne's secondary promise;

but tho' he continued to utter with an effort of Boyish Bravery "Oh! I don't mind it" it was very evident by the unceasing agitation of his features that he minded it as much as ever. Emma did not think, or reflect; — she felt & acted —

"I shall be very happy to dance with you Sir, if you like it." said she, holding out her hand with the most unaffected good humour. — The Boy in one moment restored to all his first delight looked joyfully at his Mother, and stepping forwards with an honest & simple Thank you Ma'am was instantly ready to attend his new acquaintance. The gratitude of M.ʳˢ Blake was more diffuse; — with a look most expressive of unexpected pleasure, & lively Gratitude, she turned to her neighbour with repeated & fervent acknowledgements of so great & condescending a kindness to her boy. — Emma with perfect truth could assure her that she could not be giving greater pleasure than she felt herself — & Charles being provided with his gloves & charged to keep them on, they joined the Sett which was now rapidly forming, with equal complacency. — It was a Partnership which c.ᵈ not be noticed without surprise. It gained her a broad stare from Miss Osborne & Miss

The device of patching, like the evidence of local and intense revision, appears to rule out the idea that Austen wrote her fictions in several drafts: her surviving manuscripts represent early and late versions compacted into a single space. Evidence suggests she used paper sparingly. She was a wartime writer, with paper expensive and in short supply; but her economy may also have served another purpose. Her well-known description of her way of working – 'the little bit (two Inches wide) of Ivory on which I work with so fine a Brush, as produces little effect after much labour' – is usually read as a clue to explain her narrow subject matter: what she describes elsewhere as '3 or 4 Families in a Country Village is the very thing to work on'.[17] It fits even better her ivory-coloured paper and her method in filling it. The constrained spaces of the little booklets are a material manifestation of her frugal art, her famous economy as a writer, and an essential discipline for her way of seeing and writing (fig. 6.10).

Austen was an inveterate and accomplished recycler – not just of paper, but of stories, themes and even minor details. The way she patches and fills her small manuscript pages provides an emblem of the processes of her imagination as she crosses and re-crosses her little plot of fictional ground to bring one novel out of another. The method contributes powerfully to our sense of familiarity with her world. In this, too, *The Watsons* is no exception. It tells the story of 19-year-old Emma Watson, adopted in childhood by a rich aunt and uncle and now, following her uncle's death and her aunt's imprudent remarriage, returned after '[a]n absence of 14. years' (booklet 8 [p. 3]) to her birth family. This family consists of an invalid clergyman father and three unmarried older sisters, living in genteel poverty in a country rectory. Two brothers – an apprentice surgeon and a lawyer who has been shrewd enough to marry his employer's daughter – are making their way in the world.

The novel opens on classic Austen territory as Emma Watson prepares for her first ball. At the ball she attracts the attention of two potential suitors: Lord Osborne, 'a very fine young man; but there was an air of Coldness, of Carelessness, even of Awkwardness about him, which seemed to speak him out of his Element in a Ball room … he was not fond of Women's company, & he never danced'; and Mr Howard, 'an agreeable-looking Man, a little more than Thirty', a clergyman (booklet 4 [p. 1]). But *The Watsons* is barely begun before it is abandoned: the characters are introduced; the ball comes and goes, to be followed by the unwelcome intrusion of Lord Osborne on the Watsons' meagre family dinner; the vulgar Mr and Mrs Robert Watson arrive on a short visit. There is just enough story to point up Emma Watson's discomfort in her surroundings and to hint at a courtship plot. The manuscript ends abruptly with Emma rejecting an invitation to return with her brother to Croydon. Its final words are: '& the Visitors departed without her.—' (booklet 11 [p. 1]).

Balls are the active agent, the yeast, in Austen's novels, moving the plot along with their opportunities for observing and animating relations between the sexes. Every novel, with the exception of *Sanditon*, left unfinished at her death, has a ball or, in the

Figure 6.7 Booklet of *The Watsons*, formed from a half sheet of standard writing paper, folded and cut in half again, one half nested inside the other to form eight pages (four leaves). Oxford, Bodleian Library, MS. Eng. e. 3764

case of *Persuasion*, an informal dance. The ball in *The Watsons* is Austen's most minutely described, filling almost a quarter of the manuscript. Would it have been pruned in revision; and if so, which details might have been lost? The question invites us to consider the difference between manuscript and print. Until it leaves the writer's laboratory, no part of a manuscript is invulnerable to change; nothing is settled. And unlike print, the author's presence hovers over its surface. The collusion between art and life that makes manuscript 'a present-at-hand thing' is especially intense in *The Watsons*.[18] Years later, Cassandra Austen shared with her nieces 'something of the intended story'. Emma Watson's father

> was soon to die; and Emma to become dependent for a home on her narrow-minded sister-in-law and brother. She was to decline an offer of marriage from Lord Osborne, and much of the interest of the tale was to arise from [the older] Lady Osborne's love for Mr Howard, and his counter affection for Emma, whom he was finally to marry.[19]

Why was *The Watsons* abandoned? Writing in 1883, Fanny Caroline Lefroy, Austen's great-niece and an important source of information for the first generation of professional, non-family biographers, had this to say: 'Somewhere in 1804 [Jane Austen] began "The Watsons", but her father died early in 1805, and it was never finished.'[20] *The Watsons* seems set to be a study in the bleak realities of dependent women's lives, with little of the romantic illusion we associate with the earlier fictions, *Sense and Sensibility* and *Pride and Prejudice*. Virtually penniless, the Watson sisters see their precarious grasp on respectability daily weakened by an invalid father whose death will deprive them of their home. Elizabeth Watson, the eldest, knows that her only hope of escaping destitution or the charity of unwilling relations lies in marriage, and there is nothing romantic in her vision. Her words are very moving:

> … you know we must marry.—I could do very well single for my own part.—A little Company, & a pleasant Ball now & then, would be enough for me, if one could be young for ever, but my Father cannot provide for us, & it is very bad to grow old & be poor & laughed at.—I have lost Purvis, it is true but very few people marry their first Loves. I should not refuse a man because he was not Purvis—. (p. 4 – booklet 1 [p. 1])

Figure 6.8 Manuscript page from Mary Shelley's *Frankenstein*. Note the wide margin available for revision. Oxford, Bodleian Library, MS. Abinger c. 56, fol. 21r.

In a manuscript filled with deletions and interlinear additions, with evidence of second thoughts, it is worth remarking that this passage flows easily, with almost no correction (fig. 6.11).

Before Austen brought her new novel to its domestic crisis, real events overtook fiction, and her own father, George Austen, died suddenly after a short illness in

2 (45

It was on a dreary night of November
that I beheld ~~the frame on which~~ my man compleated; ~~and~~
with an anxiety that almost amount
ed to agony. I collected ~~instruments of life~~
around me ~~and endeavour~~ that I might infuse a
spark of being into the lifeless thing
that lay at my feet. It was already
one in the morning, the rain pattered
dismally against the window panes, &
my candle was nearly burnt out, when
by the glimmer of the half extinguish
ed light I saw the dull yellow eye of
the creature open — It breathed hard,
and a convulsive motion agitated
its limbs.

~~But how~~ How can I describe my
emotion at this catastrophe, or how deli
neate the wretch whom with such
infinite pains and care I had endeavoured
to form. His limbs were in proportion
and I had selected his features & as
beautiful ~~handsome~~. ~~Handsome~~ Beautiful; Great God! His
yellow ~~dun~~ skin scarcely covered the work of
muscles and arteries beneath; his hair
of a lustrous black, & was flowing and his teeth of a pearly white
ness but these luxuriances only ~~formed~~
formed a more horrid contrast with
his watery eyes that seemed almost of
the same colour as the dun white
sockets in which they were set,

"I do not mean to distress you, but you know somebody must think her an old fool.—

...humble friends, there was no-one who would have thought of her." Emma was glad when they were joined by the others; it was better to look at her Sister-in-law's finery than listen to Robert, who had equally irritated & grieved her.—

Mrs. Robert exactly as smart as she had been at her own party, came in with apologies for her dress—"I would not make you wait, said she, so I put on the first thing I met with. I am afraid I am a sad figure. My dear Mr. W. (to her husband) you have not put any such powder in your hair." "No—I do not intend it. I think there is powder enough in my hair for my wife & sisters." "Indeed you ought to make some alteration in your dress before dinner when you are out visiting, tho' you do not at home." "Nonsense." "It is very odd you should not like to do what other gentlemen do. Mr. Marshall &

Mr. Hemming change their dress every day of their lives before dinner. And what was the use of my putting up your last new coat, if you are never to wear it." "Do be satisfied with being fine yourself, & leave your husband alone."—To put an end to this altercation & soften the evident vexation of her sister-in-law, (who was in no spirits to make such remarks) Emma began to admire her gown. It produced immediate complacency. "Do you like it? said she. I am very happy. It has been exceedingly admired; but sometimes I think the pattern too large. I shall wear one tomorrow that I think you will prefer to this. Have you seen the one I gave Margaret?"

Dinner came, & except when Mrs. R. looked at her husband's head, she continued gay & flippant, chiding Elizth for the profusion on the table, & absolutely protesting against the entrance of the Turkey—which formed the only exception to "You see your dinner." "I do beg & entreat that no Turkey may be seen today. I am really frightened out of my wits with the number of dishes we have already. Let us have no Turkey I beseech you." "My dear, replied Elizth the Turkey is roasted, & it may just as well come in as stay in the kitchen. Besides, if it is cut, I am in hopes my Father may be tempted to eat a bit, for it is rather a favourite dish."

I thought Turner had been reckoned an extraordinary sensible, clever man. How the Duce
came he to leave make such a will?" — "My
Uncle's sense is not at all impeached in my o-
pinion, by his attachment to my Aunt. She
had been an excellent wife to him. The most
Liberal & enlightened minds are always the most
confiding. — The event has been unfortunate;
~~for me~~ but my Uncle's memory is impaired to
me by such a proof of tender respect for my
Aunt." — "That's odd sort of Talking! — He
might have provided decently for his widow,
~~every thing~~ that he had to dispose of, or any part of it
without leaving ~~it all~~ at her mercy. — "My
Aunt may have erred — said Emma warmly —
she has erred — but my Uncle's conduct was
faultless. I was her own Niece, & he left to
her the power & the pleasure of providing for
me." — "But unluckily she has left the pleasure
of providing for you, to your Father, without
the power. — That's the long & the short of the
business. After keeping you at a distance from
your family, for ~~such a~~ length of time as must
do away all natural affection, & breeding you
up (I suppose) in a superior Style, you are
returned upon their hands without a sixpence."
"You know, replied Emma struggling with her
tears, my Uncle's melancholy state of health —
he was a greater Invalid than my Father. He could
not leave home." "I do not mean to make you cry —
said Bob rather softened — & after a short silence,
by way of changing the subject, he added

January 1805. Within two months, the Austen women (two ageing unmarried daughters and their mother) had given up their house in Bath and moved into cheaper lodgings. From this point to the ends of their lives they would remain financially dependent on Jane's brothers' generosity. *The Watsons* may have begun, perhaps almost unconsciously, as Austen's attempt to assert through her art her power over her own circumstances: she was in her late twenties, with a rejection of marriage and the security that represented recently behind her. That story is well known: on 2 December 1802 a family friend in very comfortable circumstances, Harris Bigg-Wither, had proposed to Jane and been turned down.[21] Immediately afterwards, or so it seems, she revised *Susan* (the novel that became *Northanger Abbey*), sold it and began *The Watsons*. The dark social criticism of *The Watsons* marked a stage in Austen's maturing as a novelist that must have required her to delve deeper into herself than she had done before. Did it remain unfinished because, with her father's death, life had pushed the experiment too far?

There is another possibility: that *The Watsons* simply ran out of fictional steam; that, despite Cassandra's sharing of the 'intended story', it had no real growth left in it. Is Emma Watson too healthy (unlike Fanny Price, heroine of *Mansfield Park*), too faultless (unlike Emma Woodhouse), and too young and confident (unlike Anne Elliot of *Persuasion*) to merit deeper acquaintance? In her short history she appears to rise too easily above the obstacles life throws at her. This raises a third possibility: is *The Watsons* in fact a novella or long short story, like the unfinished 'Kitty, or the Bower' in *Volume the Third*? Look closely at the manuscript: it is written continuously, without chapter divisions. There is a short rule drawn across the page mid-way through booklet 7, which suggests a division in the story at this point, and another short rule mid-way through booklet 10; but no stronger structural markers. If we think of it as a novella, our expectations change; a ball and its consequences become an appropriate study in and for themselves.

The Watsons is a puzzle among Austen's works, and all the richer for being so. It represents a shift in her way of writing that anticipates the introspection and tougher realism about women's lot that we associate with the mature novels; her next full-length fiction would be the sober and moralizing *Mansfield Park*. In *The Watsons* we seem to hear echoes or anticipations of several novels: a general similarity in the economic pressures on the Watson girls and the Bennet girls of *Pride and Prejudice*; a family likeness between Lord Osborne and Mr Darcy, and between Mr Howard and Austen's tutor-like lovers, from Henry Tilney to Edmund Bertram and Mr Knightley. Emma Watson promises to be a new kind of heroine whose translation from one home to another will be the ground of her identity, as it will be for Fanny Price and later still for Anne Elliot. There is no hint of an interesting pathology to explore in Emma as there will be in Fanny and Anne; but it is worth asking whether Austen could have reached the emotional complexity that Fanny Price and Anne Elliot both exhibit without the experiment in social meanness and the painful reaching into life's depths that is *The*

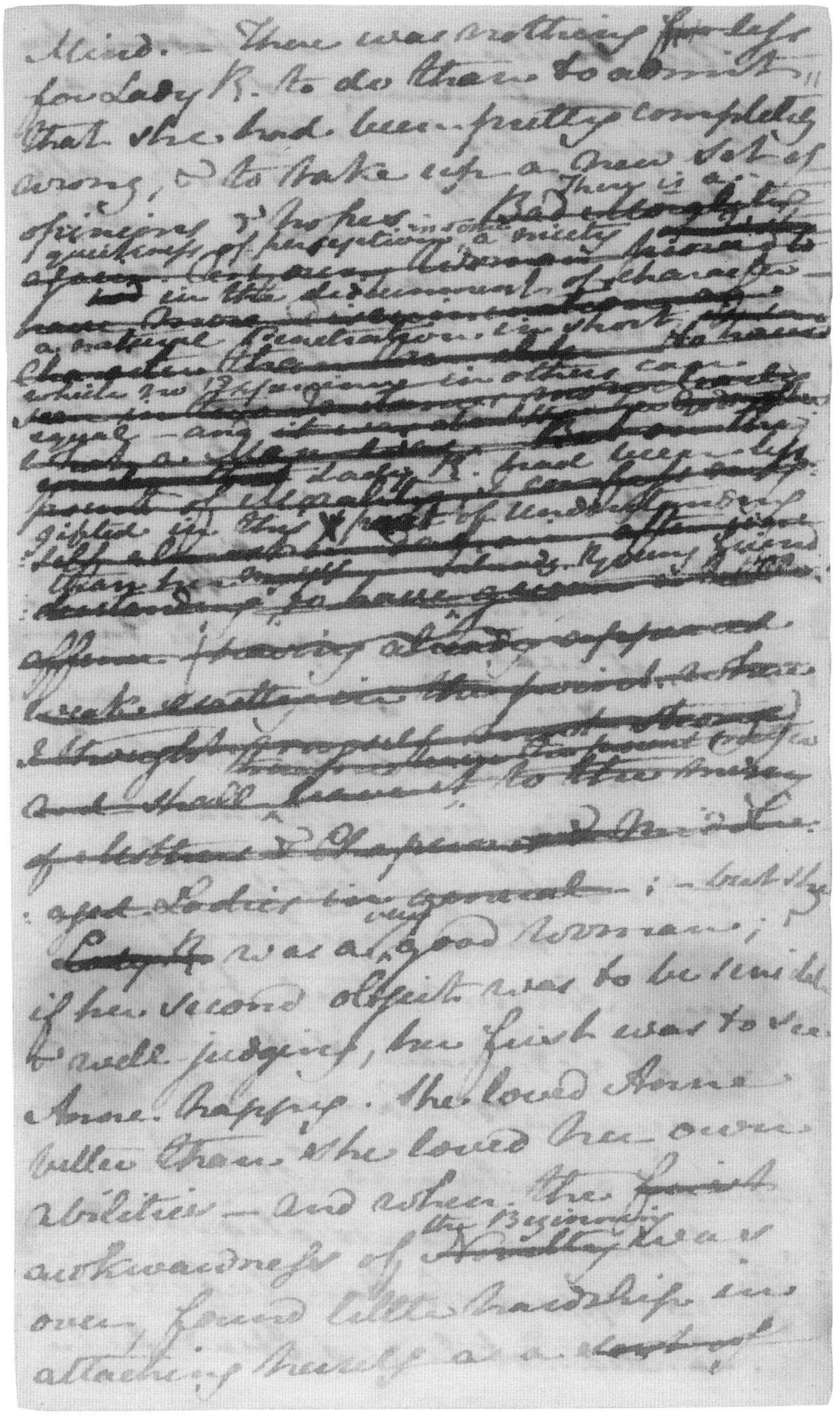

Figure 6.10 A tightly filled and rewritten page of *Persuasion*. At 15.5 x 9cm, 6.12 x 3.5 inches, it is even smaller than *The Watsons*. London, British Library, MS. Egerton 3038.

A little Company, & a pleasant Ball now & then, would be enough for me, if one could be young for ever, but my Father cannot provide for us, & it is very bad to grow old & be poor & laughed at. — I have lost Paris, but very few people marry their first Loves. I should not refuse a man because he was not Paris — Not that I can ever quite forgive Penelope. —" Emma shook her head in acquiescence. — "Penelope however has had her Troubles" continued Miss W. — She was sadly disappointed in Tom Musgrave, who afterwards transferred his attentions from me to her, & whom she was very fond of; but he never means anything serious, & when he had trifled with her long enough, he began to slight her for Margaret, & poor Penelope was very wretched —. And since then, she has been trying to make some match at Chichester; she won't tell us with whom, but I believe it is a rich old Dr. Harding, Uncle to the friend she goes to see; — & she has taken vast deal of trouble & given up a great deal of Time to no purpose as yet. —

Watsons. Like its manuscript, its story contains precious clues to how Jane Austen wrote.

What of *Sanditon*, the most poignant Austen manuscript of all? If, as Keats opines, there is a means by which the reader might recover the writer from the page, the clue is never so urgently desired as when deciphering late writing. Here, if anywhere, we expect the relationship between the self that makes and the thing made to appear most timely; we expect to find intimations of Austen's end in the manuscript long known simply as 'the last work'. Jane Austen bowed out of *Sanditon* in the course of chapter 12, its final words – 'Poor Mr Hollis!—It was impossible not to feel him hardly used; to be obliged to stand back in his own House & see the best place by the fire constantly occupied by Sir H. D.' – followed by the date 'March 18'. Exactly four months later, on 18 July, she died. Austen-Leigh worked up the evidence to a fine sentimental pitch, describing the manuscript's 'latter pages … first traced in pencil, probably when she was too weak to sit long at a desk' and its final dating as fixing 'the period when her mind could no longer pursue its accustomed course' like 'the watch of the drowned man indicates the time of his death'.[22] But the facts are other: only thirty-one lines of booklet 2 were traced first in pencil, and the manuscript continues for a further fifty pages in ink in a firm hand, while the date on the opening page of the third booklet ('March 1ˢᵀ') makes it clear that the last forty pages were all composed in under three weeks (fig. 6.12). There is the awkward matter, too, of one of its central topics – hypochondria: *Sanditon* is a study of people who imagine they are ill by a woman we know was dying. But did she know this? And, supposing she did, why should she reconcile her art to her life? Why should 'bodily condition and aesthetic style' conform?[23] Austen's last work has always seemed to its readers loaded with contradiction: last, but surprisingly reminiscent of the zany humour and freakishness of her teenage squibs. Then there is the fact of its final booklet, at eighty pages her fattest. Only forty pages are written over; with so many pages still to be filled, do we have here a sign that this most economical of writers refused to go gently? Rather than timeliness and thrift, do we find in the materials, as in its subject matter, evidence of defiance and refusal, of something unresolved, in this last work?

1   *The Letters of John Keats 1814–1821*, ed. Hyder Edward Rollins, 2 vols, Harvard University Press, Cambridge, MA, 1958, vol. 2, p. 73.

2   Marianne Knight's memories of her aunt Jane Austen were first published in Constance Hill, *Jane Austen Her Homes and Her Friends* (1902), John Lane, London and New York, 1904, p. 202. Both nieces' accounts are included in Deirdre Le Faye, *Jane Austen: A Family Record*, Cambridge University Press, Cambridge, 2004, p. 206.

3   Cassandra Austen's Note of the Date of Composition of Jane Austen's novels, probably written after July 1817, reproduced in photo-facsimile in Jane Austen, *Minor Works*, ed. R.W. Chapman, Oxford University Press, Oxford, 1954, facing p. 242.

Figure 6.11 *The Watsons*: Elizabeth Watson on the perils of being poor. New York, Pierpont Morgan Library, MS. MA 1034.

4   Isaac Disraeli, 'Autographs', in *A Second Series of Curiosities of Literature*, 2nd edition, 3 vols, John Murray, London, 1824, vol. 2, pp. 208–9, 210.

5   Edinburgh, National Library of Scotland, Adv. MS 1.1.0, *Waverley*, to which is attached *Catalogue of the Original Manuscripts … All in the Hand-writing of Sir Walter Scott, Bart.*, 1831, 2r.

6   Total proceeds have been estimated as £317 by Edgar Johnson, *Sir Walter Scott: The Great Unknown*, 2 vols, Hamish Hamilton, London, 1970, vol. 2, p. 1189.

7   Cassandra Austen's copy of the manuscript of *Sanditon* is held at Jane Austen's House Museum, Chawton, Hampshire. Austen's nieces' recollections appear in John H. and Edith C. Hubback, *Jane Austen's Sailor Brothers: Being the Adventures of Sir Francis Austen, G. C. B., Admiral of the Fleet, and Rear-Admiral Charles Austen*, John Lane, London, 1906, p. viii; and see Le Faye, *Family Record*, p. 268.

8   *The Watsons* is a divided manuscript: its opening twelve pages are held in the Morgan Library, New York, MS MA 1034; the Oxford portion is Bodleian MS Eng. e. 3764.

9   James Edward Austen-Leigh, *A Memoir of Jane Austen, to which is added Lady Susan and Fragments of Two Other Unfinished Tales by Miss Austen*, 2nd edition, Richard Bentley & Son, London, 1871, p. 295.

10   In Henry Austen's 'Biographical Notice of the Author' (1818), attached to the posthumously published *Northanger Abbey*, in Austen-Leigh, *Memoir*, ed. Sutherland, pp. 138 and 141.

11   Austen-Leigh, *Memoir*, ed. Sutherland, p. 140; Jane Austen, 16 September 1813, letter 86, and 30 November 1814, letter 114. For Jane Austen's professional dealings as novelist, see Jan Fergus, 'The Professional Woman Writer', in Edward Copeland and Juliet McMaster (eds), *The Cambridge Companion to Jane Austen*, 2nd edition, Cambridge University Press, Cambridge, 2011, pp. 1–20; and Kathryn Sutherland, 'Jane Austen's Dealings with John Murray and his Firm', *Review of English Studies*, n. s. vol. 64, 2012, pp. 105–26.

12   Austen-Leigh, *Memoir*, ed. Sutherland, p. 77.

13   *The Englishwoman's Domestic Magazine*, vol. 2, 1866, p. 238.

14   The patches are to be found at Bodleian MS Eng. e. 3764, booklets 7 [p. 7], 9 [p. 2] and 10 [p. 3]. Digital images and transcriptions of the manuscript can be examined freely at *Jane Austen's Fiction Manuscripts: A Digital Edition*, ed. Kathryn Sutherland, 2010, <http://www.janeausten.ac.uk>. All further references to *The Watsons* will be by booklet and inferred page number in the digital edition.

15   Austen-Leigh, *Memoir*, ed. Sutherland, pp. 81–2.

16   Her manuscript page is, in addition, roughly the size of the printed page of the duodecimo format in which her novels were first published.

17   To James Edward Austen, 16 December 1817, letter 146, and to Anna Austen, 9–18 September 1814, letter 107.

18   The phrase is Sally Bushell's in *Text as Process*, University of Virginia Press, Charlottesville, 2009, p. 229.

19   Austen-Leigh, *Memoir*, 1871, p. 364.

20   [Fanny C. Lefroy] 'Is it Just?', *Temple Bar*, vol. 67, 1883, p. 277.

21   For biographical details for this period, see Le Faye, *Family Record*, pp. 135–59.

22   Austen-Leigh, *Memoir*, 1871, p. 181; Austen-Leigh, *Memoir*, ed. Sutherland, p. 127.

23   On this relationship, see Edward W. Said, *On Late Style*, Bloomsbury, London, 2006, p. 3.

Figure 6.12 The last full page of the manuscript of *Sanditon* (16.2 x 10 cm; 6.4 x 4 inches), written 18 March 1817. Cambridge, King's College.

them, & every thing had a suitable air
of Propriety & Order. — Lady D. valued herself upon her liberal Establishment,
& had great enjoyment in the Importance
of her Style of living. — They were shewn
into the usual sitting room, well-proportioned & well-furnished; — tho' it was
Furniture rather originally good & extremely
well kept, than new or shewey — and
as Lady D. was not there, Charlotte had
leisure to look about, & to be told by
Mrs P. that the whole-length Portrait
of a stately Gentleman, which placed
over the Mantlepiece, caught the eye
immediately, was the picture of Sir H.
Denham — and that one among many
Miniatures in another part of the
room, little conspicuous, represented Mr
Hollis. — Poor Mr Hollis! — It was
impossible not to feel him hardly

7

The Novel in 1817

Freya Johnston

The year 1817, the *annus horribilis* of the Prince Regent, later George IV, began with an extravagant gastronomic spectacle and closed with the botched and unnecessary deaths of his only daughter and grandson. Although he lived on until 1830, George's monstrously hollow regency (he was only ever impersonating a king, before and after his accession to the throne in 1820) effectively wobbled to a halt in 1817. In that year, his kingdom reached the end of a line. Amongst the legacies of his humble servant and perky Hampshire subject, Jane Austen, is a blankly open letter to George, the sham ruler to whom she had been encouraged to dedicate *Emma* (1815):

TO

HIS ROYAL HIGHNESS

THE PRINCE REGENT,

THIS WORK IS,

BY HIS ROYAL HIGHNESS'S PERMISSION,

MOST RESPECTFULLY DEDICATED,

BY HIS ROYAL HIGHNESS'S

DUTIFUL

AND OBEDIENT

HUMBLE SERVANT,

THE AUTHOR

Echoing the stylized brevity of the dedications to friends and relatives that garland her earliest works of fiction, Austen's twenty-nine-word address to the regent manages to deploy 'Royal Highness' three times within its contracted span. The seemingly deferential attitude of the whole piece is an exercise in studied colourlessness. But the

Figure 7.1 Brighton Pavilion Kitchen from John Nash's *Views of the Royal Pavilion* (1826). Royal Pavilion & Museums, Brighton & Hove.

repeated phrase suggests that something else is bubbling under the surface. For it is in this period of grotesque royal profligacy that the laughably overblown verb 'to Royal Highness' comes into being, as in Joseph Forsyth's *Remarks on Antiquities, Arts, and Letters, during an Excursion in Italy*: 'they Royal Highnessed each other incessantly'.[1] Such pointlessly finessed and overdone phrasing, and the buoyantly gleeful sense of its redundancy, sprang from the honorifics that were bitterly and strategically deployed by Princess Caroline as weapons in open correspondence with her husband, whom she repeatedly, menacingly addressed as 'Your Royal Highness'. Deference to such a husband, to such a ruler, could be expressed only through gritted teeth. It is appropriate that *Emma*, a novel about the misguided arrogance of youth and its collisions with illegitimacy and poverty, should begin not only with a title that is obediently named after its highly superior heroine but also with a dedication to a spoilt, undisciplined and headstrong man, the epitome of a character who gets his own way.

On 18 January 1817, the recently completed Great Kitchen at Brighton Pavilion played host to celebrity chef Marie-Antoine Carême. In honour of Grand Duke Nicholas of Russia, Carême had prepared a vast, extravagant dinner of more than one hundred separate dishes, including a 4-foot-high marzipan Turkish mosque (fig. 7.1). The Prince Regent apparently exclaimed: 'It is wonderful to be back in Brighton where I am truly loved.' (The expression is wooden, but to recognize that stilted quality of utterance might lead us to think that the quotation is therefore accurate.)[2] Disturbing evidence of rather different feelings towards the prince was soon to be provided by the satirist Humphry Hedgehog in *The Pavilion; or, A Month in Brighton*, a novel whose appearance had been repeatedly threatened: 'Certainly the new Characters brought out feel very sore, and they have resorted to every mean measure to suppress the tale, but without effect'; 'The Publisher cannot but notice the attempts that are daily made to stop the circulation of this work—however indignant the new Characters that are brought out may feel, it is nothing more than their due, and all their envy, hatred and malice now only helps the sale'.[3]

Hedgehog's socio-political tale, which in the phrasing of the *Morning Chronicle* 'brought out' real characters in high life, exposing them against their will to public view in order to excoriate their vices, is a strangely febrile and nightmarish mixture (fig. 7.2). *The Pavilion* narrates the visit of 'Prince Gregory' to Brighton: his terrible profusion has caused distress and galvanized mobs who are poised to strike back, trembling on the brink of insurrection. The country is in 'an oppressed and degraded situation'. Prince Gregory unwisely ventures out into Brighton incognito, on a quixotic ramble contrived 'to give him that insight into public opinion, which he so much wished to obtain'. Frolicking in the midst of such deprivation, gorging on dainties while his subjects protest and starve in front of his face, the prince is an emblem of corruption and disgrace.[4]

None of this makes for a very enjoyable read, and not only because Hedgehog (probably the oddball provincial bookseller and printer, John Agg) was too busy

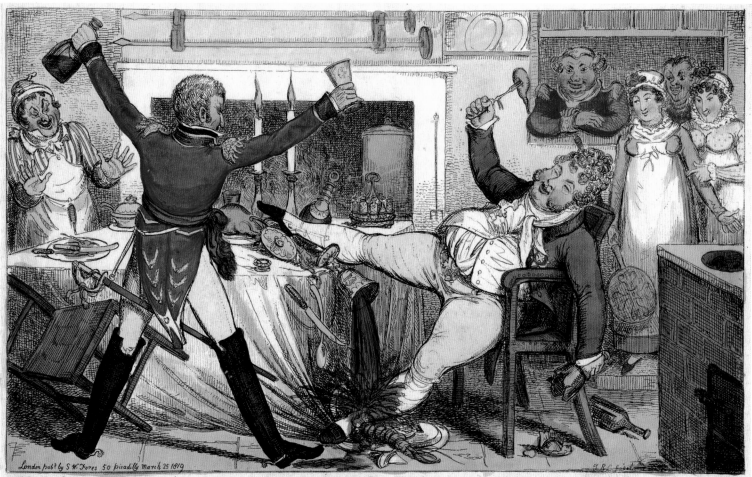

London pub'd by S W Fores 50 picadilly March 25 1819

High life below Stairs ! a new *Farce* as lately perform'd at the Theatre Royal Brighton for the edification & amusement of the Cooks, Scullions, Dishwashers, Lick-
-trenchers, Shoe-blacks, Cinder sifters Candle snuffers &c &c of that Theatre, but which was unfortunately Damn'd the first night by Common Sense !

fomenting local spats to think about his prose style for long.[5] Native fairy-tale elements, including the figure of the prince who slithers about in disguise to find out what people really think of him, collide queasily with grubby modern gossip and sudden electric glimpses of real human suffering. This transient, hard-nosed, investigative romp of a novel, a descendant of Tobias Smollett and harbinger of George Orwell, presents a cynical view of the social and political landscape in 1817, and of the corresponding task of the author when confronted with flagrant injustice and suffering:

> readers … may enquire what object the succeeding pages have in view. In the midst of the most aggravated public distress, when penury and woe walk the streets hand in hand, and thousands are actually starving, the prodigalities of those great ones of the earth, who ought to be the stewards and almoners of Providence, present a fair field for satire to hold daily tournament in.[6]

The seemingly incongruous medieval flavour of this passage attests to the universal influence of Walter Scott, whose novels blazed across the publishing stage in 1817. Throughout the early decades of the nineteenth century there were recurrent novelistic and political tussles about the desirability or otherwise of returning to the manners and morals of earlier, and specifically medieval, times: should the novel take refuge in a distant past, or should it rather chart, clear-sightedly, the morals and manners of the degenerate or superior present? Could a work of fiction combine those strains, whether in order to reflect critically or sadly or comically on the past or the present, or in some cases both?

Like other novels published this year, Hedgehog's slim and urgent book about a slow, fat man leaking poison is full of imminent danger and endless talking. The exchange of opinions was the lifeblood of fiction in 1817, and some of those opinions concerned the proverbially low status of fiction itself. By this stage, as everyone knows, the novel was nothing new. But it continued to display what Thomas Love Peacock called, in a peculiar and inventive tale published that year, 'the fertility of fiction'.[7] Many early nineteenth-century novelists proved willing, perhaps even desperate, to push the capacities and rethink the shape and purpose of book-length fiction. The results of that experimentation include farcical, sentimental, historical, political and philosophical novels; fictions of dialogue and broad, sweeping narrative; novels with a public, social, outward-facing stance and novels of domestic manners and private feelings; books which set out to expose individuals and fortified texts which sought to remain studiously impersonal. Some writers of fiction were confident enough behind those defences to tackle ways other than their own of conceiving and interpreting character, as in Azilé d'Arcy's five-volume *Prejudice; or Physiognomy*,[8] a laborious attack on Johann Kaspar Lavater's popular pseudoscientific method of deducing personality from external facial appearance.[9]

Some common threads unite the novels of 1817: much interest, contempt, alarm and every so often a titbit of sympathy is shown regarding the social and domestic roles, duties and characters of women, especially regarding marriage and education. The virtues and vices of the great are scrutinized and contrasted with more absorbing and engaging sets of possibilities than those embodied in the Prince Regent. A manifestly troubled social landscape surges into view, alongside delight in the sheer beauty of nature. Many novels experiment with dialogue, tinkering freely with the ways in which it may be understood and misunderstood, whether on account of its specialist jargon or because it is presented on the page as another kind of dialect to which only particular groups of readers and listeners will have immediate access. People are talking and talking, but they cannot always be heard. The sheer geographical and imaginative span embraced by the novel, and the fidelity of individual writers to local and national manners and customs, are strikingly rich and bold ingredients and the cause of amazement and delight in many readers.

Perhaps what unites the majority of novels appearing in 1817 is a concern, whether overt or implicit, thematic or formal, with history. Was the novel best approached as an authentic narrative of things as they are, or were? Should the incidents of fiction be founded in reality, or at least in probability? Novels consumed by the public in 1817 ranged from angry portrayals of present-day injustice to outlandish romances of the distant past – a past which might nevertheless be understood in direct relation to social problems of the here and now. By this point, a new kind of poetic-novelistic antiquarian romance (such as Thomas Moore's *Lallah Rookh*), weaving gritty factual detail into sophisticated forms of narrative elaboration, was beginning to thrive.[10] Such works made a virtue of their mixed provision: Moore's spliced four narrative poems with a connecting tale in prose. The many forms and voices of the novel in 1817 are charged with myriad collisions between past and present. The results are sometimes comic, sometimes tragic; by turns whimsically indifferent to and fiercely involved in the world outside and around them. This is a kind of novel which has Charles Dickens on its horizon.

Viewed from the perspective of publishing history, most novelists and most novel-readers paid a considerable price for their involvement with the genre. Production was expensive and returns were low. Austen's *Northanger Abbey* and *Persuasion* appeared together in four volumes at the very end of 1817 (the title page is dated 1818) in a print run of only 1,750 copies, of which 282 remained unsold three years later.[11] James Raven singles out, as distinguishing features of novels at this time, 'their high retail price, the production of ephemeral editions in very small print runs, and the poverty and exploitation of novelists'.[12] The ways in which all or part of a typically three-volume novel might fall into the hands of a reader were varied and circuitous. The majority of literate people, unable or reluctant to purchase such works, might borrow them from employers, friends, relatives or from circulating libraries (some publishers

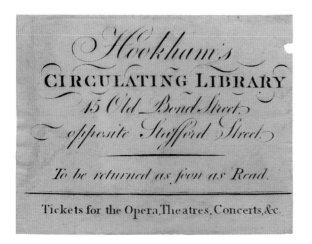

such as William Lane, founder of the Minerva Press, had their own affiliated circulating libraries) (figs 7.3–7.5). Book clubs and reading societies also helped these luxury goods to reach a wide audience, although novelists were bound to have mixed feelings about that; Austen wrote to her niece Fanny Knight on 30 November 1814 (letter 114) that people were 'more ready to borrow & praise, than to buy'.

Once acquired, the precious volume or volumes might then be read in silence or aloud; alone or within a circle of family and acquaintances. Novels were often enjoyed or endured more than once, even if not in their entirety. This repeated experience of the same work of fiction, whether loved or liked or indifferently received, may have been a response not only to the luxury status of novels as printed artefacts. The readers of 1817 may well have felt entitled to graze freely upon whatever material they were lucky enough to get their hands on. Looked at another way, this variegated landscape also testifies (contrastingly) to the shambolically episodic character of many such works of fiction. If readers already assumed that such works were written piecemeal or to a formula, they may also have wondered why they should bother to plod dutifully from beginning to end. Then again, such works may have dispensed with structural integrity on the assumption that no reader would respect or even notice it. Novelists may in their turn have been writing on the assumption that their works would quickly be gutted in reviews for the long quotations or elegant extracts judged to be worthy of attention and preservation.

Some novels issued in England in 1817, including the less celebrated titles, were swiftly translated for and transported to European audiences, and went on to be published in America. Edward Moore's *The Mysteries of Hungary* was translated into French in the same year, 1817, in which it appeared in England. Frances Moore's *Manners: A Novel* appeared in America and England in that year, too. Peacock's *Melincourt* (with no generic affiliation or subtitle) was published in England and America in 1817 and translated into French in 1818; Maria Edgeworth's two-for-one *Harrington, A Tale; and Ormond* was also published in America and translated into French (both in 1817), as was Anna Maria Porter's *The Knight of St John*. Within two years of its 1817 publication in the United Kingdom, Walter Scott's *Rob Roy* had appeared in America and been translated into French and German (fig. 7.6). Austen's *Persuasion and Northanger Abbey* had to wait a little longer to reach these audiences; a French translation of *Persuasion* was published in 1821, and three years later of *Northanger Abbey*; in 1822, a German version of *Persuasion* appeared. Ten years after that, a Philadelphia edition of *Persuasion* arrived, and of *Northanger Abbey* in 1833.

There was a steady growth in novel publication between the 1750s and the 1800s, then a dropping off in the 1810s: it must have been faintly dispiriting to Jane Austen,

pp. 150–1 **Figure 7.3** Circulating Library from *Poetical Sketches of Scarborough*, with plates by Rowlandson (1813). Oxford, Bodleian Library, G.A. Yorks 4° 253, plate at p. 140.

Figure 7.4 Hookham's Circulating Library, *c.*1800. Oxford, Bodleian Library, John Johnson Collection, Circulating Libraries 1 (71c).

Figure 7.5 Book-plate from Soulby's Circulating Library, 1772–1816. Oxford, Bodleian Library, John Johnson Collection, Circulating Libraries 2 (32).

if indeed she was aware of it, that she began to publish her fiction in the first decade to experience a strictly numerical downturn in novels in more than half a century. Of the fifty-five or so new novel titles to be published in 1817, the vast majority appeared in London. Just over 60 per cent of novels published between 1770 and 1819 advertised the author's name on the title page. Austen's first novel was demurely identified as 'By a Lady', while her subsequent fiction used the formula pointing readers back to earlier titles 'By the author of …'. There was a 'major explosion' of novels 'By a Lady' in the 1780s (when Austen was writing her teenage spoofs), with a quarter being signed in this way in 1785. By the 1790s, this had dropped to 5 per cent and after that it was a 'thin trickle'. Amongst the novelists of 1817 whom we still remember, Peacock and Austen chose not to reveal their own names on the title page. Others, like Scott, preferred the shield of a pseudonym; Elizabeth Thomas churned out nine Minerva Press novels between 1806 and 1818, in the bustling homely guise of Mrs Bridget Bluemantle.

Many genres nestled beneath the blanket term of what we now call the 'novel'; depending on the inclinations of the author in question, it can be tricky or fruitful or pointless to attempt to establish the demarcations between self-styled tales, histories, adventures, romances and 'novels' proper. Austen categorized all the works of fiction that she published in her lifetime as *A Novel*, and was already practising this titular flourish as a teenager. Book-length fiction published by women in the 1810s did tend to sport a generic marker of some kind: this was often nothing more or less boldly descriptive than *A Novel*, as in works of 1817 by Selina Davenport, Azilé d'Arcy, Elizabeth Thomas and Henrietta Rouviere Mosse.

Any novelist, then as now, would have keenly awaited a review; if their work was noticed at all, they could expect a shortish notice and plot summary, followed by long extracts of what were characterized to readers as admirable or interesting or especially woeful passages. Indeed, the practice of lavish excerpting, whether in the body of the text or stashed in a footnote, whether for the purpose of castigating or praising the author, is so standard that when some reviewers fail to supply extracts they mention it as a departure from the norm. Judgements are often summary and harsh, and there is a general atmosphere of exhausted saturation. The tone of relief and gratitude when something fresh and well written arrives on the scene is therefore all the more striking.

Thomas Love Peacock's well-received second novel, *Melincourt*, was published in the same month of 1817 as Humphrey Hedgehog's *The Pavilion* and offers a contrasting version of the novelistic satire of opinion, with a far wider gallery of characters and a far more sophisticated armoury of stylistic and comic tools at its disposal. Female novelists, female

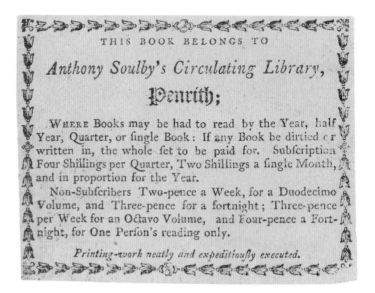

dialogue and female education all feature prominently, while the greatest joke in this novel of talk is that the hero, a chivalric orangutan who strides triumphantly across a scene of human degeneracy, cannot speak at all. One reviewer was impressed with the sheer number of useful things contained within this small book. The terms of his praise suggest that we might all do better to read magazines rather than fiction, unless fiction possesses the miscellaneous, ludic quality of such publications. The two forms of writing, novelistic and journalistic, were in fact already related, and would go on to become even more richly associated, again in the figure of Charles Dickens, who began his career by publishing Peacock's essay, 'Recollections of Childhood', in *Bentley's Miscellany*:

> *Melincourt*, under the form of a novel, is a work unique in its kind: it is a repository of morality and erudition, and of keen and gentlemanlike satire on passing events, and on such who deserve the utmost severity of its lash. … Nothing escapes the searching eye and just reflection of this inimitable author, yet there is so much playful elegance, so much sterling wit mingled with sarcasms, that even the party most satirized, will scarce be able to suppress a smile at the strong likeness, while, if any, of what the writer humorously styles, that 'expensive article, conscience,' is left, he must own the ridicule to be just.[13]

Melincourt includes the most extreme examples of Peacock's satirical, bureaucratic tendency to give sources, in footnotes, for the things his characters say. In ch. 6, Sir Telegraph Paxarett and Mr Sylvan Forester argue about the origins and nature of Sir Oran Haut-Ton. One note supplies four quotations to endorse Mr Forester's general comment that 'the most enlightened and illustrious philosophers agree in considering him [that is, the orangutan] as the natural and original man' (vol. 1, pp. 68–70).

The fallibilities with which Peacock is concerned are primarily those of the mind. Having said that, his stories are highly flirtatious and, like many other novels of this period, they end in marriage. Another such novel of 1817 is Frances Holcroft's four-volume *Fortitude and Frailty: A Novel*, a work that opens with a chapter of light, sarcastic dialogue between a plotting brother and sister; the brother, Leoline Hargrave (with a 'propensity to sneering satire'), is determined to bag a teenage heiress to save himself the bother of earning a living.[14] Many novels, this one included, remain saturated in the names and conventions of Austen's acknowledged favourites and models among the eighteenth-century novelists of her youth: of Samuel Richardson's epistolary fiction ('Clarissa', 'Hargrave'), as refracted through Austen's near-contemporary Frances Burney and the innocently observed manners of the town. The contrasting influence of Richardson's old nemesis, Henry Fielding, continues to make itself strongly felt, too – perhaps especially in Maria Edgeworth's *Ormond*, with its great healthy indecorums and strapping, obstreperous women, and in Walter Scott, whose picaresque hero Rob Roy echoes the loose morals and lurid exploits of Fielding's Tom Jones.

Figure 7.6 Walter Scott, half-length portrait, seated, facing right, with dog. Etching by William Nicholson, 1817. Library of Congress, Prints & Photographs Division.

Published mid-way through 1817, *Leap Year: or, a Woman's Privilege* was the fifth novel to be completed in as many years by the enterprising and resourceful Selina Davenport. Most of her works were published by the Minerva Press, a business known for producing sentimental and Gothic fiction, especially by women. In this year alone, the same press also published (amongst other titles) Elizabeth Thomas's *Claudine, or Pertinacity. A Novel*; Henrietta Rouviere Mosse's *A Bride and No Wife. A Novel*; Catharine Selden's *Villa Santelle; or The Curious Impertinent. A Romance*; and Edward Moore's *The Mysteries of Hungary. A Romantic History, of the fifteenth century.* Davenport, who was separated from her husband, began her career in fiction as a means of supporting herself and her two daughters. Her life is an instructive example of how a determined female author might set out to earn an income from novels in the early decades of the nineteenth century, and of the sorts of connections she might need to cultivate en route. Novel-writing was one of several money-making ventures in which Davenport was involved (and perhaps doomed to be the least successful, given how poorly novelists were remunerated). After publishing eleven lengthy, sensational tales for and about women – tales contrived in the first place to keep herself and her own daughters alive – she gave up fiction and turned her hand to running a small shop in Knutsford, Cheshire, the town on which Elizabeth Gaskell went on to base her *Cranford* in the fiction of that name, published in 1851.

In 1817, Maria Edgeworth's double publication *Harrington, A Tale; and Ormond, A Tale* aided the launch of the historical novel in Europe. Scott read and learnt from her how a novelist might introduce one cultural tradition to another, whether across a long period or in a tense contemporary setting. The Edgeworth family's connections with pre-revolutionary French society fed directly into *Ormond*, a novel Edgeworth wrote in haste as her father was dying. The novel mingles fashionable Parisian society with settings on the wild west coast of Ireland, while its companion piece, *Harrington*, offers a fiction of English life in which Edgeworth tries rather clumsily to make amends for an anti-Semitic passage in *The Absentee* (1812). These were her last novels for adults for sixteen years. Generally speaking, *Ormond*, with its rich cast of Irish characters, was far better received than *Harrington*. Many readers felt a degree of resistance to Edgeworth's attempt to counter prejudice against Jews and specifically to counter the impression that Edgeworth herself was anti-Semitic. The ensuing debates about the tale and its transparent message bring into sharp focus the knotty issue of whether novels ever could point a moral of this kind successfully, and indeed the question whether that is what fiction should ever be used to do.

There is a sort of didacticism in works like Edgeworth's 1817 tales that reviewers are beginning to find ill-suited to the imaginative strains of the novel, not that such reviewers do not hold fiction to account. Dozens of reviewers of the time are keen to point out grammatical errors in female writers, including those of the most extravagant historical fiction. The following passage comes from a brief commentary on Anna

Maria Porter's *The Knight of St John: A Romance* (September 1817):

> A strain of noble though romantic sentiments pervades this work; many of
> the scenes are pleasing and well-imagined; … Yet, as a whole, this romance is
> somewhat deficient in interest, and disfigured by puerilities: …
> Some incorrect expressions must also be noticed, such as, in vol. iii. p. 14.,
> '*fetching* a sigh:' p. 17. 'the *thick* of the fight:' p. 26. '*without* the siege were raised,
> he knew the fort must fall:' p. 346. 'plunging into the *thick* of the combatants:' p.
> 140. '*La Citte* notabile,' instead of La Citta, &c. &c.[15]

In the preface to her *Villasantelle; or The Curious Impertinent. A Romance*, Catharine
Selden describes herself as a 'historian'.[16] She is in fact the author of the kind of curious
and impertinent Euro-Gothic romp that Catherine Morland, the heroine of Austen's
Northanger Abbey, would eat for breakfast. Two Spanish men – one of them the noble
young Castilian hero of the title, Henriquez de Villasantelle – are travelling in Italy.
The fatally inquisitive youth cannot but pursue two fair strangers (virtuous Victoria
and evil, sleazy Isabel) through settings that include gloomy apartments, sepulchral
vaults and subterraneous passages. A body goes missing; there are lots of monks;
some coincidental encounters; a long gallery full of armour (some of which moves);
a bloodstained floor; moonlight; cloaks and veils; murder; abandoned morals; more
moonlight; unjust imprisonment; shocking revelations (including, at the end, those of
paternity) and confessions – in the moonlight – ending (but of course) with the eternal
happiness of the hero and his Victoria.

Back home in England, Princess Charlotte's death after fifty hours in labour with
a stillborn nine-pound son on 5 November 1817 let rip a national outpouring of grief
and rage. Sir Richard Croft, the royal surgeon, committed suicide. Into this strange
atmosphere came Frances Brooke's *Manners*, a society novel which failed to convince the
reviewers that lower-class Irish characters possessed any such thing, and another fiction
involving England and Ireland, William Godwin's *Mandeville: A Tale of the Seventeenth
Century in England*.

At some time in the second half of 1817, Henry and Cassandra Austen negotiated
with John Murray for the publication of *Northanger Abbey* (evidently their choice of title,
since it was previously known as *Susan*, and by Austen in 1817 as *Catherine*), together
with *Persuasion* (fig. 7.7). Henry Austen's 'Biographical Notice', dated 13 December 1817,
appeared as a preface to the four-volume edition (two volumes for each of the novels);
and in his 'Notice' Austen's name appeared in print for the first time as the openly
acknowledged author of the six novels. These two works were first advertised in *The
Courier* of 17 December 1817 for publication on 20 December, *Northanger Abbey* being
described as a 'Romance' and *Persuasion* as a 'Novel', although this distinction does not
appear on the title pages. The advertising copywriter may have read the novelist Clara

NORTHANGER ABBEY:

AND

PERSUASION.

BY THE AUTHOR OF "PRIDE AND PREJUDICE,"
"MANSFIELD-PARK," &C.

WITH A BIOGRAPHICAL NOTICE OF THE
AUTHOR.

IN FOUR VOLUMES.

VOL. I.

LONDON:

JOHN MURRAY, ALBEMARLE-STREET.

1818.

Reeve's definition of the difference:

> The Romance is an heroic fable, which treats of fabulous persons and things.—The Novel is a picture of real life and manners, and of the times in which it is written. The Romance in lofty and elevated language, describes what never happened nor is likely to happen.—The Novel gives a familiar relation of such things, as pass every day before our eyes, such as may happen to our friends, or to ourselves; and the perfection of it, is to represent every scene, in so easy and natural a manner, and to make them appear so probable, as to deceive us into a persuasion (at least while we are reading) that all is real, until we are affected by the joys or distresses, of the persons in the story, as if they were our own.[17]

But perhaps Henry and Cassandra slipped up when they plumped for *Northanger Abbey*. Between 1784 and 1818 thirty-two novels contained 'Abbey' in the title; many others were as liberally sprinkled with convents, monasteries, priories, abbots, friars and nuns. Readers waking up to all this once again at the dawn of 1818 may well have thought the title indicated no more than a rerun of a hackneyed plot, something along the lines of the 'romances' mentioned by Reeve. And *Northanger Abbey* really is, in some ways, hackneyed. Like *Persuasion*, but for different reasons, it keeps one foot in the past: the turn of the nineteenth century, the period of Austen's mid-twenties. By 1816, Bath itself had faded a little, too (this makes it just the right place for Anne Elliot, apparently past her sell-by date, and her father, clutching his anti-ageing face cream).[18] With the joint publication of her last completed novel, *Persuasion*, alongside one of her earliest works of fiction, *Northanger Abbey*, readers at the end of 1817 had the chance to compare and contrast two very different treatments of the past. In *Persuasion* they would find Austen's most overt and sustained reference to historical events in living memory, the Napoleonic Wars, while in *Northanger Abbey* history appears in the not-entirely-fresh form of a spurious antiquity and the dappled perversions of Gothic fiction.

Fanny Price may have alluded to him as a consolation, but Austen viewed her contemporary novelist Walter Scott through the sharper eyes of a competitor.[19] It is fitting as well as irksome to recall that her final novels appeared in the same month as the fifth of his *Waverley* novels; as novelists, Scott and Austen both had a keen interest in the success and profits of their work. On the last day of 1817, eleven days after *Northanger Abbey and Persuasion* had appeared, *Rob Roy* was published. The first edition of 10,000 copies sold so quickly that a new impression of a further 3,000 copies was needed after only two weeks. This was the clear and unequivocal bestseller, the runaway racehorse novel of 1818. Austen, had she lived to see in the new year and the fate of her remaindered volumes, might have had cause to repeat her comment in a letter to her niece Anna on 28 September 1814 (letter 108):

Figure 7.7 Title page of *Northanger Abbey* and *Persuasion* (John Murray, London, 1818). Oxford, Bodleian Library, Dunston B 121.

Walter Scott has no business to write novels, especially good ones.—It is not fair.—He has Fame and Profit enough as a Poet, and should not be taking the bread out of other people's mouths.—I do not like him, and do not mean to like Waverley if I can help it—but fear I must.

No such fear need tarnish the celebration of her novels in 2017: Jane Austen has not been left on the shelf.

1 Joseph Forsyth, *On Antiquities, Arts, and Letters, in Italy*, 4th edition, John Murray, London, 1835, p. 461. Forsyth is describing a tour undertaken in 1802–3.

2 See Ian Kelly, *Cooking for Kings: The Life of Antonin Carême, the First Celebrity Chef*, Short Books, London, 2003.

3 *Morning Chronicle*, 10 March 1817; *Morning Chronicle*, 19 May 1817.

4 Humphry Hedgehog [John Agg], *The Pavilion; or, A Month in Brighton The Pavilion*, 2 vols, London, 1817, vol. 1, pp. 63, 107.

5 According to the British Book Trade Index, (<http://bbti.bodleian.ox.ac.uk/>), Agg began his fervid professional life as an apprentice bookseller and printer in Evesham in Worcestershire, operating between 1790 and 1825. His writings often landed him in the hot water that was his natural element, and by 1814, he was in the King's Bench Prison for libel.

6 Hedgehog, *The Pavilion*, vol. 1, pp. 10–11.

7 [Thomas Love Peacock], *Melincourt. By the author of Headlong Hall*, 3 vols, T. Hookham, Jun., and Co., and Baldwin, Cradock and Joy, London, 1817, vol. 3, p. 73.

8 Minerva Press for A.K. Newman and Company, London, 1817.

9 See Johann Kaspar Lavater, *Physiognomische Fragmente zur Beförderung der Menschenkenntnis und Menschenliebe*, 4 vols, Weidmanns, Erben, und Reich, Leipzig, 1775–8.

10 Thomas Moore, *Lallah Rookh. An Oriental Romance, With Illustrative Notes*, Longman, Hurst, Rees, Orme, and Brown, London, 1817.

11 William St Clair, *The Reading Nation in the Romantic Period*, Cambridge University Press, Cambridge, 2004, p. 580.

12 James Raven, 'Production', in Peter Garside and Karen O'Brien (eds), *The Oxford History of the Novel in English*, vol. 2: *English and British Fiction*, Oxford University Press, Oxford, 2015, pp. 4–28 (p. 28).

13 *La Belle Assemblée*, n.s. vol. 15, April 1817, pp. 188–90.

14 Frances Holcroft, *Fortitude and Frailty: A Novel*, 4 vols, W. Simpkin and R. Marshall, London, 1817, vol. 1, p. 40.

15 Review of Anna Maria Porter's *The Knight of St John, A Romance*, 3 vols, Longman, Hurst, Rees, Orme, and Brown, London, 1817, in *The Monthly Review*, 2nd series, no. 85, March 1818, pp. 328–9 (p. 329).

16 Catherine Selden, *Villasantelle; or The Curious Impertinent. A Romance*, A. K. Newman and Co., London, 1817, Preface, p. ii.

17 [Clara Reeve], *The Progress of Romance through Times, Countries and Manners … in a Course of Evening Conversation*, 2 vols, printed for the author, Colchester, 1785, p. 111.

18 [Jane Austen], *Persuasion*, ch. 16.

19 [Jane Austen], *Mansfield Park*, ch. 9.

Jane Austen
Imagined

8

A Life in Portraits

Susan Owens

'What an exquisite possession a good picture of her would be! I would give any money for it.'

Emma, ch. 6

Imagining the missed opportunities for a professional portrait of Jane Austen is a sobering pastime. While it is regrettable that only a single likeness of Shakespeare exists that is generally thought to have been painted from life, that the same is true of Austen is staggeringly unfortunate.[1] By the early nineteenth century, British art was enjoying an unprecedentedly high status, and a generation of brilliantly talented artists was energetically reinvigorating portraiture. Drawings were particularly popular, offering a wide variety of more intimate, informal likenesses at a significantly lower cost than oil paintings.

So, to give the imagination free rein, who could have portrayed Jane Austen? One candidate was the highly successful portrait miniaturist and draughtsman Richard Cosway, who would surely have responded to her 'full round cheeks', her 'well formed, bright hazel eyes' and her 'brown hair forming natural curls close round her face'.[2] Another was Thomas Lawrence, although it is difficult to imagine his dazzling brand of Regency glamour greatly appealing to Austen herself. The fashionable portrait draughtsman John Downman would have revelled, albeit in a more restrained way, in Austen's taste for 'pretty caps', and his technique of applying watercolour to the back of the thin paper sheet to give a subtle rosy flush to cheeks would have flattered the 'rich colour' of her 'clear' complexion.[3] But perhaps Henry Edridge would have been the best match of all. One of his meticulous full-length portrait drawings, executed in pencil with grey wash and judicious touches of colour, would have complemented Austen's tall, slender figure, its calmly dignified mood suiting her natural reserve.[4]

The lack of an 'official' portrait of Austen is especially ironic, as the second half of the eighteenth century had seen a huge growth of interest in celebratory portraiture. By the late Georgian and Regency period, in what Samuel Taylor Coleridge disparagingly called 'this AGE OF PERSONALITY', portraits of eminent men (and, occasionally, women) helped to create and to commemorate contemporary heroes to

Figure 8.1 Cassandra Austen (1773–1845), *Portrait of Jane Austen*, c.1810. Graphite and watercolour. © National Portrait Gallery, London.

an unprecedented degree.[5] This was expressed at all levels, from Cassandra Austen's amusing thumbnail illustrations to Jane Austen's teenage spoof 'The History of England' (1791), to volumes of prints illustrating British history through images of its protagonists, to Lawrence's portraits of twenty-eight celebrated figures who helped to secure the overthrow of Napoleon, commissioned by George IV, for what would become the Waterloo Chamber at Windsor Castle. The Royal Academician George Dance made over 200 profile drawings of London's artistic establishment and other 'Eminent Characters' that were etched by William Daniell and published with brief biographical notes from 1802 onwards, while in 1822 the booksellers Thomas Cadell and William Davies attempted a hugely ambitious survey of leading figures of the day in their *British Gallery of Contemporary Portraits, being a series of engravings of the most eminent persons now living or lately deceased, in Great Britain and Ireland; from Drawings accurately made from life, or from the most approved original pictures.*

Jane Austen was not, of course, amongst these 'eminent persons'. In fact she would have to wait until 1873 for a comparable honour, when her portrait was included in Evert A. Duyckinck's *Portrait Gallery of Eminent Men and Women of Europe and America*. And far from deriving from a drawing 'accurately made from life', this print was loosely based on the stipple engraving produced by Richard Bentley and included as the frontispiece for the 1870 *Memoir* – that was based on the watercolour by James Andrews commissioned the previous year – that was based on an amateur sketch made around 1810 by Cassandra Austen. Sixty-three years and a process of idealization later, Austen's portrait had been reimagined to include the trappings of authorship: an inkwell and a manuscript.[6] It is a history that proves an old maxim correct: that what is desired tends, eventually, to appear.

'There is my sister ...' (Emma, ch. 6)

The best-known image of Jane Austen is the drawing made by her sister Cassandra, fairly shortly after their move to Chawton, when Jane was about 35 years old (fig. 8.1). This is one of only two extant drawings Cassandra made of Jane.[7] Was she so sparing with her brushes? Or did Cassandra, like Emma Woodhouse, have a portfolio full of portrait drawings, long since lost, that included more of her sister?

It would have been entirely fitting if she had. During this period, paintbrushes up and down the country were being poised over sketchbooks, picturesque views composed and friends' faces scrutinized. For the upper and middle classes, drawing and watercolour painting were viewed as accomplishments rather than idle pastimes, for which reason they were considered to be beneficial activities – especially for the young. According to her brother Henry, 'in her earlier days' Austen herself drew, and 'evinced great power of hand in the management of the pencil'; while Jane's own favourite niece, Fanny Knight, is depicted with her head bent diligently over her paint

Figure 8.2 Cassandra Austen (1773–1845), *Portrait of Fanny Knight*, c.1810. Watercolour. © Jane Austen's House Museum.

box in a watercolour by Cassandra, looking the very picture of exemplary occupation (fig. 8.2).[8] According to Thomas Smith, the author of *The Young Artist's Assistant* (1824), painting in watercolour was superior to other diversions such as playing cards or reading a novel because it was 'certain to bring neither regret, anxiety, fatigue of body, nor enervation of the mind'.[9] Landscape views were the most popular subjects and are the focus of the great majority of didactic drawing manuals, but amateur artists also ventured into portraiture and used themselves, each other, friends and family as models – 'a likeness', as Austen put it, 'pleases every body' (*Emma*, ch. 6). While the skill required to achieve a likeness, and a pleasing one at that, might have daunted some amateurs, drawing portraits had the advantage of adding a sociable dimension to amateur art practice. Indeed, Cassandra's watercolour depicts Fanny engaged in making a portrait.

In describing the contents of Emma Woodhouse's portfolio as she prepares to draw Harriet Smith's portrait, Austen gives us a valuable contemporary insight into an amateur artist's scope and equipment:

> Emma wished to go to work directly, and therefore produced the portfolio containing her various attempts at portraits, for not one of them had ever been finished, that they might decide together on the best size for Harriet. Her many beginnings were displayed. Miniatures, half-lengths, whole-lengths, pencil, crayon, and water-colours had been all tried in turn. (ch.6)

Emma's experimentation with a range of different formats is indicative both of her spirited confidence and of her familiarity with pictures by professional artists. While a miniature implies a close-up portrait of the face, usually in an oval format, a full-length portrait, while seemingly more ambitious, suggested more of an emphasis on the subject's costume. It is just this kind of attractive 'whole-length' portrait drawing, in fact, that appears in the 'Friendship Book' of the Revd James Stanier Clarke (fig. 8.3), and which has even been mooted as a portrait of Austen herself.[10]

Emma's range of media was limited to an amateur's usual tools of 'pencil, crayon, and water-colours'. Pencils would have been similar to those used today. Since the late seventeenth century rods of graphite (an allotrope of carbon) had been inserted into pine, deal or cedar-wood casings, but it was only in the late eighteenth century that Nicolas-Jacques Conté's experiments with mixing finely ground graphite powder with clay and water and baking it in long, narrow moulds led to the production of so-called 'black lead' pencils in a range of hard and soft grades. Emma's 'crayon' would have been a stick of ground pigment, usually consisting of black, red or white chalk, mixed with a filler such as clay, a binder such as gum arabic (the dried sap of acacia trees), and with the addition of wax or oil to give hardness and density.[11] Crayons were either wrapped in paper to protect the hands, or held in a brass or steel implement known as a porte-crayon which had a split end into which they were inserted, and a sliding ring to hold them firmly in place.

Figure 8.3 James Stanier Clarke (1766–1834), *Portrait of a lady*, watercolour. Private collection.

Watercolour was the amateur's medium *par excellence*. In 1781 the artists' supplier William Reeves revolutionized watercolour painting when he invented hard, soluble cakes of watercolour which replaced the messier loose ground pigments that artists had previously used. These attractive cakes, which were usually stamped with the manufacturer's logo, fitted snugly into paint boxes which were often furnished with all the paraphernalia that could be desired, from camel hair and sable brushes (made with the hair of the Asiatic marten, which was particularly easy to handle) to tiny sponges for soaking up excess wash. In his manual, Thomas Smith lists the twelve colours he judged suitable for the amateur: Indigo, Prussian Blue, Venetian Red, Lake, Yellow Ochre, Gamboge, Raw Umber, Vandyke Brown, Burnt Sienna, Burnt Umber, Sepia and Lamp Black.[12] Watercolour was considered to be clean and neat enough for use by the amateur artist, with none of the pungent smell and potential for mess of oil paints, which were generally the preserve of professional artists. Finally, special drawing paper was sold: 'wove' paper, which became available in the 1780s, offered a smooth surface without the ridges that characterized ordinary writing paper, and various kinds of coloured papers and sketchbooks were also marketed.

By the early years of the nineteenth century drawing materials such as these, alongside periodicals, fashion plates and decorative prints, were available from shops that had emerged to cater for amateur artists, the most fashionable of which were in London: Rudolph Ackermann's 'Repository of Arts' on the Strand and S. and J. Fuller's 'Temple of Fancy' on Rathbone Place. A contemporary illustration of the former's interior reveals what an enticing cornucopia it was (fig. 8.4). Ackermann advertised a wide range of equipment, all intended to appeal to the amateur artist, from his own 'Superfine Water Colours' to embossed 'fancy papers'.[13]

In her half-length portrait, Cassandra shows Jane sitting with her arms folded and her head turned to her right, wearing a simple dress over a short-sleeved chemise and a cap. No background is included save for the back of her chair, which is visible to the left. Like the portrait drawings in Emma's portfolio, this one appears to be unfinished. Cassandra has sketched the contours of her sister's features and figure lightly with a soft pencil, and she has used watercolour sparingly and with delicacy to define her face and hair. She has used a warmer brown for Jane's eyes than for her hair and eyebrows and a pale pink for her cheeks, to which she has mixed a darker colour to indicate shadows. An oval line, lightly but positively

Figure 8.4 Unknown artist after Augustus Charles Pugin (1769–1832) and Thomas Rowlandson (1757–1827). *Rudolph Ackermann's Repository of Arts on the Strand*, 1809. Etching and aquatint with hand-colouring. Oxford, Bodleian Library, John Johnson Collection, Ackermann box.

drawn to form an elegant border, suggests that Cassandra perhaps initially intended this to be more than an off-the-cuff sketch.

Why did Cassandra apparently abandon this drawing before completing it? Was it not a good enough likeness?[14] Was she unhappy with the expression she had caught on Jane's face? Was Jane? It certainly does not conform to the normal conventions of amateur drawings of this period; Jane is clearly not self-consciously posing like Harriet Smith, 'smiling and blushing, and afraid of not keeping her attitude and countenance' (ch. 6). Far from it. Could Cassandra even have taken her sister's likeness 'by stealth', just as Emma was obliged to when she drew her father, on account of his nervousness? What we have here seems to be a more characteristic expression, one into which the face might compose itself when preoccupied. Although Cassandra's portrait is clearly the work of an amateur, the face is delicately and painstakingly drawn and sensitively coloured, which suggests that she took great care over it. It is possible that she caught an expression on Jane's face that no professional artist could – one which, being comfortably at home and in the company of her much-loved sister, she relaxed into. With her slightly raised eyebrows and pursed lips, Jane looks as though she is lost in thought.

But are we right to interpret it as unfinished? An alternative view to the portrait having been abandoned is that Cassandra never intended to take it any further. After all, as it stands it conveys the most important information – had Jane's dress been coloured in or given a pattern, or her arms and hands tinted with flesh tones, or the background elaborated, it would arguably have added little to the portrait either in terms of aesthetic quality or data. The oval line Cassandra drew round the image might have been intended to indicate the extent of a card or paper mount to be placed over the drawing sheet before it was put into a frame. Today the National Portrait Gallery presents the portrait in just this manner: framed, and with the edges of the paper covered by a border of gold mount-board with an oval aperture. By concealing much of the blank paper of the background, this method of display makes the drawing appear more 'composed'.

Moreover, during this period there was a fashion for a light touch in portrait drawing; completeness, in the sense of an all-over uniformity of finish, was not necessarily desirable. Fashionable portrait draughtsmen such as Cosway and Lawrence tended to draw the face in detail, usually in graphite enhanced with watercolour or chalk, but only lightly to indicate the figure and dress with loose, graceful lines. The portrait drawing (as opposed to the oil painting) was allowed a certain latitude, to be informal and lively – to look as though it had been dashed off in a few minutes' brilliant inspiration. It is worth noting that Austen herself appreciated the charm of the unfinished drawing, permitting the narrator to remark of Emma's portfolio of incomplete sketches: 'There was merit in every drawing – in the least finished, perhaps the most' (ch. 6).

Figure 8.5 Cassandra Austen (1773–1845), *Portrait of Jane Austen*, 1804. Pen and ink and watercolour. Private collection.

An unconventional portrait

Cassandra had made another drawing of her sister five or six years earlier, in 1804 (fig. 8.5). Quite different from the later example, here we have a back view of Austen painted in watercolours. She is sitting outdoors, next to a tree on what appears to be a high earthy bank offering a vantage point, straight-backed and alert, and with her left hand resting lightly on her left knee. She wears a form of poke-bonnet whose large, shady peak conceals what would otherwise have been visible of her face; only the curve of her pink cheek is seen. Austen's niece Anna Lefroy described the drawing in a letter of 1862 to James Edward Austen-Leigh, who was then collecting material for his memoir, as: 'a sketch which Aunt Cassandra made of her in one of their expeditions – sitting down out of doors on a hot day, with her bonnet strings untied'.[15] Perhaps Austen's pose in this 'portrait' was also a characteristic one. Shortly after her death, her brother Henry recalled that she 'was a warm and judicious admirer of landscape, both in nature and on canvass [*sic*]'.[16]

This drawing is more conventionally 'finished' than the later one, in the sense that watercolour has been used to colour the whole image. But not entirely – there is a second major omission in that the view at which Austen gazes so raptly is also left out. Is she looking over panoramic country? Or out to sea?[17] As a result, the 'portrait' is teasing and ironic, withholding the two vital bits of visual information that one would expect to find in such an image. It is possible that Jane shared Mr Woodhouse's aversion to sitting for a likeness, and that the 1810 portrait was made surreptitiously, when Jane's mind was elsewhere. Would Jane only submit to Cassandra painting her from behind, on the condition that her face was not shown, while she rested and enjoyed the view? Was the absence of a view part of the joke of an enigmatic 'portrait'? Or, perhaps, it had simply started to rain.

Cassandra was also basing her composition upon specific sources among the fashion plates that, enjoying huge popularity at this time, were enthusiastically collected. One frequently seen convention of these plates was to represent the dress from behind so as most clearly to represent its silhouette and details. Some plates were so fantastic they bordered on caricature, while contemporary satirical prints mercilessly sent up the perceived absurdities of fashionable costume, from overly revealing muslin dresses to elaborate, all-concealing poke-bonnets (tellingly, these were known in France as *invisibles*).[18] Cassandra's particular source for this teasing 'portrait' of her sister might well be a plate from Nikolaus von Heideloff's phenomenally successful *Gallery of Fashion*, 'the first English magazine to be devoted entirely to fashion, and the first to be issued with all its plates in colour', which could be purchased from places such as Ackermann's Repository of Arts.[19] 'Bathing Place: Morning Dress', a plate published in 1797, shows two women standing on a high bank on a windy day, looking out to sea (fig. 8.6): their dresses billow in the breeze, and their faces, like Jane's, are completely hidden by the vast brims of their bonnets.[20]

Figure 8.6 Nikolaus Wilhelm von Heideloff (1761–1837), *Bathing Place, Morning Dress*, published in the *Gallery of Fashion*, September 1797. Etching and aquatint with hand-colouring. © British Library Board.

L'aimable Jane

Two enigmas

A silhouette portrait, which dates from the period 1810–15, was found pasted into the back of Volume 2 of a copy of the second edition of *Mansfield Park* (1816) (fig. 8.7). At the top of the sheet someone had inscribed the words '*L'aimiable Jane*'. Whether or not this particular portrait represents Austen herself must remain a moot point; it would, however, be remarkable if no silhouette of her had ever been made, given the ubiquity of this form of portraiture during her lifetime.[21] Silhouettes became popular during the second half of the eighteenth century and remained so until the arrival of photography in the 1840s. Although at first it was expensive to have a silhouette made – in the 1790s one could cost as much as ten shillings – by the 1810s the price had dropped significantly, and the simplest kind could be had for as little as a shilling or two. Professional studios were established in many towns and cities, but were particularly numerous in spa towns like Bath and seaside resorts. This example has tentatively been attributed to a Mrs Collins, who worked in Bath in the late eighteenth and early nineteenth centuries.[22] While having a portrait painted, or even drawn, might require several sittings, a silhouette could be cut in a matter of minutes and taken home the same day. Their affordability, and the speed with which they could be produced, meant that silhouettes were often exchanged as gifts and tokens of friendship. Sitting for a silhouette was regarded as a pleasant diversion, and if the pictures themselves were ephemeral – and one can only assume that a relatively small proportion has survived of the huge numbers that were produced – it was no great matter. For most people, they were the souvenir of a day.[23]

The popularity of the silhouette was based partly on the fashion for the antique. The profile was associated with classical antiquity – by suppressing detail and colour, it offered a pared down and idealized aesthetic suggesting qualities of nobility and authority. There was an additional dimension that made them especially intriguing: silhouette portraits were thought to be particularly expressive of character. The Swiss pastor Johann Caspar Lavater's *Essays on Physiognomy, Designed to Promote the Knowledge and Love of Mankind*, first published in Germany in 1772 and translated into English in the 1780s, was largely illustrated with silhouettes.

Had the silhouette not been inscribed with the words '*L'aimiable Jane*', would anyone have thought to identify the sitter as Austen? Almost certainly not. It is ironic that examples of a species of portrait thought to express character so distinctly can so easily slip into anonymity. It is also the presence of an inscription that has, in recent years, raised the possibility of another likeness of Austen: in this instance, a portrait drawing with the words 'Miss Jane Austin [*sic*]' written on the back (fig. 8.8).[24] This drawing is on vellum – treated calf skin – which is more durable than paper, for which reason it has traditionally been used for legal documents. Vellum has also long been valued by artists for its exceptionally fine, smooth surface and its suitability for delicate kinds of drawing, particularly portraits. The principal drawing material is black crayon

Figure 8.7 Unknown artist, *Portrait of a lady*, c.1810–15. Hollow-cut silhouette. © National Portrait Gallery, London (NPG: 3181).

(not graphite, which has a telltale sheen), and tonal areas have been augmented with subtle passages of grey wash. The artist has used the sharpened point of a crayon where precise linear detail was needed to depict jewellery and masonry, and has added touches of white bodycolour (an opaque form of watercolour) as highlights, particularly to point up the sitter's elegant lace and to make the pen nib lying on her table shine.

Details of the sitter's costume have been shown to date the drawing to the mid-1810s.[25] The heavy swag of the curtain seen in the background here had, by the Regency period, long been a conventional element in portraiture, both for its implication of gravitas and for the practical reason that it created a dark and relatively unfussy backdrop against which the face was naturally highlighted. Although somewhat gawky, and too heavily drawn to be considered fashionable, the portrait appears to be the work of a professional artist. The sitter, evidently a writer, looks up from her manuscript as though inspired. But what is she writing? St Margaret's Church and a corner of Westminster Abbey, depicted so prominently outside the window, must surely have some important significance for her – this is, after all, a carefully composed portrait, not a snapshot. Taken together, the portrait's high degree of finish, its pointed symbolism and even the direction faced by the sitter suggest that it was perhaps intended as the model for the frontispiece of a book. If this is the case, and if indeed the project was realized, the book in question has yet to be identified. If she is not Austen, could she instead be a writer of religious essays or books offering moral advice for the young of the kind that enjoyed huge popularity in the Regency period, who had some connection to one or other of these institutions? If only the words the author has just written at the top of her manuscript sheet were legible, and not represented by a generic smudge, her identity might never have been a mystery.

A transformation

The history of Cassandra's 1810 likeness of Jane is like *The Picture of Dorian Gray* in reverse. While in Oscar Wilde's novel, the oil painting, kept under lock and key, reflects Gray's debauchery by growing old and ugly, the portrait of a sharp-eyed, tight-lipped author with a slightly ironical lift to her eyebrows grows more rounded and comfortable. Her eyes become larger and softer, her lips fuller. Her chest narrows, her bust becomes more defined and her arms relax out of that defensive cross. Rather than looking off to the side, the direction of her gaze shifts and she now stares pensively into the middle distance. Jane Austen has grown prettier. She also appears to have grown younger. And is that a slight smile?

The transformative process began when the Revd James Edward Austen-Leigh, the Vicar of Bray in Berkshire and the eldest son of Jane's eldest brother, James, commissioned a watercolour when he was writing his *Memoir of Jane Austen*. He wanted a portrait of Austen to use as a frontispiece to the *Memoir*, but considered Cassandra's

Figure 8.8 Unknown artist, *Portrait of a lady*, c.1815. Crayon with grey wash and white heightening on vellum. Collection of Paula Byrne.

sketch, the only contemporary likeness, to be inadequate – he needed a better version. So in 1869 Austen-Leigh approached a local artist, James Andrews of Maidenhead, and asked him to work Cassandra's likeness up into something more acceptable. Andrews based his portrait (fig. 8.9) closely on the model he was lent; tiny holes on the original sketch that correspond to marks on his version suggest that he pinned tracing-paper onto Cassandra's drawing and used his tracing to transfer the outline to his own.[26] And yet Andrews idealized the face and made it more conventionally attractive, in particular adjusting the eyes to remove the sharp look to the side, and giving Austen slightly fuller lips, which he arranged into a smile. He then used watercolour to unite the whole, and it is this attractive, 'finished' composition which Austen-Leigh gave to the publisher, Richard Bentley.

Until photo-mechanical means of reproducing drawings and paintings were generally adopted, in order for any work of art to be printed it needed to go through the hands of a professional engraver who was obliged to transfer the image manually onto the printing plate or the woodblock. This translation from one medium to another unavoidably involved interpretation and modification – and in this case, the engraver pushed Andrews' image of Austen even further along the road towards an idealized image (fig. 8.10). This is partly down to the print technique itself: that the eyes are shaded more heavily than in Andrews' portrait is an inevitable result of the contours of the face being modelled with dots, and the monochrome nature of engraving tends to generate starker contrasts than the softer medium of watercolour. But the engraver has also introduced subtle changes of his own, most notably giving Austen's shoulders a more acute, 'milk-bottle' slope, a body shape that was considered to be attractive at the time. In comparison with the doll-like figure in the frontispiece to the *Memoir*, in Cassandra's original image Austen has a positively strapping physique.

Faint praise for the *Memoir*'s frontispiece came from Austen-Leigh's sister Caroline:

> The portrait is better than I expected – as considering its early date, and that it has lately passed through the hands of painter and engraver – I did not reckon upon finding *any* likeness – but there is a *look* which I recognize as *hers* – and though the general resemblance is *not* strong, yet as it represents a pleasant countenance it is *so* far a truth – & I am not dissatisfied with it.[27]

Caroline is, of course, being polite. Even so, her statement is significant in its suggestion that what Austen actually looked like had ceased to matter all that much – and that a pleasant countenance, animated by a certain 'look', conveyed enough of a 'truth' for the purpose.

Although we might regret that neither Cosway, Lawrence, Downman nor Edridge portrayed Austen, it is possible to find in Cassandra's modest likeness a quiet sincerity that, paradoxically, might have eluded a professional artist. Those who do respond to it

Figure 8.9 James Andrews (1807–1875) after Cassandra Austen (1773–1845), *Portrait of Jane Austen*, 1869. Watercolour. Private collection/Sotheby's.

in this way would be of a mind with Thomas Carlyle, who in 1854 remarked that even if no 'good *Portrait*' exists, then 'even an indifferent if sincere one' will serve as a 'small lighted *candle*' to illuminate a life story. 'In short', he continues, '*any* representation, made by a faithful human creature, of that Face and Figure, which *he* saw with his eyes, and which I can never see with mine, is now valuable to me, and much better than none at all.'[28] Those who do not respond in this way have the satisfaction of knowing that the image of Austen chosen for the new £10 note is based on the engraved frontispiece to the *Memoir*.

Figure 8.10 Unknown artist after James Andrews (1807–1875), *Portrait of Jane Austen for the frontispiece of the Memoir*, 1870. Stipple engraving with etching. Oxford, Bodleian Library, Rec. e.115.

1 See Katherine Duncan-Jones, *Portraits of Shakespeare*, Bodleian Library, Oxford, 2015, p. 75. Because this essay is concerned with portraits of the adult Austen, and moreover because the authenticity of the 'Rice' portrait has yet to be conclusively demonstrated, I do not discuss it in this essay.

2 Austen-Leigh, *Memoir*, ed. Sutherland, p. 70.

3 To Cassandra Austen, 15–16 September 1813, letter 87; Austen-Leigh, *Memoir*, ed. Sutherland, p. 70.

4 For more information on portrait drawings of this period, see Stephen Lloyd and Kim Sloan, *The Intimate Portrait: Drawings, Miniatures and Pastels from Ramsay to Lawrence*, National Galleries of Scotland, Edinburgh, 2008.

5 Samuel Taylor Coleridge, *The Friend*, ed. Barbara E. Rooke, 2 vols, Routledge & Kegan Paul, London, 1969, vol. 2, p. 138.

6 Evert A. Duyckinck, *Portrait Gallery of Eminent Men and Women of Europe and America: embracing history, statesmanship, naval and military life, philosophy, the drama, science, literature and art, with biographies*, 2 vols, Johnson & Gittens, New York, 1873, vol. 1, between pages 408 and 409. Curiously, this engraved portrait also furnishes Austen with a wedding ring. A related painting is in a private collection in America. The engraving was reproduced as a portrait of Austen as recently as 2016 in the *Times Literary Supplement* (Devoney Looser, 'It is a truth', *TLS*, 1 April 2016; see also the response by Deirdre Le Faye, *TLS*, 8 April 2016).

7 Or, perhaps, three – it has been suggested that Cassandra's thumbnail sketch of Mary Queen of Scots, illustrating Jane's 'The History of England', is a jokey likeness of Jane herself. See Annette Upfal and Christine Alexander, 'Are We Ready for New Directions? Jane Austen's "The History of England" and Cassandra's Portraits', in *Persuasions: the Jane Austen Journal On-Line*, vol. 30, no. 2, 2010, <http://www.jasna.org/persuasions/on-line/vol30no2/upfal-alexander.html>, accessed 12 January 2016.

8 Henry Austen, 'Biographical Notice of the Author' (1818), in Austen-Leigh, *Memoir*, ed. Sutherland, p. 139.

9 Thomas Smith, *The Young Artist's Assistant in the Art of Drawing in Water Colours*, Sherwood, Gilbert & Piper, London, 1824, p. v.

10 See Joan Klingel Ray and Richard James Wheeler, 'James Stanier Clarke's Portrait of Jane Austen', in *Persuasions: the Jane Austen Journal*, no. 27, 2005, pp. 112–18.

11 Carlo James et al., *Old Master Prints and Drawings: A Guide to Preservation and Conservation*, ed. and trans. Marjorie B. Cohn, Amsterdam University Press, Amsterdam, 1997, pp. 71–2.

12 Smith, *Young Artist's Assistant*, p. 24.

13 See <http://www.npg.org.uk/research/programmes/directory-of-suppliers/a.php>, accessed 12 January 2016.

14 Austen's niece Anna Lefroy considered it to be 'hideously unlike'. See Kathryn Sutherland's introduction in Austen-Leigh, *Memoir*, p. xlvi.

15 Quoted in R.W. Chapman, *Jane Austen: Facts and Problems*, Clarendon Press, Oxford, 1948, p. 213. I am most grateful to Belinda Austen for arranging for me to see the drawing.

16 Henry Austen, 'Biographical Notice of the Author' (1818), in Austen-Leigh, *Memoir*, ed. Sutherland, p. 140.

17 This suggestion is made by Paula Byrne in *The Real Jane Austen: A Life in Small Things*, Harper Press, London, 2013, p. 329.

18 I am grateful to Dr Sarah Grant, Curator of Prints at the Victoria and Albert Museum, for her thoughts on the close links between fashion plates, portraiture and caricature during this period. See also Catherine Flood and Sarah Grant, *Style and Satire: Fashion in Print* 1777–1927, Victoria and Albert Museum, London, 2014, pp. 14–17 and pp. 44–7.

19 *Hollar to Heideloff: An Exhibition of Fashion Prints drawn from the Collections of Members of the Costume Society and held at the Victoria and Albert Museum*, 5 December 1979 to 18 February 1980, The Costume Society, London, 1979, p. 35.

20 Paula Byrne reproduces this plate in *The Real Jane Austen*, p. 321.

21 Another silhouette, in the collection of Winchester Cathedral, was once believed to represent Austen, but on stylistic grounds it clearly dates from the late nineteenth century. See also Margaret Kirkham, 'Portraits', in Janet Todd (ed.), *Jane Austen in Context*, Cambridge University Press, Cambridge, 2005, pp. 68–79 (p. 75).

22 Ibid.

23 See Emma Rutherford, *Silhouette: the Art of the Shadow*, Rizzoli, New York, 2009, pp. 120–3.

24 The identity of the sitter in this portrait is discussed in Paula Byrne, 'Who was Miss Jane Austin? A possible alternative to Aunt Jane: the professional writer at work', *Times Literary Supplement*, 13 April 2012; in subsequent letters to the *TLS* published 20 and 27 April; in a lengthy response by Deidre Le Faye, 'Three Telltale Words', *Times Literary Supplement*, 4 May 2012; and in Byrne, *The Real Jane Austen*, pp. 306–8. The arguments put forward in a related BBC documentary, *Jane Austen: the Unseen Portrait?*, shown December 2011, are summarized by Deborah Kaplan in '"There she is at last": the Byrne Portrait Controversy', *Persuasions: the Jane Austen Journal*, no. 34, 2012, pp. 121–33. See also Deidre Le Faye, 'Imaginary Portraits of Jane Austen', *Jane Austen Society Report*, 2007, pp. 42–52 (p. 43). I am grateful to Paula Byrne for allowing me to examine the drawing and to Diane Bilbey, Acting Curator of Jane Austen's House Museum, for kindly facilitating it. I have not, however, seen the drawing out of its frame. I am also grateful to Stephen Calloway for his thoughts on the drawing.

25 See Byrne, 'Who was Miss Jane Austin?', for an account of period-specific details of dress and architecture.

26 Sotheby's, catalogue entry for the Andrews portrait, in *English Literature & History*, 10 December 2013, lot 283.

27 Letter from Caroline Austen to James Edward Austen-Leigh, undated, but written in response to the publication of the *Memoir* on 16 December 1869, in Austen-Leigh, *Memoir*, ed. Sutherland, p. 192.

28 Thomas Carlyle to David Laing, 3 May 1854, *The Carlyle Letters Online*, <http://carlyleletters.dukeupress.edu/content/vol29/#lt-18540503-TC-DL-01> accessed 2 February 2016.

9

Jane Austen at 200

Deidre Lynch

Like many traditions, the one that aligns our remembrance of renowned heroes and artists with the calendar turns out to be a modern invention. It was only during the last two centuries, as part of a still incomplete emancipation of time from the church's liturgical calendar, that the rites of commemoration accorded to venerated figures from the past came to be linked to the anniversaries of their dates of birth and death, and linked in particular to special anniversaries like the twenty-fifth or fiftieth or the centennial or bicentennial. When on 18 July 2017 we mark the 200th anniversary of Austen's early death, or when on 16 December we put our Christmas preparations on hold in order to attend a Jane Austen birthday tea or do some Jane Austen country dancing (activities apparently of particular charm for devotees located in North America and Australia), we will in various ways be attesting to the timelessness of the novels – affirming the permanence of their artistic value. In equal measure, however, we will also be participating in practices that date to Austen's lifetime specifically: practices that register the needs of a moment of political upheaval and mass migration in which history's *dis*continuities were far more conspicuous than its continuities. In 1821, the essayist Charles Lamb lamented that, in a world in which time was money, the 'red-letter days' of the old liturgical calendar had all been converted into 'dead letter days'; the nineteenth-century people who found out new occasions for festivity and new ways to deliver a shared time and shared culture, aimed to redirect if not reverse that transformation. Paradoxical by-products of the modernization process, the protocols for commemoration inaugurated by Austen's contemporaries and their Victorian successors register a widely felt desire to undo the disenchantment of the world.[1]

   As others have noted, Austen's superstar reputation is of fairly recent standing. Austen today is beyond doubt a primary object of that particular form of modern memory cult that was first manifested two centuries ago in her compatriots' founding of Burns Night and Shakespeare Birthday celebrations, their editing and re-editing of authors' works, their adaptations of those works into new media, and their erection of many, many statues. Even in time of economic recession, 'Jane-anything sells' *Newsweek* declared a few years ago, and at present the brand, by no means limited to books, has global reach.2 But Austen's attainment of such extravagant marketability and such fame was surprisingly delayed. Initially, it appeared that her reputation would be short-lived. The tardiness with which she and her fictions came at last, in the later nineteenth century, to be conscripted for modernity's new rites of collective remembrance is notable. It represents one reason why Austen's afterlife has provided an intriguing case study for historians of literary reception and celebrity culture. The other reason is, of course, her gender. It makes the novelist the anomaly in the literary history of her period – the sole survivor of what the critic Clifford Siskin calls the Great Forgetting, the episode, hinging on the masculinization of the very definition of literature, that effectively consigned to oblivion all other British women writers from the period 1700–1830.3

Austen at 200 is not only a quite different creature from Austen at 150 or Austen at 100 (this because each generation of admirers has remade her according to historically contingent needs); contemporaries themselves have differed with each other, sometimes quite vehemently, about what they want Austen to be and mean. Even while helping us to locate ourselves on the same place in a shared calendar, Austen can sometimes divide as much as unite us. In the history of her reception, as we shall see, feathers often get ruffled.

Jubilees

As we count off the twenty-first-century Austen anniversaries (whether in celebration of the staying power of *Sense and Sensibility,* which turned 200 in 2011, or the staying power of Colin Firth's Mr Darcy, a performance that marked its twentieth anniversary in 2015), contemporary devotees add a chapter to a history of memory whose beginnings Austen noticed herself. Even on her sick bed in 1817, she would have had trouble missing, for instance, the pomp accompanying the dedication, on the second anniversary of the Battle of Waterloo, of London's Waterloo Bridge. In *Sanditon,* the novel left incomplete at her death, she derives some exquisite comedy from her real estate developer character Mr Parker's regret over his decision to name the new house he has built in the novel's eponymous seaside resort 'Trafalgar House': 'Waterloo', Mr Parker says wistfully, 'is more the thing now' (ch. 4). As that slangy phrase, *the thing,* suggests, Austen was capable of regarding with a rather satirical eye contemporary efforts to perpetuate the memory of the nation's military glories – even though in *Persuasion* (completed in 1816) she had tried her hand at such commemoration herself and identified her fictional Captain Wentworth as winning his stripes as naval hero at the real Battle of San Domingo (a great British victory of 1806) (ch. 4).

Historians of collective memory agree, however, in identifying the Shakespeare Jubilee that the actor-manager David Garrick organized at Stratford-upon-Avon in 1769 as a significant turning point: an indication of how, during the nineteenth century, authors, composers and visual artists would displace warriors, monarchs and saints as *the* candidates for public memorialization.[4] Garrick missed the bicentennial of Shakespeare's birth in 1564 by five years. That bad timing aside, though, the arrangements he made to choreograph his compatriots' bardolatry effectively established a script that those seeking to perpetuate other authors' presence in the world could mobilize in their turn. Garrick's very choice of the word *jubilee* to name his project was suggestive, for instance. *Jubilee* not only linked his rites celebrating the dead author to the calendar and paved the way for their periodic repetition, but it also suggested how practices of aesthetic veneration might take their shape from religion: the medieval church had used the term *jubilee*, which originates in the Book of Leviticus, to designate years of plenary indulgence or periods of remission from punishment for sin.[5] Styling himself 'Great Shakespeare's Priest', and deliberately blurring in this ministry the lines between artistic renown and sainthood, Garrick also explicitly identified the country town of Stratford as a *pilgrimage site* for the Bard's devotees (fig. 9.1). In this manner, he predicted the kinds of literary tourism to authors' homes and haunts that would supplement or even replace literary reading for generations of bardolaters to come, as it would eventually do for Austen's devotees as well.

During Austen's lifetime other projects of commemoration were launched, including some that remedied Garrick's failure to exploit the allure of round numbers and properly mark the interval of the century. For example, in 1785, the centenary of George Frideric Handel's birth was heralded with three nights of performances that took place in Westminster Abbey and involved the largest orchestra and choir ever convened. By contrast, Burns night suppers, still held worldwide on the Scottish poet's birthday every 25 January, began in Greenock in Scotland in 1802, only six years after his death; Burns was also the first British poet to get a statue. On the 300th anniversary of Shakespeare's birth, 23 April 1816, as Austen was writing *Persuasion*, the Theatre-Royal at Covent Garden, London, staged the pageant that was to have been the centrepiece of Garrick's 1769 Jubilee, though called off on that occasion because of rain. This time round, in the pageant's spectacular, all-singing, all-dancing conclusion, after forty actors dressed in Shakespeare costumes paraded across the stage, a statue of Shakespeare himself appeared amongst them, pulled into position in a car drawn by seven Muses. Its coronation by personifications of Fate and Time brought down the curtain.[6]

As a practitioner of the lowly genre of the novel, who never in her lifetime saw her name printed on a title page, Austen was awkwardly situated in relation to this commemoration industry in its initial phase. A writer so circumstanced was not ordinarily someone who could anticipate crowning by Fate and Time. With fewer than half the new novels published between 1800 and 1829 carrying the names of their authors, writers of prose fiction were in general unlikely to achieve immortality through their works. (At this point, many still deemed novels sub-literary, light entertainment to be enjoyed once and then disposed of.)[7] The fiction of Walter Scott was, in those decades, the exception when it came to negotiating the transition from bestseller to classic status – though it lost prestige at a devastatingly rapid rate at the start of the twentieth century, just the time when Austen was being reinvented as *the* classic English novelist. As a specialist in historical fiction – a genre Austen eschewed – Scott was already involved in reconnecting contemporary readerships to the past: that fact helped make his books a natural reference point for promoters of the new memory culture, and, by means of re-editions, adaptations and monuments (a very big one in Edinburgh especially), commemorators maximized his oeuvre's public presence through the nineteenth century.[8]

Austen's case was different for most of the nineteenth century, and complicated not just by her choice of genre but also by her gender. As we shall see, one complexity in her posthumous fortunes was that the relatives who became the guardians of her reputation seemed to suspect that to appear in a coronation scene like the one Garrick had scripted for Shakespeare might be a rather unladylike thing for their maiden aunt to do.

Figure 9.1 *Mr. Garrick reciting the ode, in honour of Shakespeare, at the Jubilee at Stratford*, 1769. Royal Collection Trust/© Her Majesty Queen Elizabeth II 2016.

Beatification

One indication that Austen's current renown was not always on the cards, that she might well have ended up (like Scott now) a niche writer read mainly in university classrooms, is that two years after the posthumous publication of *Northanger Abbey* and *Persuasion*, her fiction began to go out of print. In 1820 her publishers John Murray and Thomas Egerton starting remaindering their unsold copies of Austen's works. It took the novels' inclusion in the 1830s in the 'Standard Novel' series of publisher Richard Bentley – and after that a number of re-editions in the mid-nineteenth century, in America as well as Britain – for Austen's reputation to begin that climb up the charts that nowadays looks unstoppable (fig. 9.2).

The efforts Austen's siblings and, more so, their children and those children's children made to keep her books in the public eye were foundational for this increase in her popularity: in her recent assessment of Romantic-period literary reputations, H.J. Jackson proposes that one of the lucky breaks that could help ensure lasting fame for authors of this period occurred if those authors turned out to have champions, stakeholders with an interest in the survival of their literary estates, who would look out for them.[9] Even so, it is curious to watch the Austen stakeholders tie themselves in knots as they both work to secure public acclamation of the novelist and insist even while doing so that she was too modest and femininely delicate ever to have wanted applause. Starting with Austen's brother Henry, who in 1818 published the brief Biographical Notice that belatedly affixed a name to her works, the relatives who reintroduce Austen to her readership project an image of the author as a homebody more committed to her needle than her pen, a diffident amateur and, above all, a moral paragon. 'It was with extreme difficulty that her friends … could prevail on her to publish her first work'; and 'in public she turned away from any allusion to the character of an authoress', wrote Henry, seemingly unaware of the dissonance he produced as he combined statements like those with the laudatory declaration that his sister 'never dispatched a note or letter unworthy of publication'.[10]

Scholars frequently propose the year 1870, when the Austen nephew James Edward Austen-Leigh published a full-length, ultimately much-reviewed biography of his aunt, as a turning point in the novelist's afterlife. The great Austen critic Brian Southam, for instance, influentially divided the history of the novelist's critical reception into two parts, before and after 1870. True, for all its prosiness and saccharine piety about Aunt Jane, the biography did succeed in making the author who was its subject available for the love that readers already bestowed on her novels. With the assistance of the particulars about the life that the *Memoir* provided, the reading public at last felt compelled to draw a connection between the woman and her works. Still, the members of the Austen clan who explained the 'great advance in her fame' by reference to the *Memoir* might have been indulging, venially, some family pride; with this claim, they touted how well the clan had guarded the novelist's memory.[11] When we take our cue

Figure 9.2 Frontispiece illustration from Bentley's 'Standard Novels' edition of *Emma*, 1833. Oxford, Bodleian Library, 256 f.3148.

from them and emphasize the difference the *Memoir* made to Austen's afterlife, we should also recall that Richard Bentley would not have risked publication had he not anticipated the *Memoir*'s having a ready-made audience.

What *is* new in 1870 is that Austen-Leigh is often palpably ambivalent about reaching out to this audience – more precisely, about broadening it. Austen-Leigh is at once a popularizer and, registering a new trend in the history of Austen's reception, a snob. As though hoping to spare his aunt from being saddled by popularity of the *wrong* sort, he seems in the *Memoir* to have already decided that he will never succeed in changing the mind of 'the multitude' to whom the novelist's 'works appear … tame and commonplace' – a verdict that he goes on to contrast with that of 'superior judges', the discriminating few.[12] This move likely represents a defensive reaction to the emergence during the Victorian period of a mass reading audience. Powered by educational reforms that also date to 1870, new sorts of people were in Austen-Leigh's day beginning to demand their say in the literary field, and his generation witnesses a boom in affordable books and magazines produced to satisfy the growing demand. In the new context created by this development, worries about whether the wrong sort of people, with the wrong motives, were signing on as Austen's audience would become increasingly frequent.

In other respects, though, the *Memoir* reads quite similarly to Henry Austen's Biographical Notice, which after 1870 it replaced within Bentley's editions. Austen-Leigh continues and indeed heightens his Uncle Henry's hagiographic tone. The *Memoir* is delicately balanced between canonizing Austen as an author and – reflecting the Victorians' cult of domestic womanhood – canonizing her as a saint. Henry Austen (then recently ordained) had concluded the Biographical Notice in 1818 by reassuring readers of *Northanger Abbey* and *Persuasion* that his late sister's 'opinions accorded strictly with those of our Established Church'. James Edward Austen-Leigh (another clergyman) strikes a comparable note. The *Memoir* opens, for instance, inside a church – Winchester Cathedral, the setting for his aunt's funeral. In its conclusion, it rounds back to her Christian deathbed. 'Her life had been passed in the performance of home duties and the cultivation of domestic affections, without any self-seeking or craving after applause', Austen-Leigh writes as he puts the finishing touches on his hagiography.[13]

Austen was left undepicted – as were almost all other female luminaries – when the British Empire went statue-mad during the Victorian period. But in keeping with this emerging tradition of Saint Jane, the novelist was in 1900 commemorated with the stained glass window that still looms above her grave in Winchester Cathedral, a memorial paid for by a public subscription and designed by the prominent designer C.E. Kempe, whose object it was 'to illustrate the high moral and religious teachings' of her works (fig. 9.3). Kempe's design aligns Austen with both Saint John, picturing the latter with the Gospels opened to the line 'In the beginning was the word', and Saint

Figure 9.3 The stained glass window dedicated to Jane Austen in Winchester Cathedral. Courtesy of Dr John Crook.

Augustine (whose name in abbreviated form is, as the window's official description informs us, 'St. Austin').[14] The 23 April birthday ascribed to Shakespeare, though only speculatively, aligns him with Saint George, commemorated on that date. The Bard aside, though, few authors have been sanctified in quite this manner.

The sanctification of Austen met with opposition, certainly. In 1861 an anonymous essayist in the *Englishwoman's Domestic Magazine* complained of the primness of the Biographical Notice's portrait of Austen and remarked that 'we can think of her as nothing less than an angel writing novels with a quill plucked from one of her own wings'.[15] But as Austen and her works came to the forefront of public awareness in the closing decades of the nineteenth century and opening decades of the twentieth, several members of that public mobilized the language of the sacred to describe their relationship to her. They defined themselves as her worshippers, and the novels as her miracles.

For 'her adorers', wrote the American novelist W.D. Howells in 1901, 'she is a passion and a creed, if not quite a religion'.[16] In 1902 the second Earl of Iddlesleigh published an article titled 'The Legend of St. Jane' which identified Austen as 'the most fascinating of saints' and then, drawing up an itinerary for literary pilgrims, focused on the 'sacred spots', 'where our divinity visited Earth'.[17] In the early years of the Jane Austen Society (founded 1940) a regular column on 'Relics' appeared in its bulletins: the Society turned readily to an idiom originally associated with the cult of the saints to report on the whereabouts of precious bits and pieces associated with the Austens' domestic lives and – in the case of the lock of hair that appeared on the cover of the 1953 report – bits and pieces of the writer herself (fig. 9.4). This idiom of the sacred, used partly facetiously, has persisted into this century – so much is suggested, at least, by Karen Joy Fowler's 2004 novel *The Jane Austen Book Club*, where the twenty-first-century Californian characters set about putting their lives in the hands of their divinity. They equip themselves with a kind of divination toy, a Magic 8 Ball filled with quotations from Austen's books, and then consult their oracle, trusting that her position in the afterlife has made her omniscient and omnipotent regarding matters of the heart. 'We'd let Austen into our lives and now we were all married and dating', reports the narrator in the jubilant tone of the true believer.[18]

Heritage and home

In the Bentley reissue of Austen's works in 1833, a preface identified Austen as literature's pre-eminent novelist of home. (Those of us who recall that Longbourn and Hartfield and Mansfield Park are uniformly places that young women might wish to escape might find this description counter-intuitive.) During the late Victorian era

Figure 9.4 A lock of Jane Austen's hair. © Jane Austen's House Museum.

and, especially, during the war years of the early twentieth century, the home evoked in those books was bit by bit reinvented as an object of nostalgia, a place of refuge and calm that a modern generation had lost. Once again, in the *Memoir* Austen-Leigh had led the way by insisting on the historical remoteness of the world his aunt inhabited and the gulf between her time and his audience's. 'There is no doubt that if we could look into the households of the clergy and the small gentry of that period, we should see some things which would seem strange to us, and should miss many more to which we are accustomed', he writes; he goes on to enumerate the quaint customs of Austen's generation, the way Regency people conducted themselves at table, for instance, and the contrast between their scantily furnished rooms and the cluttered Victorian parlour.[19] In this framework Austen may retroactively be discovered as a historical novelist in her own right, though of a different breed from Scott's. She is depicted, that is, as bearing witness to a bygone time of graceful living and good manners, this even while – as in the common refrain to which many commentators of the period resort – she seals herself off from history's unpleasantnesses (like war or class conflict).

When her works are read in this nostalgic way, commemoration of Austen can be difficult to disentangle from the forms of English nationalism and heritage politics that emerged in the closing decades of the nineteenth century. In this framework Austen and/or her heroines become poster girls for a mythic England. The books are understood to return their readers to a past when this nation was also more truly English, less riven by social tension, more centred on country life and, not incidentally, more white.

One manifestation of this nationalization was a new emphasis on Austen as a novelist of place: the chronicler of the English country house. As Alexandra Harris observes, cultural commentary from the early twentieth century was intent to an unprecedented degree on rooting literature in particular topographies, and intent, by extension, on conceiving of reading as a 'process of literary pilgrimage'.[20] The reading of Austen was certainly reconceived along those lines. Thus the 1902 book by Constance Hill, *Jane Austen: Her Homes and Her Friends*, which combines biography with a description of the journey the author and her sister take through Hampshire lanes en route to 'Austen-Land' (fig. 9.5). Following Austen to all the places where she dwelt, the book, copiously illustrated, is organized by place: the author's birthplace, Steventon Parsonage (though by 1901 only the house's pump remained), Bath, Lyme Regis, Stoneleigh Abbey and Godmersham Park, and then Chawton at last.

A saint requires a shrine, but the programme of Austen tourism that the Hill sisters tout was not easy to launch. It was not exactly clear what sightseers might have to see until, in 1947, T. Edward Carpenter, an enthusiastic member of the newly founded Jane Austen Society, purchased and restored Chawton Cottage. By the mid-twentieth century, however, the memory culture centred on Austen had at last caught up with that centred on Scott and Shakespeare and Burns. Indeed, the twenty-first-century

Austen tourist's trail is more extensive still: now it includes the mansions that have served in the film adaptations as stand-ins for the novels' great houses – and which, in the case of Lyme Park/Pemberley especially, have in some sense had the starring roles (fig. 9.6).

The conservatism so often audible in the commentaries presenting Austen as the English nation's number one cultural asset provoked dissent across the Atlantic. In the same 1901 book in which he announced his adherence to the Austenite creed, W.D. Howells also declared that Austen in her way had 'asserted the Rights of Man as unmistakably as the French revolutionists whose volcanic activity was of about the same compass of time as her literary industry' – a statement claiming the books for a New World rather than an Old.[21] Reading this statement now, one senses that battle lines are being drawn. In the decades around 1901 several English commentators begin to include foreigners of all stripes in that 'multitude' who, as Austen-Leigh had put it, failed to get the novels.[22] Even if her growing popularity meant that the novelist was becoming 'everybody's dear Jane' (in Henry James's phrase), nonetheless there were still (are still) plenty of people claiming that only the native-born English could appreciate properly her quiet charm, or subtle wit, or analyses of class politics … or … or … or.[23]

But Austen's reception history also suggests that she and her works have never quite functioned, even within England, as a straightforward emblem of national unity. Even as the number of her admirers increased, that Victorian account of the fiction as a kind of art novel appealing only to a coterie of connoisseurs was carried forward into the twentieth century. (This despite the astounding sales, for instance, of the edition of *Pride and Prejudice* with illustrations by Hugh Thomson that was produced in 1894 – 11,600 copies that year alone, a figure exceeding the total number of all the novels the author sold while alive.) Beyond doubt a national treasure, populist in her reach, Austen in the second century of her afterlife is also persistently associated with collectives existing on a smaller scale than the nation state – associated with the club, for instance, or secret society. Many admirers have insisted, that is, that there is something private and personal in their admiration: a response that registers, perhaps, the effects of insidership and secret sharing engendered by her narratives' irony. These admirers have imagined their Austen love as taking them out of the wider world and into a smaller, more select and closer-knit circle (a 'loyal tribe' or 'true lovers' knot' – to cite some characteristic terms from these testimonies). In 1913 Virginia Woolf wrote, for instance, of how formerly a taste for Austen had been 'a gift that ran in families … and a mark of a rather peculiar culture'.[24] There is a touch of nostalgia in this observation, for an era when the novels didn't have to be shared with quite so many; one hears, too, a possessive note.

Figure 9.5 Finger-post pointing to 'Austen-Land' in Constance Hill, *Jane Austen: Her Homes and Her Friends* (John Lane, London and New York, 1902). Oxford, Bodleian Library, 2569 e.141, tail-piece to ch. 1.

Figure 9.6 Lyme Park, a.k.a. Pemberley in the 1995 BBC adaptation of *Pride and Prejudice*. Wikimedia Commons.

Minefields

In 1924, in a short story about Austen admiration in the trenches of the Great War, Rudyard Kipling masterfully negotiated exactly these tensions in the readerships' self-descriptions. The poem with which 'The Janeites' begins when Kipling publishes the story in book form refers to 'England's Jane', yet here the common bond that Austen and her works sponsor is also that uniting the tiny secret society (four members all told) that gives the story its name. Amidst the chaos of the Western Front, the Janeites, a small subset of an English artillery battery, find ways to keep conversing about the writings of that 'Secret Society Woman' whom they idolize.[25] With Austen's help, they assert cultural continuity at a moment of maximal disruption (fig. 9.7).

Is an Austen novel a refuge from war? Kipling's story may easily be read as saying just that. In the final plot turn, its narrator's acquaintance with the characters of *Emma* proves to be the pass that gets him into a hospital train and away from hostilities, so that he can survive to tell the tale. In the war year of 1917, just as the centennial of Austen's death was being commemorated, many English readers testified to how (in part thanks to the novelist's own remove from the conflicts of her time) her books provided a respite from their distresses: the Oxford don H.F. Brett-Smith, who chose reading matter for the military hospitals, prescribed Austen's fiction to the severely shell-shocked. (The fiction was mobilized for therapeutic uses in the next war as well: the story is often told, for instance, of Winston Churchill's rereading of *Pride and Prejudice* in a dark hour of 1943.)[26] But the reverse might equally be true: far from being escapist reading, the Austen novel might itself represent a combat zone. Kipling's narrator, after all, nicknames the artillery battery's guns after her fiction's nastier characters: Mr Collins, Lady Catherine de Bourgh and General Tilney.

'Reading Austen is a freaking minefield', complains a character in the 2007 film adaptation of Fowler's *Jane Austen Book Club* – a line encapsulating the arguments that she and her fellow club members have over Austen's meanings, and one which a decade on still gets retweeted and cited on blogs and Pinterest sites. The line resonates, one assumes, in part because Howells' 'quiet little woman' has been the occasion for some of the noisiest disputes in the culture wars that have polarized academics and journalists in the United States for the last three decades. In the meantime, the so-called special relationship between the United States and the United Kingdom that Churchill celebrated back in 1946 has on occasion looked jeopardized by our transatlantic quarrels over who has title to and authority over this woman and her works.

The issues in dispute are legion. In that respect alone, they indicate something that is worth making explicit: that many of the truths universally acknowledged about what Austen stands for tend to look rather more like patchy guesswork as soon as one scrutinizes, as here, the vagaries of the reception history during the last two centuries. To conclude, let us consider a couple more flashpoints.

Figure 9.7 Illustration for Kipling's story 'The Janeites', on the cover of *The Storyteller*, May 1924. Oxford, Bodleian Library, Per 2561 d.46.

One debate currently ruffling feathers unfolds between those who understand Austen's novels as love stories written by a real romantic in several senses of the term, and those who praise (or condemn) the books instead as the ironic anti-romances of a spinster who chose not to define herself as marriage material. Twenty-first-century readers approaching Austen's fiction may be forgiven for imagining the novelist as the mother of contemporary 'chick lit' – with Helen Fielding's *Bridget Jones's Diary* (1996) as her eldest child. (One of Kipling's Janeite artillery-men invoked a contrasting literary genealogy and famously declared Austen the mother of Henry James.) The film industry that packages the adaptations as romantic comedies, 'date films', primes these readers to suppose that Austen's marriage plotting is the essence of her books – that, or this love goddess's creation of hunky heroes (figs 9.8 & 9.9). It is salutary to recall, however, that such a supposition inverts the axioms about Austen that circulated through the first part of the twentieth century. In sociological works like Q.D. Leavis's *Fiction and the Reading Public* (1939) and books of literary criticism like Mary Lascelles' *Jane Austen and Her Art* (1939), Austen was heralded for her refusal of the romantic sentimentality that infused mass culture, for having the backbone and common sense that the (sappy, girly) practitioners of popular fiction lacked.

This is certainly not to say that to read the books properly we must isolate them from contemporary mass culture and treat them as period pieces, time capsules from the Regency. Far less is it to say that Austen herself requires protecting from the current preoccupations of an over-sexed generation of teenagers – or of queer theorists in departments in English. Indeed, it might be worth trying, as Austen enters her third century, to emulate the many readers who have treated the works as *new* writing rather than an object of a memory cult, and, being new, as relevant to and competitive with the fiction being published at their contemporary moment. George Saintsbury, for instance, at the close of the nineteenth century stated that Austen '"set the clock", so to speak, of pure novel writing, which was to be nineteenth century time to the present hour'. The prose is complex, but this appears to claim Austen for the future as well as the past of the novel.[27] Long before the updatings that have accompanied the novels' translation into other media and that have delivered Emmas in southern California and Elizabeth Bennets in Amritsar, other commentators followed Saintsbury and noted the contemporary feel to the fiction.

In their accounts, Austen, thanks to this quality, is not simply ahead of *her* time but, more precisely, more modern than her *posterity*. 'You could not shock her more than she shocks me', wrote W.H. Auden in 1936 in a poem that continues, 'Beside her Joyce seems as innocent as grass': as Auden reads her, Austen is not a figurehead for a threatened tradition, but more modern than the modernist Joyce.[28] Keeping in mind this reading of the works seems a good method to ensure that in 2117 admirers yet unborn will be celebrating Jane Austen at 300 – and arguing over her.

1   Charles Lamb, 'Oxford in the Vacation', in *The Essays of Elia*, J. M. Dent, London, 1906, p. 9.

2   Quoted in Janet Todd, *Jane Austen: An Introduction*, 2nd edition, Cambridge University Press, Cambridge, 2015, p. 142.

3   Clifford Siskin, *The Work of Writing: Literature and Social Change in Britain*, 1700–1830, Johns Hopkins University Press, Baltimore, MD, 1998, pp. 193–209.

4   'Where military heroes were remembered for specific deeds and events located in the past, artists and writers were remembered for works that were still "alive" in the present, that is, still capable of generating affect, provoking pleasure, and inviting re-enactment', Ann Rigney, 'Burns, 1859', in Joep Leerssen and Ann Rigney (eds), *Commemorating Writers in Nineteenth-Century Europe*, Palgrave, Basingstoke, 2015, p. 50.

5   Coppélia Kahn and Clara Calvo, 'Introduction: Shakespeare and commemoration', in Coppélia Kahn and Clara Calvo (eds), *Celebrating Shakespeare: Commemoration and Cultural Memory*, Cambridge University Press, Cambridge, 2015, pp. 6–7.

6   Vanessa Cunningham, *Shakespeare and Garrick*, Cambridge University Press, Cambridge, 2008, pp. 115–17.

7   See H.J. Jackson, *Those Who Write for Immortality*, Yale University Press, New Haven, CT, 2015, pp. 63–106.

8   Leerssen and Rigney notice 'a certain preference in the "cult of centenaries"' for writers – Shakespeare, Scott, Schiller – who themselves were already involved in 'the business of narrating history'; see their Introduction to *Commemorating Writers in Nineteenth-Century Europe*, p. 12.

9   Jackson, *Those Who Write for Immortality*, p. 91.

10 'Biographical Notice' to *Northanger Abbey* and *Persuasion*, reprinted in Austen-Leigh, *Memoir*, ed. Sutherland, pp. 140 and 141.

11 Quoting William Austen-Leigh and Richard Arthur Austen-Leigh's claim in *Jane Austen, Her Life and Letters: A Family Record*, Smith, Elder, & Co., London, 1913, p. 404.

12 Austen-Leigh, *Memoir*, ed. Sutherland, p. 104.

13 Ibid., p. 130.

14 See Claudia L. Johnson, *Jane Austen's Cults and Cultures*, University of Chicago Press, Chicago, IL, 2012, pp. 38–43.

Figure 9.8 Kate Beaton, 'Jane Austen Comics'. © Kate Beaton.

AUSTEN MANIA

IT'S A LARGE BOOK

EMILY HAS SOME ADVICE

WHERE THIS IS GOING

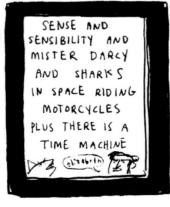

Figure 9.9 Kate Beaton, from *Hark! A Vagrant*, considering the topic of Jane Austen fandom. Drawn and Quarterly Comics, Montreal, 2011, p. 87. © Kate Beaton.

15 Cited in Kathryn Sutherland, *Jane Austen's Textual Lives: From Aeschylus to Bollywood*, Oxford University Press, Oxford, 2005, p. 72.

16 W.D. Howells, *Heroines of Fiction*, Harper and Brothers, New York, 1901, vol. 1, p. 41.

17 B.C. Southam, 'Introduction', in *Jane Austen: The Critical Heritage*, vol. 2, Routledge & Kegan Paul, London, 1987, p. 57.

18 See Sarah Raff, *Jane Austen's Erotic Advice*, Oxford University Press, New York, 2014, p. 31 and Deidre Lynch, 'The Cult of Jane Austen', in Janet Todd (ed.), *Jane Austen in Context*, Cambridge University Press, Cambridge, 2005, pp. 111–20.

19 Austen-Leigh, *Memoir*, ed. Sutherland, p. 36.

20 Alexandra Harris, *Romantic Moderns: English Writers, Artists and the Imagination from Virginia Woolf to John Piper*, Thames and Hudson, London, 2010, pp. 160–1.

21 Howells, *Heroines of Fiction*, p. 49.

22 For instance, a clueless Frenchman, unable to keep up when the conversation turns to Austen, figures in the preface to Anne Thackeray Ritchie's *A Book of Sibyls*, Smith and Elder, London, 1883, p. iv.

23 Henry James, *The Question of our Speech; The Lesson of Balzac: Two Lectures*, Houghton Mifflin, Boston, 1905, p. 62.

24 Woolf is cited in Brian Southam, 'Introduction', in *Jane Austen: The Critical Heritage*, vol. 2, p. 46; Sheila Kaye-Smith and G.B. Stern write of their readers as 'a true lovers' knot around us' in *Talking of Jane Austen*, Cassell, London, 1953, p. 189.

25 Rudyard Kipling, 'The Janeites', in *The Writings in Prose and Verse*, Scribner's, New York, 1926, vol. 31, p. 165.

26 On the shell-shocked, see Sutherland, *Jane Austen's Textual Lives*, p. 53; on Churchill, see Johnson, *Jane Austen's Cults and Cultures*, pp. 151–2.

27 George Saintsbury, *A History of Nineteenth-Century Literature*, Macmillan, London, 1895, p. 130.

28 W.H. Auden, 'Letter to Lord Byron', in Edward Mendelson (ed.), *Collected Poems*, Vintage, New York, 1991, p. 84.

Suggested Further Reading

1 Teenage Writings: Amusement, Effusion, Nonsense

Alexander, C., and J. McMaster (eds), *The Child Writer from Austen to Woolf*, Cambridge University Press, Cambridge, 2005.

Doody, M.A., *Jane Austen's Names: Riddles, Persons, Places*, University of Chicago Press, Chicago, IL, 2015.

Grey, J.D. (ed.), *Jane Austen's Beginnings: The Juvenilia and Lady Susan*, UMI Research Press, Ann Arbor, MI, 1989.

2 Making Music

Duquette, N., and E. Lenckos (eds), *Jane Austen and the Arts: Elegance, Propriety, Harmony*, Lehigh University Press, Bethlehem, PA, 2013.

Gammie, I., and D. McCulloch, *Jane Austen's Music*, Corda Music Publications, St Albans, 1996.

Selwyn, D., *Jane Austen and Leisure*, Hambledon, London, 1999.

3 Jane Austen's Pelisse-Coat

Arnold, J., *Patterns of Fashion 1: Englishwomen's Dresses and Their Construction c.1660–1860*, Macmillan, London, 1972.

Byrde, P., *Jane Austen Fashion: Fashion and Needlework in the Works of Jane Austen*, Moonrise Press, Ludlow, 2008.

———, *Nineteenth Century Fashion*, Batsford, London, 1992.

Downing, S.J., *Fashion in the Time of Jane Austen*, Shire Publications, Oxford, 2010.

4 The Art of the Letter

Favret, M.A., *Romantic Correspondence: Women, Politics, and the Fiction of Letters*, Cambridge University Press, Cambridge, 1993.

Galperin, William H., *The History of Missed Opportunities: British Romanticism and the Emergence of the Everyday*, Stanford University Press, Stanford, CA, 2017.

Le Faye, Deirdre (ed.), *Jane Austen's Letters*, 4th edition, Oxford University Press, Oxford, 2011.

Modert, Jo (ed.), *Jane Austen's Manuscript Letters in Facsimile*, Southern Illinois University Press, Carbondale, IL, 1990.

O'Neill, L., *The Opened Letter: Networking in the Early Modern British World*, University of Pennsylvania Press, Philadelphia, PA, 2015.

5 Women Writing in Time of War

Butler, M., *Jane Austen and the War of Ideas*, 1975; reissued with a new introduction, Clarendon Press, Oxford, 1987.

Favret, M.A., *War at a Distance: Romanticism and the Making of Modern Wartime*, Princeton University Press, Princeton, NJ and Oxford, 2010.

Russell, G., *The Theatres of War: Performance, Politics, and Society*, 1793–1815, Clarendon Press, Oxford, 1995.

Uglow, J., *In These Times: Living in Britain Through Napoleon's Wars 1793–1815*, Faber & Faber, London, 2014.

6 Making Books: How Jane Austen Wrote

Fergus, J., 'The Professional Woman Writer', in Edward Copeland and Juliet McMaster (eds), *The Cambridge Companion to Jane Austen*, 2nd edition, Cambridge University Press, Cambridge, 2011, pp. 1–20.

Southam, B.C., *Jane Austen's Literary Manuscripts: A Study of the Novelist's Development through the Surviving Papers*, 1964; revised edition, Athlone Press, London, 2001.

Sutherland, K., 'Manuscripts and the Acts of Writing', in *Jane Austen's Textual Lives: from Aeschylus to Bollywood*, Oxford University Press, Oxford, 2005, pp. 118–97.

———, 'Jane Austen's Dealings with John Murray and his Firm', *Review of English Studies*, n. s. vol. 64, 2012, pp. 105–26.

7 The Novel in 1817

Garside, P., and K. O'Brien (eds), *The Oxford History of the Novel in English*, vol. 2: *English and British Fiction*, Oxford University Press, Oxford, 2015.

Kelly, G., *English Fiction of the Romantic Period 1789–1830*, Routledge, London, 1989.

Maxwell, R., and K. Trumpener, *The Cambridge Companion to Fiction in the Romantic Period*, Cambridge University Press, Cambridge, 2009.

St Clair, W., *The Reading Nation in the Romantic Period*, Cambridge University Press, Cambridge, 2004.

8 A Life in Portraits

Lloyd, S., and K. Sloan, *The Intimate Portrait: Drawings, Miniatures and Pastels from Ramsay to Lawrence*, National Galleries of Scotland, Edinburgh, 2008.

Noon, P., *English Portrait Drawings and Miniatures*, Yale Center for British Art, New Haven, CT, 1979.

Rogers, M., *Master Drawings from the National Portrait Gallery*, National Portrait Gallery, London, 1993.

Sloman, S., and T. Fawcett, *Pickpocketing the Rich: Portrait Painting in Bath 1720–1800*, Holburne Museum of Art, Bath, 2002.

9 Jane Austen at 200

Dow, G., and C. Hanson (eds), *Uses of Austen: Jane's Afterlives*, Palgrave Macmillan, London, 2012.

Johnson, C.L., *Jane Austen's Cults and Cultures*, University of Chicago Press, Chicago, IL, 2012.

Lynch, D. (ed.), *Janeites: Austen's Disciples and Devotees*, Princeton University Press, Princeton, NJ, 2000.

_____, 'Sequels', in Janet Todd (ed.), *Jane Austen in Context*, Cambridge University Press, Cambridge, 2005, pp. 160–8.

Wells, J., *Everybody's Jane: Austen in the Popular Imagination*, Bloomsbury, London, 2011.

Contributors

Jeanice Brooks is Professor of Music at the University of Southampton. Her current book project, 'At Home with Music: Domesticity and Musical Culture in Georgian Britain', delves into the material aspects of domestic music-making in the years around 1800.

Hilary Davidson is a dress historian, curator and lecturer working between Sydney and London. She is an Honorary Associate at the University of Sydney and is completing a book on clothing in the British Regency world for Yale University Press.

Freya Johnston is Fellow and University Lecturer in English at St Anne's College, Oxford. She is general editor of the *Cambridge Edition of the Novels of Thomas Love Peacock*, Cambridge University Press, 2016–, and co-editor, with Kathryn Sutherland, of *Jane Austen's Teenage Writings*, Oxford University Press, 2017.

Thomas Keymer is Chancellor Jackman Professor in the Arts and University Professor of English at the University of Toronto, where he directs the graduate programme in Book History and Print Culture. His books include *Sterne, the Moderns, and the Novel*, Oxford University Press, 2002; *Poetics of the Pillory: English Literature and Seditious Libel 1660–1820*, Oxford University Press (forthcoming), and, as editor, the pre-1750 volume of the *Oxford History of the Novel in English*, Oxford University Press (forthcoming).

Deidre Lynch is Ernest Bernbaum Professor of Literature in the Department of English at Harvard University. Her books include *Loving Literature: A Cultural History*, University of Chicago Press, 2015; *Janeites: Austen's Disciples and Devotees*, Princeton University Press, 2000; and editions of Austen's *Persuasion* and *Mansfield Park*.

Susan Owens, formerly Curator of Paintings at the Victoria and Albert Museum, is a writer and art historian.

Kathryn Sutherland is Professor of Bibliography and Textual Criticism, University of Oxford, and Professorial Fellow in English at St Anne's College, Oxford. Her books include *Jane Austen's Textual Lives: from Aeschylus to Bollywood*, Oxford University Press, 2005. She is editor of the free-to-access *Jane Austen's Fiction Manuscripts, A Digital Edition*, 2010 (<www.janeausten.ac.uk>), and of editions of *Mansfield Park* and J.E. Austen-Leigh's *A Memoir of Jane Austen*.

Index

Illustrations are denoted by the use of *italics*. JA refers to Jane Austen. Entries within single quotation marks refer to works by Jane Austen.